Newspaper Abstracts of FREDERICK COUNTY Maryland

1816-1819

F. Edward Wright

WILLOW BEND BOOKS
2007

WILLOW BEND BOOKS
AN IMPRINT OF HERITAGE BOOKS, INC.

Books, CDs, and more—Worldwide

For our listing of thousands of titles see our website
at
www.HeritageBooks.com

Published 2007 by
HERITAGE BOOKS, INC.
Publishing Division
65 East Main Street
Westminster, Maryland 21157-5026

Copyright © 1993 F. Edward Wright

All rights reserved. No part of this book may be reproduced or transmitted in any form or by any means, electronic or mechanical, including photocopying, recording or by any information storage and retrieval system without written permission from the author, except for the inclusion of brief quotations in a review.

International Standard Book Number: 978-1-58549-073-8

Contents

Preface v

Political Examiner & Public Advertiser 1

Star of Federalism 27

The Republican Gazette and General Advertiser 45

Frederick-Town Herald 73

Index 161

Preface

This book is a continuation of our earlier abstracts of newspapers of Western Maryland. Earlier publications include *Western Maryland Newspaper Abstracts (1786-1810)*, in three volumes; *Newspaper Abstracts of Allegany and Washington Counties, 1811-1815*; *Newspaper Abstracts of Frederick County, 1811-1815*; *Marriages and Deaths in the Newspapers of Frederick and Montgomery Counties, Maryland, 1820-1830*; and *Marriages and Deaths in the Newspapers of Allegany and Washington Counties, 1820-1830*. These were published by Family Line Publications. In addition, L. Tilden Moore has complied *Abstracts of Marriages and Deaths and Other Articles of Interest in the Newspapers of Frederick and Montgomery Counties, Maryland, 1831-1840*.

This book was based in its entirety from the microfilm collection of the Maryland Historical Society. The newspapers abstracted are *Political Examiner & Public Advertiser, Star of Federalism, The Republican Gazette and General Advertiser*, and *Frederick-Town Herald*. All of these newspapers were published in the city of Frederick, then called Frederick-town.

As each successive newspaper was abstracted, those items which duplicated earlier ones were omitted.

F. Edward Wright
Westminster, Maryland
1993

Abbreviations

adm'r, admr. - administrator (of an estate)

atty. - attorney

co. - company or county

dau - daughter

dec'd. - deceased

extr. - executor (of an estate)

inst. - instant (current month)

no. - number

st. - streeet

ult. - ultimor (previous month)

Political Examiner & Public Advertiser

Wednesday, 4 Nov 1818

1. 4 Nov 1818. Spring Goods received from Philadelphia. John BAILY.
Doct. Jacob BAER, having returned to Frederick, offers his professional services to citizens of the city and its vicinity.
Fall and Winter just received from Baltimore. George TRISLER.
John HOFFMAN has just received an assortment of Cheap Goods and Auction bargains.
Edmund BOWNEY, wishing to move westward, offers for sale 150 acres on the Shenandoah river, 3 miles from Charlestown; includes a 3 story stone merchant mill.
Peter TOOLE and Patrick M'QUAID, having learned the cloth manufacturing business in Europe, have rented the Union Factory, 1 1/2 miles from Mr. Middletown Valley, from Mr. Remsburg.
William R. ELVINS & Co., Clock & Watch Makers, have commenced business in North Market St.
House and lot for sale by Sarah LARNED, extx., by authority of will of Augustus LARNED, dec'd., in Newtown.
Frederick Co. lime-stone for sale, Surry Farm, for sale, property of Otho H. WILLIAMS, dec'd., near Woodsborough, 589 acres. William E. WILLIAMS.
Peter SOERS, offers at private sale, his two farms adjoining lands of James JOHNSON and Thomas DRAPER, about 9 miles from Frederick-town, 320 acres; also a tanyard, plus 100 acres of mountain land; apply to Gideon BANTZ, Frederick Town. Peter SOWERS.
Henry STEMBEL, Middletown, will sell two-story brick house and lot in Bentz-town, adjoining the Poor House at the west side, now occupied by John STEMBEL.
NORRIS & GAITHER, have just returned from Baltimore with assortment of goods.
Eli P. BENTLEY, next door to the Bank of Frederick Co. has just received from Philadelphia and assortment of Fall Goods.
Thomas W. MORGAN and Daniel ARTHUR, candidates for sheriff.
100 logs of prime Mahogany for sale. William CAMP, No. 25 Wat St.
William WERTENBAKER, will rent blacksmith shop on the Harper's Ferry Road, about 5 miles from Frederick-town.
Bank of Westminster announces that an instalment of $2.50 on every share of stock is required. John WALSH, Cashier.
Tacitus CA..IT, Laurel Hill, PA, offers reward for negro man, ISAAC, formerly the property of Isaac ZIMMERMAN, near this place, from whom said negro was purchased April last, and made his escape; he has a wife at Col. Luckett's on the Potomack.
John L. LEVY, admr. of Mary Ann LEVY.
Andrew THOMSON has rye malt and hops for sale at the Frederick-town Brewery.

2. 4 Nov 1818

BAUER & MANTZ have received from the factory of Wm. BAER, & Co., Baltimore, a large supply of close, cooking and coal stoves.

Peter NICHOLS, woolen, draper, mens' mercer and taylor, next door to Mrs. KIMBOLL's Tavern, Frederick Town, has received black, blue and fancy coloured cloths, vesting, gilt buttons, twist buttons, silk velvet.

William GUNTON, Druggist, 3 doors east of Mrs. KIMBOLL's, has received from Philadelphia, assortment of genuine drugs and medicines, and fancy articles.

Frederick Town races will be run. Thomas CARLTON, M. K. HAMMET.

Frederick NUSZ, North Market St., Frederick-town, has gold and silver watches, gold and silver spectacles.

SPRENGLE and MARKEY, black and white smiths, continue business at their shop north market St., a few doors above the Examiner office, nearly opposite George TRISLER'S store.

Bennett's Creek Property for sale, Frederick Co., 90 acres, merchant mill, plaister mill, saw mill, blacksmith & cooper's shops. Apply to Dr. Belt BRASHAER, Otho SPRIGG, or C. B. ROSS. John K. COOK.

Clock and watch making, Woodsborough, in the house formerly occupied by Mr. BARNETT. Daniel MARTZ.

Hugh BLAIR, Williamsport, has walnut plank for sale.

Philip DIETRICK, has taken up stray hogs at his plantation near Joshua DORSEY's, on Irael's Creek.

Houses and lots for sale in Hyatt's Town, Montgomery Co. Baruch HALL, one mile this side of Hyatt's Town.

Persons holding subscription papers for Gatson's Scripture Account of the Faith and Practice of Christians, will please forward them to George KOLB, Frederick-town.

Thomas BURGEES, Sen., cautions persons from taking assignment of a note of hand given to John TURNER, of Philip, living in Hampshire Co., VA.

Thomas WOOD offers for sale a grist mill with 3 acres in the settlement of Little Pipe Creek, about 1 mile from the Turnpike road.

Died on Saturday on 24th inst., Mrs. Mary RITCHIE, in her 87th year.

Died Wednesday night, in this town, Miss Elenor TURNER, dau of Thomas TURNER, of George Town, D.C.

James DUNLAP, taylor, Graceham, Frederick Co., continues the business.

A teacher wanted immediately. Apply to Otho SPRIGG or Davis RICHARDSON.

Stockholders of Frederick Co. Bank, are notified that instalment of $2.50 is required. Geo. BEAR, Cash'r.

Otho SPRIGG, admr. of Captain Thomas SPRIGG.

James ROBERTSON gives highest price for good clean merchantable wheat.

3. 4 Nov 1818

John B. WEBER to serve Oysters at his old stand next door to the office of the Political Examiner, and continues to make hot and cold punch, egg nog, with an assortment of other liquors of the first quality. He still attends to the business of a public crier.

The lottery will be completed on 5 Nov. John P. THOMSON, Samuel BARNES, agents.

Looking glasses for sale at the store of Mr. HAUSER; also quantity of hardware, salts with stands, cut glass, etc. Joseph HOW.

Public sale at late dwelling of Hannah STEINER, dec'd., all personal estate, 202 shares in Westminster Bank, all the real estate of Christian STEINER, consisting of 3 small tracts, one near Monocacy, one about 1/4 mile from Frederick-town on Baltimore turnpike road and two lots in Haller's Town; also house and lot no. 271 in Patrick St., late residence of Hannah STEINER.

100 acres for sale, 1 1/2 miles from Emmitsburgh on road from Emmitsburgh to Hagers Town, adjoining lands of the heirs of Wm. SHIELDS, dec'd., dwelling house and kitchen, barn and other out houses, with saw mill, and complete powder mill, with 16 pestles. William SHIELDS.

Tobias BELT, near Berlin, Maryland Tract, offers reward for mare which strayed from Carroll's Manor.

Nathan HAMMOND, near Frederick-town, offers reward for Negro man named HARRY, about 30 years of age, 5 feet 8-9 inches, purchased from the heirs of Mr. BENTZ near Frederick-town about 3 years ago; has brother living in Frederick-town with Mr. William HANE.

Joseph M'GREED offers reward for horse stolen from COOKERLY'S tavern on Liberty road. Return horse to Thomas ELLIOTT, Baltimore, William MYERS, Liberty or to Joseph M'GREED, living near Smithfield, Jefferson Co., OH.

4. 4 Nov 1818

Nicholas HACKE has returned from Europe and received since by the Clara and Witbelen(?) from Bremen, an assortment of German goods. Apply at the store, No. 120 North Howard St.

William M'FARLAND has commenced the fulling and dying at his Factory on the new road from Frederick-town to New Castle, 4 miles from Middletown. Cloth will be received at Wm. WERTENBAKER's tavern on road from Frederick to New Town (Trap), at John GETZENDENNER's on the turnpike, and at John HOUCK's on the new road from Frederick to the factory.

William BROWN, having gotten the Fleecy Dale Woolen Factory again in complete operation, and taken Mr. C. MORSE into partnership, solicits public patronage.

Michael STRAVER offers tract for sale, 125 1/2 acres on the Tuscoroa, 4 miles from Frederick-town.

Lewis HEARN, admr. of Daniel HEARN.

Jas. F. HUSTON, Frederick-Town retailer of medicines prepared by W. T. CONWAY, Boston.

John HOFFMAN, extr. of Hannah STEINER.

Best quality Oysters - George J. LOUX, upper end of Market St.

Jacob MALAMBRE states that he was robbed of several articles of clothing from his house. For reward apply at the factory, at the 45 miles stone in Patrick St.

Sale of property in accordance of the will of Edward BOTELER, sen., 200 acres 8 miles south west of Frederick-town, and several lots. Edward S. BOTELER, extr.

WILLIAMS & STINCHCOMB continue to purchase wheat. Waggons coming to the mill will, in case of high water, be put over the river free of expense, and have every attention paid them at the Ferry, by the old, careful Ferryman, John NEWPORT.

5. 6 Jan 1819.

Jonah BUFFINGTON and John RENNER, admrs. of John ECARD.

Miss Zulma MARCILLY has opened a millinery store in Patrick St. next door to John HOFFMAN.

Notice to stockholders of the Rockville and Washington turnpike road company that the second instalment of $4.00 must be paid at Davis' Hotel. John DAVIS, President, John P. INGLE, Treasurer. Sheriff's sale at the house of Nicholas TURBUTT of Negro boy named HENSON, late the property of Nicholas CLOPPER, seized and taken by virtue of two writs of fieri facies, one at the suit of Thomas COOK use of Joseph M. CROMWELL and one at the suit of James DIGGS, use of Joseph M. CROMWELL. Peter MARTIN for Wm. M. BEALL, jun., Sheriff.

Peter BRENGLE, candidate for sheriff.

Corporation taxes are due. Joseph SCHELL, Collector.

Eli P. BENTLEY cautions persons from trusting his servants without an order.

Benj. WINTER wishes to purchase 8 or 10,00 bushels of oats.

Jacob HOFFMAN, Middletown, to sell brick house and lot in Bentz-town, adjoining poor house at the west side, now occupied by John STEMBLE.

Petition will be presented to Frederick Co. court to open a road from M'FARLAND'S Factory to the widow CRAFT'S merchant mill, from thence to Middletown, on the bed of the old road, between Adam ROUTZANG and Samuel BRANDENBURG. The contemplated road will run through the public alley, adjoining the property of Adam HERRING and Aaron SUMAN.

6. 6 Jan 1819

Abraham GRIFFITH, on Carroll's Manor, two miles from Buckey's Town, seeks journeymen cabinet makers.

John ZIMMERMAN and G. M. EICHELBERGER, extrs. of Isaiah HARR.

John COOK, attorney at law, Rockville.

Thomas W. MORGAN, auditor, warns creditors of William B. LUPTON, dec'd., to exhibit claims.

Monocacy Bridge Lottery meeting at house of Francis SPALDING, C. BURNIE was called to the chair and Mr. G. M. EICHELBERGER, appointed secretary.

David HAINES, at the head of Sam's Creek, offers reward for missing horses.

Thomas CARLTON, desirous of closing his business, will sell property at his house in Frederick-town.

Jos. HYATT cautions persons from receiving a land warrant granted to him for militia services, the warrant having been lost.

George LITTLEJOHN offers reward for Negro man named Harry WARREN, about 30 years of age, 5 feet, 8 inches; can read and write; may have been enticed away by a white man named James GOULDING, an Irishman, about 5 feet, 6 inches high, well made, has traveled a great deal.

Nimrod OWINGS, Fountain Rock, near Frederick-town, offers reward for dark mulatto slave, PHILIP, about 19 years of age. His mother, SARAH, was set free by the late Edward OWINGS and now resides in the city of Baltimore.

Sale of farm lately owned by Joshua DORSEY, 777 1/2 acres in Baltimore Co. on the branches of Patapsco Falls. Lands will be shewn by James HOOD or Benjamin DORSEY, sen. living adjoining this farm. For William CAMPBELL, Wm. C. RUSSELL.

Sale of tan yard in Greensburg, Green Co., PA. John EBERT.

Petition to be presented for road to begin at Henry GAVER's new house on the new cut road from Frederick-town to HUGHES' coaling ground in Washington Co.; to run from thence to intersect the turnpike road at Middletown between the buildings of Valentine BOWLUS and Jacob CRITZER.

7. 6 Jan 1819

L. A. BEATTY has taken up stray sheep, 4 miles from Frederick.

Ferdinand ONEALE, Samuel GRIFFITH and Ann STEWART, both now confined in public jail for debt, to be discharged and a trustees will be appointed.

Chancery sale at the tavern now occupied by Adam BAUGHMAN, near Harper's Ferry - 343 acres in Washington Co., including a merchant mill, dwelling, cooper's shop, distillery, tavern stand. Property will be shewn by Jonah BUFFINGTON. Richard BROOKE, trustee.

Wm. WORMAN has again got his mill into operation, 4 miles below Liberty, on the Liberty road.

Edward KENNEDY has taken up a stray mare. Certified by J.P., Belt BRASHEAR.

Tavern stand for sale on road from New-town (Trap) to Sharpsburg. Conrad FLOOK.

Rewards offered two men who escaped from Frederick jail: George C. CAMPBELL, about 5 feet, 7 inches, 36 years of age, brown hair, large nose and red face, some of his teeth out, a mill-wright and miller, formerly residing in Philadelphia; and Samuel MACHER, about 5 feet, 6-7 inches high, 27 years of age, has large whiskers, dark brown hair, rather slow of speech; has a $20 counterfeit note on one of the Philadelphia banks.

8. 13 Jan 1819

Chancery sale of 7 1/2 acres, 5 miles from Liberty, adjoining lands of John KINZER. Surratt D. WARFIELD lives near it.

Town lot for sale pursuant to will of Barnet RENN, dec'd, lot no. 5 in that addition to Frederick-town called Bentztown, conveyed by Caspar MYER to Barnet RENN on 2 Oct 1759. Apply to Barnard RENN, extr. or Henry KEMP.

Frederick ROW, Emmittsburg, offers reward for apprentice to cabinet making business named Henry RODGERS, about 20 years of age, 5 feet, 3-4 inches, sandy complexion.

100 cords of oak wood for sale, about 5 miles from Frederick-town, on the Turnpike Road. Lewis CREAGER.

9. 27 Jan 1819

Large frame house for sale in Chambersburg, near the stone bridge adjoining lots of A. FLEEK and M. GIBBENS. Henry KLUNK, Andrew KLUNK.

Fall Goods from Philadelphia. John BAYLY.

Persons indebted to estate of Jacob HOCKENSMITH are requested to make immediate payment. John HOCKENSMITH and Wm. HOCKENSMITH, extrs.

Chancery sale of wood-land, 1 mile from Frederick-town, for the benefit of George SCHNERTZELL's heirs. George BALTZELL, trustee.

Independent hosemen are to attend at the Union Tavern. A. QUYNN, Sec'y.

Sale at the late residence of Jeremiah BELT, dec'd., on the Merryland Tract, 27 Negroes, cattle, grain, etc. Tobias BELT, extr.

Statement of the amount of Internal Duties imposed by the United States (excepting those on Household Furniture, on Watches and on Stamps) paid by each person in the 7th Col. district of Maryland during the year 1818: Frederick BAUCHMAN, 108.42; Walter BEAVINS, 196.97; Abraham D. CLOPPER, 325.44; John DOUP, 85.48; Joshua DELAPLANE, 816.44; Thomas DRAPER, 365.20; Geo. M. EICHELBERGER, 171.90; Frederick EICHELBERGER, 562.30; George GUMP, 32.15; John GRAYBILL, 344.21; Jacob HILTIBRAKE, 21.31; Peter HOUK, 43.20; John HOFFMAN, 87.08; Perry HILLEARY, 458.44; John JONES, 63.36; Jacob KELLER, 57.??; Gilbert KEMP, 256.89; James MATHEWS, 56.60; Joseph MATHIAS, 50.28; Philip MATTERN, 24.62; George RAMSBURGH, 88.76; Henry REPP, 218.16; Henry STRAY, 22.03; Jacob STONECIPHER, 104.97; Michael SPRENGLE, 28.03; Philip STRIDER, 635.83; George UMBAUGH, 269.54; Pierce WOODS, 242.33; Horrace WEST, 197.64; Nathan WILLYAR, 27.54.

Sale of farm on which Robison EASTBURN now resides, 240 acres.

Sale by power of attorney from Miss Victoire VINCENDIERE, at Joseph TALBOTT'S tavern, 300-400 acres on road from Frederick to George-town. Apply to major Peter MANTZ or to subscriber, Leonard JAMISON.

Equity case: Edward GARROTT vs. Ann admx. of Jos. GARROTT and others. Ordered that sale of real estate of Joseph GARROTT be ratified.

Sheriff's sale of estate of Adam SMITH, west part of lot no. 38 in Woodsborough. David HINES for Wm. M. BEALL, jun., sheriff.

Sale of tract in Washington Co., 1 mile from John ROHRER'S Factory, 21 acres with log dwelling house. Abraham SHOWERS.

10. Wednesday 3 Feb 1819.
George WISSINGER has taken up a stray mare. Certified by J.P., John S. FRAZIER.
Sheriff's sale of estate of John GIBSON, 9 acres, 90 perches, part of Mountain Tract, taken at the suit of William GIBSON, use of James DUNLAP, within one mile of Graceham.
Chancery sale at the tavern of William COOKERLY, farm, 127 acres, adjoining lands of Adam BURRIER, Major SOLLERS and Mr. POMFREY. Apply to Adam BURRIER or John STEPHANUS who resides on it.
Tavern for rent in Emmittsburg, formerly occupied by Solomon KEPPART, dec'd., at present by William FARQUHAR. Peter BOYLE.
Sale of farm on which he now resides 8 miles from Frederick-town adjoining farms of Messrs. J. HOLTZ, COCKEY and POE, 318 acres; also Fleecy Dale merchant and saw mills on Bennett's Creek. Philemon CROMWELL.

11. 10 Feb 1819.
Died in the vicinity of Bladensburg, Saturday morning, General Armistead T. MASON, of Loudoun Co., VA, aged about 33 years, killed in a duel, fought with muskets at short distance [12 feet]. Former Senator from Virginia, leaves mother, wife and child. The following issue identifies his opponent as John M'CARTY. They were cousins; and the sister of one was married to the brother of the other.
Sheriff's sale at the house of George HAMMOND, Negro man, late the property of George HAMMOND, taken at the suit of John WAGNER, and of Polly HAMMOND, use Philip HAUPTMAN.
Chancery sale at the house of John DILL, Frederick-town, tract 1 1/2 miles from Frederick on Noland's Ferry road, belonging to the heirs of Baltzer FOUT, dec'd., 186 1/2 acres; lies between lands of Doct. SHAAFF and Col. M'PHERSON. It is now occupied by John HELDERBRAND. Frederick A. SCHLEY, Richard POTTS, trustees.
Dorothea SHAFER has opened the Fountain Inn, Frederick.
Singleton DUVAL, Attorney at Law, with office a few yards north of Mr. DILL'S tavern.

12. 17 Feb 1819
Married Thursday evening, 4th inst., by Rev. James L. HIGGINS, Basil DORSEY, to Miss Harriet, dau of Rev. Joshua JONES, all of this co.
F. and G. ENGELBRECHT, inform customers of their late father that the tayloring business will be continued by them.
Sale of real estate of John ECARD is postponed. Property will be for rent; apply to Jonah BUFFINGTON, near Harper's Ferry.
Margaret ENGELBRECHT and George ENGELBRECHT, extrs. of Conrad ENGELBRECHT.
Superfine cloth on hand at the house of Jacob STEINER, Market and Patrick sts. RUSSELL & STEINER.
Daniel BUSSARD, Baltimore Co., offers reward for John JOHNSON, bound to the tanning business, 17 years of age, slim visage, quick spoken.

Sale of land 3 miles from Frederick-town, 80 acres. Wm. GOLDSBOROUGH.
Philip BLESSING offers for sale, 3 1/2 miles from New Town, Trap, horses, cattle, sheep, etc.
Henry HALLER admr. of Tobias HALLER.
Henry POFFINBARGER, 4 1/2 miles from Middletown, offers reward for stolen horse.
Trustee's sale (chancery) of the real estate of Jacob DELAUTER, dec'd., in neighborhood of Godfrey LEATHERMAN and Mr. GROSNECKLE, in the northern part of Middle Town Valley. Property will be shown by George DELAUTER, living on the premises.

13. 24 Feb 1819

Fire on Sunday night last, of barn and hay-stack on the farm occupied by Mr. REED, 1/2 mile from town.
Sale of land at the house, late residence of widow RENN, 23 1/2 acres, part of Mount Pleasant, and Deer Spring, 5 miles from Frederick-town, adjoining lands of Jacob SHELLMAN and lands lately bought by Henry THOMAS; also 19 acres of timber land, part of the Resurvey on part of Mount Pleasant, adjoining lands of Henry THOMAS and lands of Michael and George ZIMMERMAN. Also 25 acres 2 1/2 miles from New Town (Trap) and on both sides of the Bridle road, adjoining the lands of Frederick BERGER and lands formerly belonging to Andrew KESSLER. Lands will be shewn by Isaac RENN, who lives near the land, and the mountain land can also be shewn by Thomas PERREL who lives adjoining thereto. Henry KEMP, extr. of George RENN.
Marshall's sale by virtue of a decree of the court of the United States for the fifth circuit in the Virginia district in a suit in chancery wherein Mary WORMLY, wife of Hugh Wallace WORMLEY, by George S. STROTHER her next friend, and John S. S. WORMLY, Mary W. WORMLY, Jane B. WORMLY and Anne B. WORMLY, infant children of the said Mary and Hugh WORMLY by the said George F. STROTHER, their next friend, plaintiffs - against Hugh Wallace WORMLEY, Thomas STRODE, Richard VEITCH, David CASTLEMAN and Charles M'CORMICK, defendants - of 300 acres, and also the reversion of 50 acres, in Frederick Co., VA, on north side of the Shenandoah river. Wm. MANN, D.M. for Andrew MOORE, M. V. D.
Dissolution of partnership of Joseph ADLUM and David B. DEVITT.
Sale of tavern stand in Woodsborough. Joseph HEDGES, near Woodsborough.

14. 3 March 1819

Married Sunday evening, 21st, by Rev. HELFENSTEIN, Ezra DILL, to Miss Margaret MORGAN, all of this city.
Died Friday last, John BRUNER, of this co.
Councilmen elected: Ward 1 - Peter DEGRANGE; Ward 2 - Jacob STEINER; Ward 3 - Michael BUCKEY; Ward 4 - Michael HAUSER; Ward 5 - George A. EBERT; Ward 6 - Frederick STONER; Ward 7 - William KOLB.
APPOINTMENTS:
Orphans Court: John M'PHERSON, Ignatius DAVIS and Peter MANTZ.

Levy Court: Alexander WARFIELD of Chas., Benjamin BIGGS, Stephen STEINER, James MORRISON, William MURPHY, Jacob MATTHIAS, William B. HEAD.

Justices of the Peace: David BOWLUS, F. B. SAPPINGTON, Belt BRASHEAR, William GRIMES, jun., Jason PHILLIPS, Henry WILLIAMS, Joseph Sim SMITH, Joseph TANEY, William B. HEAD, William P. FARQUHAR, Henry KOONTZ, jun., Davis RICHARDSON, William DURBIN, jun., James MURPHY, Levin HAYS, George KOLB, Michael HAUSER, Jonathan M. DANIEL, Benjamin BIGGS, John S. FRAZIER, Jacob CLABAUGH, Vachel W. RANDALL, David BUCKEY, Dennis POOLE, John BALL, Peter ERB of Christopher, Abraham ALBAUGH, Jonathan NORRIS, Samuel P. RICHARDSON, Patrick RIED, sen., Thomas C. SCOTT, William COGHLIN, Andrew SMITH near Middletown, Samuel OGLE, Greenbury MAJORS, Joshua JONES, Washington VANBIBBER, Jacob MATTHIAS, George KEILER, Surat D. WARFIELD, William HART, George PRICE, John GLISAN, Joseph PENN, George CREAGER, Thomas GIST, Jesse WRIGHT, William HODGKISS, John COSKERY, Henry KEMP, Elie TOWNE, Francis HAMBLETON, Joseph TANEY, jun., George Jacob CONRAD, Joel JACOBS, James M'ATEE, Joshua C. GIST, jun., John SMELZER, Elias H. HARDING, David MARTIN, John REITZELL, Thomas HAMMOND, Thomas POWEL, Elihel ROCKWELL, Thos. W. MORGAN, Patrick OWINGS, Alexander M'ILHENNY, Joachim ELDER, Doct. Jacob BAER, George ROHR and Lewis MOTTER.

James ROBERTSON has on hand at his mill, a large quantity of plaster, ground and ready to put on the land.

Statement by John SHIELDS, of Cock Co., TN, by his letter of attorney, dated 1801, appointed William SHIELDS of Frederick Co., MD, his attorney for the recovery of debts due him and to convey his lands in Frederick Co.

Lewis BIRELY, candidate for sheriff.

Sale of 90 - 100 acres on the premises, the late dwelling of Edward THOMAS, late of Frederick Co., dec'd., on main road from Hook's Gap to the mouth of Monocacy. William R. KING and Richard T. HEBB, extrs.

Sale of Negroes by E. C. & R. POTTS, extrs. of Doctor William POTTS.

15. 10 March 1819

Henry SCHNEBLY, Washington Co., admr. of John SCHNEBLY, Montgomery Co.

Dissolution of partnership of Patrick M'QUAID and Mr. TOOL. The Union Factory, property of Mr. REMSBURG, 2 miles from Middletown Valley, will be kept in operation by Patrick M'QUAID. He will receive cloth for fulling or wool to be manufactured at James TORRANCE's in New Town (Trap) and Thomas POWEL's store, Middletown.

Samuel GEYER, New Market, offers reward for James GARDINER, apprentice to the saddling business, about 15 years old, freckled face and red hair.

Henry BLACK admr. of Adam BLACK.

1000 cords of tanners bark will be wanted next spring. John MANTZ.

Annual election of Directors of the Bank of Westminster will be held. Jesse SLINGLUFF, Pres.

New Grocery Store at the store lately occupied by Henry THOMAS, nearly opposite Joseph TALBOTT'S Hotel. HAUSER & LEVY.

Sale of lands adjoining Creagerstown, sundry houses and lots in said town and all of the quit rents at the house late Mr. HAAS' tavern, in Creagerstown, 215 acres. Samuel GRIMES, residing in Creagerstown, will show the property. Also moiety held conjointly with HOLTZMAN's heirs. John RITCHIE, extr.

Mill, houses, lands, tavern stand (occupied by Adam BAUGHMAN) and distillery for sale - 343 acres. Property will be shewn by Jonah BUFFINGTON, residing near the premises. Richard BROOKE, trustee.

The horse, Richmond, will stand at the farm of Christian KEMP.

16. 17 March 1819

Sale of furniture by M. E. Bartgis, declining the tavern business. Exhibition of air balloons, by Mr. NAPEY.

Chancery court: John BLACK, Adam BLACK, Jacob SINGER, and Eve, his wife, complainants against Michael BLACK, Henry BLACK, and Elizabeth, Ann, Mary, Catharine and Jacob WHITMORE, defendants. Complainants and defendants hold parcels of lands in Frederick Co., as tenants in common: part of tract called Brotherly Love, 100 acres; part of Pleasant Hill, 32 acres; tract called Sycamore Island, 5 acres. Henry BLACK and Elizabeth, Anne, Mary, Catharine and Jacob WHITMORE are under age of 21. All defendants except Henry BLACK reside out of the state of Maryland.

Trustee's (chancery) sale of house and lot, property of Edward SELMON, dec'd., in the rear of the Lutheran Church. Raymer KOLB lives in said property.

Mount Hampton farm for sale, formerly the property of late capt. Thomas SPRIGG, dec'd., 6 miles from Frederick-town. Otho SPRIGG.

Equity case: CARBERRY and others vs. SCHNERTZELL and MORE. That the sale of property be ratified.

Chancery sale of land and mills, 162 acres, 1 1/2 miles from Middleburg on the Beaver Dams, formerly the property of David ROOP, dec'd., adjoining lands of John DEAL and Hammond RAITT. John KINZER lives near the property.

Sale of James WAGERS' property is postponed. Benjamin HAGAN, for Wm. M. Beall, jun., sheriff.

Tract for sale on road from Frederick to George-town. 1 1/2 miles from Middlebrook mills, adjoining John BUXTON' tavern, 146 acres. Joseph FUNK.

Sale of 215 acres in Frederick Co., 1 mile from Creager's Town, farm where Wm. B. HEAD lives.

17. 24 March 1819

Republican Meeting at the house of Nicholas TURBUTT, in Frederick-town - Doctor William TYLER called to the chair; John J. M'CULLEY appointed secretary.

William MARKS has started a new line of post coaches from Baltimore to Frederick-town.

Ground plaster - WILLIAMS & STINCHCOMB, Ceresville.

Dissolution of partnership of John THOMAS and William C. EMMIT.

Jacob GESEY makes and repairs mill spindles, cast steal picks and casing hammers, at his shop on Fishing Creek near Cronise's mill on the Emmitsburg road.

Chancery sale of tract of land, 360 acres, part of the Merryland Tract, late residence of capt. Jeremiah BELT, dec'd. Tobias BELT, extr.

18. 31 March 1819

Chancery sale at the house of John AGNEW in Emmittsburg, lot of 2 acres with log dwelling house and blacksmith shop. Michael BLESSING, trustee.

John STIER, inn-keeper, continues to carry on the plough making in Middletown.

James WILLIAMS, near Battle-town, Frederick Co., VA, will sell Virginia farm, 240 acres, on the line of Frederick and Jefferson counties.

Auction and commission store. HOUSTON & RUSSELL.

Line of mail stages will leave Mrs. KIMBOLL's tavern in Frederick-town every Sunday, Tuesday and Thursday and arrive at Col. M'GUIRE's in Winchester, VA, the same days...

Equity sale by decree of Washington Co. Court of 217 acres belonging to the heirs of Christopher ERNSBERGER, late of Washington Co., dec'd. F. ANDERSON, trustee.

19. 7 April 1819

A waggoner of this co, a coloured man, in attempting to cross the Monocacy with his team was drowned Monday last with three horses. The horses belonged to John HUGHES, near this town.

Auction Thursday next at the Auction Rooms, Market St.: cut goods, remnants, books, dutch quills, brushes, etc. J. LARKIN, auct'r.

John REESE and Jacob REESE, extrs. of Adam REESE.

Spring Goods - John THOMAS.

Notes are due from the sale of Mrs. Mary Ann LEVY's goods. John L. LEVY, admr.

Sheriff's sale of estate of Jacob GIBBONS, house and lot contiguous to west end of Frederick-town, heretofore conveyed by Stephen STEINER to Stephen KLINE - taken at the suit of Stephen STEINER.

20. 14 April 1819

Married Thursday last, by Rev. HAUSE, George SALMON, of this city, to Miss Catherine SMITH, dau. of Captain Daniel SMITH, of this co.

Married Thursday evening, 25th ult. by Rev. James L. HIGGINS, Henry WEBB, to Miss Eve FINE, dau of Philip FINE, all of this co.

Died Monday morning last, at his residence near Frederick, of a pulmonary disease, Charles HAMMOND, in his 38th year, leaving wife and two small children - *Herald*.

A. BONAFFON, professor of dancing, has opened a dancing school at the house of Mrs. SHAFER, sign of the Fountain Inn.

John L. POTTS offers reward for Joe THOMAS, slave of Mrs. E. POTTS, tolerably white in complexion, straight hair, about 5 feet high, carriage driver.
Sale of farm, 6 miles from Washington and Georgetown, 137 acres. Thomas PATTERSON.

21. 21 April 1819

Elected directors of the Bank of Westminster: Jesse SLINGLUFF, President; William DURBIN, Ludwick WAMPLER, Henry KUHN, George COLEGATE, Benjamin RUTHERFORD, John C. COCKEY, Gideon BANTZ, Thomas BOYER, John FISHER, Joseph SWEARINGEN.

Adam STEWART of this city has invented a machine for making bricks.

LANE & RUTHERFORD have removed their store from the corner of Patrick & Market Sts. to their house in Patrick St., one door below the currying shop of Isaac MANTZ.

Jane DIGGS, near Allen's Fresh, Charles Co., MD, offers reward for Negro fellow HENRY; 5 feet, 6 inches, about 21 years of age.

The horse Tom will stand this season for mares at Surrey farm, with a mile of Woodsboro.' George YANTES, manager.

Abaello, a maltese Jackass will cover mares this season at Ceresville farm. Daniel ELLIS, manager.

George GULICK, near Aldie, Loudoun Co., VA, offers reward for Negro man, Ned BIAYS, active, shrewd, intelligent, about 5 feet, 7-8 inches, 30 years of age; raised near Centreville (VA) by James P. CARTER.

22. 28 April 1819

At a Republican Meeting it was resolved that Thomas C. WORTHINGTON, John HOFFMAN, Henry KUHN, Nicholas HOLTZ, Samuel BARNES, John REMSBERG, George W. ENT, Moses WORMAN, John KUNKLE, Jacob GETZENDENNER, Jacob SHRIVER, Jacob HEFFNER, Gideon BANTZ, John GITTINGER and George ZEALER, be a committee to represent the second election district.

Died on 23rd inst. at Belmont, in his 33rd year, Alexr. C. HANSON, Senator of the U.S. from this state.

Notice of meeting of stockholders of Frederick Co. Bank. George BAER, Cashier.

Sale of 3336 acres on Cove Creek, Harrison Co., VA George BAER.

Sale of half lot, no. 104, lying between Adam SCHISSLER and late Edward SALMON's property. Michael HAUSER.

Conrad KELLER forewarns persons from harboring black boy, about 18 years of age, bound till he is 21, by name of Lat JONES; his father and mother live in Frederick-town.

Tract of land for sale on which he lives, 1500 acres, joining town of Warrenton, Fauquier Co., VA George B. PICKETT.

23. 5 May 1819

Republican Meeting at the house of William PERRY, Capt. Robison EASTBURN called to the chair, and Geo. TITLOW appointed secretary.

Resolved that Frederick STEMBEL, sen., Lewis BIERLY, John STOTTLEMEYER, General Joseph SWEARINGEN, Thomas POWELL, esq., Capt. Jacob ALEXANDER, Godfrey LEATHERMAN, Nicholas BOWLUS, Dr. Lewis CREAGER, John R. MAGRUDER, Capt. Robison EASTBURN, George MARKER, sen., Jacob STALEY, Capt. Daniel SHAWEN, Capt. Jacob COLEMAN and John Philip COBLENTZ, be a committee to represent the third election district, in the general committee.

At a Republican meeting at the house of John L. CREEGER of L., Lawrence CREEGER was called to the chair and Jacob FIRER appointed secretary. Resolved that Lawrence CREEGER, Colonel Jacob CRAMER, Capt. Samuel DUVALL, Zebulon KUHN, J. CREEGER of L., Abraham GRUSHON, Peter HAWMAN, John MOYER, Jacob WELLER, merchant, George HERMAN, Ignatius BROWN, Jacob WILLYARD, Adam SNECK, Henry CREEGER of John, Joseph CREEGER, Jacob CRIST, Jacob FIEROR, Jacob WICKHAM, George OATS, jun., George MARKER, John GRUSHON, sen., Dr. Jacob CHARN, Jacob CRISE, John OTT and John DERR, be a committee to represent the 4th District.

Republican Meeting at the house of Mr. BOHN, in Emmitsburg, George TROXEL called to the chair, and George M. EICHELBERGER appointed secretary with Pierce WOODS, John EYLER and Geo. M. EICHELBERGER elected.

Republican Meeting of the 9th district at the house of Mr. INGMAN, Arthur TANZEY called to the chair and Dr. John H. M. SMITH appointed secretary. It was resolved that Thos. DUVALL, Jacob HOUCK, John SMITH, sen., John H. M. SMITH, Wm. DOWNEY, John BURGESS, John SMITH of Geo., Richard CLARK, Justus KOHLENBURG, Arthur TANZEY, Plummer IAMS, Benjamin WRIGHT and Luke DAVIS be a committee to meet the general committee.

Died on Thursday last in his 82d year, Capt. John ADLUM, for upwards of 50 years a respectable inhabitant of this place.

Sale by order of the Orphans' Court at late residence of Charles HAMMOND, dec'd., personal property of dec'd, including 13 Negroes. Thomas HAMMOND, admr.

24. 5 May 1819

Chancery sale at tavern of John S. HALL in New Market, of house and lot, late the property of Abraham B. WOODWARD and in which said Woodward now resides. Frederick A. SCHLEY, trustee.

Andrew THOMSON now has ready for delivery, Bottled Porter.

Henry STRAUSE offers for sale property occupied by him, 450 acres, 1 1/2 miles of Rockville, Montgomery Co. Persons may also apply to captain Matthew MURRAY, Hagerstown.

Chancery sale farm, property of Jonas URNER, dec'd., 238 1/2 acres, adjoining lands of Jacob SNODER and Paul MOURER - on road from Liberty to Baltimore. Also 48 3/4 acres of timber land; Samuel URNER lives on the farm.

Sale at the store room (New Town, Trap) lately occupied by Prestley WARFIELD, dec'd., all the store goods belonging to the dec'd. John COST, Thomas JOHNSON, admrs.

Lots of wheat in the ground for sale, on that part of Doctor POTTS' estate adjoining WORMAN and CRONISE's mill. These lots have been laid off and accurately staked by major Peter MANTZ. R. POTTS.

25. 12 May 1819

Married Tuesday evening, 4th inst., at St. Peter's Church, Baltimore, by Rev. HENSHAW, William BRADFORD, of Frederick-town, to Miss Jane RINGGOLD, of that city.

Married Thursday evening lat by Rev. Jonathan HELFENSTEIN, Jesse WRIGHT, jun. of New Market, to Miss Margaret MANTZ.

Died at his residence in Frederick, Saturday night last, in his 44th year, Richard BROOKE, Esq., member of the bar of this state; received the holy sacraments of the Roman Catholic Church.

Died Monday, 3d of May, Lewis HILL, in his 33d year, resident of this co.

Died at Gisborough, Friday last, John T. SHAAFF, M. D., aged 56 years. After completing his professional education in Europe he began the practice of Medicine in this city. *Md. Gaz.*

Philip LOWE, saddler, has removed his shop from Market St. to the store house lately occupied by LANE & RUTHERFORD.

Peter NICHOLS, woollen draper, men's mercer and tailor, next door to Mrs. KIMBOLL's tavern, has just received from Baltimore an elegant assortment of Sheppard's extra cloths, cassimeres, and fancy vesting.

Doct. George HUGHES offers his professional services to the people of New Market and vicinity.

Dissolution of the partnership of David WEBSTER and Samuel WEBSTER.

Samuel WEBSTER will carry on the business of Shoes. He has on hand an assortment of boots, shoes, trunks, &c.

26. 19 May 1819

Republican Meeting of District 8 at Brooke BAKER's tavern, in Woodsborough, Joseph HEDGES called to the chair, Dr. Henry STALEY appointed secretary. Resolution adopted that John KINZER, Dr. Henry BAKER, James RICE and Robert FULTON be a committee to represent the district.

Died on 5th instant, Benjamin BIGGS, Esq., in his 59th year.

Died Tuesday last in her 47th year, Mrs. Sophia KOLB, wife of Michael KOLB [of a pulmonary complaint - See *Gazette*].

Gerard ALEXANDER, Jun., wishing to remove to the western country this fall, will sell the farm on which he resides, in Prince William Co., 1500 acres; also 800 acres in Centreville area.

David SHRIVER, Superintendant of the U.S. road, east of Washington, Pa, will attend at his office in Brownesville, PA, for purpose of receiving proposals for constructing any part of the U.S. road between Union-town and Washington, PA.

Isaac CRUM has had a number of sheep destroyed by dogs.

G. F. TEUTO & Co. - New Confectionery,. next door to Henry KUHN, Esq., Market St.

Doct. G. WEISE, druggist, chemist and apothecary at the above place (lately from Europe) has on hand all the various drugs and medicines.

Jas. H. WILLIAMSON has rented Friendship Factory of captain John S. LAWRENCE on Linganore, 5 miles from Liberty town, and 1 mile from Peter SHRINER's mill, where he will manufacture merino and other wool, having engaged Mr. HARDING who has been head workman at fulling, dying and dressing in the above factory two seasons. Leave wool to card or to manufacture, or cloth to dress, at John GREEB's tavern, 1 mile below Freedom, or at Samuel J. TUCK's at Allen's mills, or at James RICE's.

Perry RICE has taken up a stray colt.

27. 26 May 1819

The body of James ADAMS, a native of England, respectable farmer from Cadworth, England, found Sunday, 9th inst., near Cumberland in this state, apparently robbed and murdered by three men in his company: William COTTERELL, and his two sons, William and John COTTERELL who were passengers on the same ship from England.

Died at Wheeling, VA, Monday, 17th instant, after a tedious illness, of a pulmonary affection, John A. SHELDMERDINE, of this co., in his 24th year.

Ice Creams - Mrs. WRIGHT, near Mr. TALBOTT'S tavern.

Philip CULLER, two miles of New Town, Trap, offers reward for Negro woman, named SALLY, upwards of 30 years of age, 5 feet, 3 inches; speaks a little German, seen Friday last near Robert G. M'PHERSON's farm.

Samuel BAUGHER offers reward for steers which strayed from his plantation, Monocacy manor, near Nimrod OWINGS', 5 miles from Frederick-town.

28. 2 June 1819

Republican Meeting - Recommended as delegates of Maryland: Thomas HAWKINS, William E. WILLIAMS, Plummer IIAMS, John NELSON.

Married 20th instant, by Rev. William CLINGAN, William DISON to Miss Ann DARNALD, both of Montgomery Co.

Married on Thursday, 20th inst., Peter HARDT, Editor of the *York Recorder*, to Miss Catharine SIDES, of Hanover, PA.

Married Thursday evening last, by Rev. J. HELFENSTEIN, Christopher MYERS, to Miss Margaret BROWN, all of this place.

Died on Wednesday night last, George William MURDOCH, Esq., only son of the late George MURDOCH, dec'd., in his 32d year, leaving a wife, two infant children, mother and sisters to survive him.

Sale of tract in upper part of Middle-town Valley, called Toms Safeguard, lately belonging to John TOMS, 280 acres. Richard POTTS, trustee.

The Presbyterian Church Lottery will conclude drawing this evening. S. BARNES.

Chancery sale ratified - Henry FAHNESTOCK and George FLECK vs. Michael BLESSINGER, trustee Cath. HENNING.

Equity case: Samuel JOHNSON vs. Daniel FUNDENBURG, Horatio HOBBS, John STEWARD and John PITTINGER. The case states that Daniel FUNDENBURG, one of the defendants, being the holder of a single bill, drawn in his favour by Joseph HUGHES, of Frederick Co. for $72 assigned the same to complainant who assigned and guaranteed its payment to Horatio HOBBS, John STEWARD and John PITTINGER. under the firm of Horatio HOBBS and Co. Daniel FUNDENBURG does not reside within the state of Maryland.

Carding machinery of DUSTIN & SANBURN is now in operation at the mill near David KEMP's. Leave wool at George GEBHART'S tavern, 1 mile of Noland's Ferry.

Chancery sale of real estate of Christian HOOVER, dec'd., 184 1/2 acres on Owen's creek, 1 1/2 miles from Graceham; also Graceham Mills. Daniel HOOVER, trustee.

29. 9 June 1819

Married Thursday, 27th ult. at Lancaster, PA, Walter KEMP, son of Christian KEMP, of this co., to Miss Catharine GLONINGER, dau of Philip GLONINGER, Esq. of the former place.

Married Thursday last by Rev. David MARTIN, John LANE, of Baltimore Co., to Mrs. Barbara FOUT, of Frederick Co.

Died yesterday afternoon, George William HOFFMAN, son of John HOFFMAN, Esq., aged about 25 years. His funeral from the residence of his brother, Patrick St.

Barth ZAPELONE has arrived and taken the store room of Mr. Isaac MANTZ in Patrick St. where he offers for sale collection of pictures, copperplate engravings, scripture and fancy pieces, from the best European authors, day and night telescopes, spy and opera glasses, barometers, thermometers, and other.

Sheriff's sale of house and lot of John KURTZ in Union Town, at this time occupied by Charles HERSTONS, taken at the suits of George WINTER and Jacob LANDES, admr. of John WINTER, dec'd., Nathan ZIMMERMAN, John YOTER and Patrick DINSMORE.

Doctor L. J. SMITH has taken an office near Buckeys' town, Rocky Fountain.

Chancery sale made by Richard ROBERTS, trustee for the sale of the real estate of William GIBSON, dec'd.

Lydia JOHNSON, Clarksburg, offers reward for Negro man, George THOMPSON, about 5 feet, 10-11 inches high, 23 years of age.

Robert N. MARTIN, Attorney at Law, Market St.

Wood-land for sale near the saw mill of Jacob HOLTZ on Fishing Creek. B. S. PIGMAN.

George WILLARD and Daniel WILLARD, extrs. of Elias WILLARD.

30. 16 June 1819

Married Thursday, 3d instant, by Rev. Jonathan HELFENSTEIN, Henry MILLER of Washington Co., to Miss Eve STIFER, dau of John STIFER, of Frederick Co.

Married Thursday last, by the same, John STALEY, to Miss Elizabeth MOTTER, dau of Henry MOTTER, Esq. of Frederick Co.

Died Friday, 4th inst. in his 66th year, Jacob ROHR, sen. of this place.

Died on Tuesday, 8th instant, in his 12th year, Peter, eldest son of Elias BRUNER, when a loaded waggon turned over on him. *Herald*
Peter STORM has taken up a stray horse.
John HOFFMAN admr. of George Wm. HOFFMAN.

31. 23 June 1819
Died yesterday morning in the vicinity of this town, Madame DE LA VINCENDIERE, in her 65th year, after a painful and lingering illness.
Death of George STILES, our late Mayor (Baltimore), in his 59th year, after a painful and lingering illness. *American*.
Sale of the real estate of Jacob DELAUTER, dec'd., grist and saw mill, in northern part of Middle Town, 51 1/2 acres. B. S. PIGMAN, trustee.
James KARNEY continues to manufacture at Fishing Creek Factory, merino and other wool. Deliver wool or cloths to NORRIS & GAITHER's store, Patrick St., or David BOYD's, blue dyer, 2nd St.
Sale of furniture and books of the late G. W. MURDOCH, dec'd.
Sale of personal property of Andrew HEIM, dec'd.. Andrew HEIM, John J. M'CULLEY, extrs.
Jacob RHODES, Middletown, offers reward for apprentice to tayloring business, George SMITH, about 5 feet, 7 inches high, slim made, darkish hair, walks crooked.
Richard CLARK has taken up a stray mare.
Boarding a few young men - Eli P. BENTLEY.

32. 30 June 1819
House and lot for sale which they at present occupy. Louis B. OPELO, Mary OPELO.
John MAGILL, recently arrived in this city, offers several publications.
The Sunday School Society to meet by appointment at the Episcopal Church. Rebeckah BYERLY, sec'ry.

33. 7 July 1819
Murder in St. Inigoes, MD, of Stephen MILBURN of St. George's. His nephew, Wm. MILBURN, is suspected. James MILBURN, brother of William, has been arrested in connection with the murder. *Pat.*
Died Thursday last, Levin WINDER, Esq., late Governor of Maryland.
Sale at his store room, nearly opposite the Hagers Town Bank, all the jewelry belong to the personal estate of C. L. D. GUNDERMAR, late of Hagers Town, dec'd. John P. HERR, admr.
All Saints Church, being vacant by the resignation of Rev. HATCH, the vestry have appointed 1 Sep next for the election of Rector.

34. 14 July 1819
Died Friday evening last, after a lingering illness, Mrs. Lydia BROOKE, consort of Richard BROOKE, Esq., dec'd., interred in the Roman Catholic burying ground.

Died yesterday morning, Leonard STORM, an aged and respectable inhabitant of this town.

Died near the Navy Yard, Washington, on 6th instant, after a painful and lingering illness, Mrs. Elizabeth HARRISON, wife of Dr. John HARRISON and dau of John HOFFMAN, Esq. of this co., leaving husband and children.

35. 21 July 1819

Audit of an account current between the estate of Catherine HENNING, and her trustee.

Whereas by the last will of Catherine BAYER, dec'd., a legacy was bequeathed to her grand dau, Susanna RIGGS, also a distributive share of her estate to her grand children, Maria GATES, George RIGGS, Elizabeth JENKINS, Susanna RIGGS, John RIGGS and William RIGGS, this is to notify said legatees that the money due them is ready and will be paid. John MARKELL, admr. with the will annexed, of Catherine BAYER.

John WENRICK, living within about 5 miles of Frederick Town, offers reward for apprentice to the shoemaking business, named Michael DEVILBISS, 20 years of age on 27 July, about 5 feet, 8 inches, dark complexion; had on him and took with him, pair of nankeen pantaloons, velvet pantaloons, two waistcoats, one marseilles white, the other figured, long close bodied blue cloth coat, a fine hat and an old French watch.

Joseph HEISLER and John V. CROSS, insolvent debtors, discharged from jail, seek relief from debt.

Examination at Frederick Academy. Robert ELLIOTT.

Sale of horses and cattle at the residence of the widow Elizabeth SMITH, Carrol's Manor. Leonard SMITH, Henry JENKINS.

36. 28 July 1819

Died at Abbott's Town, Wednesday, 14th inst., in his 90th year, Lewis ROSENMILLER, Sen., maternal grandfather of Rev. SCHAEFFER of this place. *Herald*.

Auction at the residence of Rev. HATCH, in Patrick St., of furniture.

Jesse LEATHERWOOD and Richard F. SHECKLES, seek relief from debts; both released from jail.

Jacob GETZENDANNER, extr. of Leonard STORM, to sell furniture and other personal estate of dec'd. in Bentz Town.

Solomon STICKLE informs shoemakers that he has commenced the Last Making in 2nd St., opposite Henry BANTZ's store.

37. 4 August 1819

Married at Baltimore, on Tuesday evening, by Rev. HARGROVE, Dr. Godfrey WEISE, of Frederick-town, to Mrs. Susanna Louisa WEISE, of that city.

Died in Washington, Friday morning last, after a long and painful illness, Dr. James H. BLAKE, in his 52d year, native of this state.

Died 4th ult. near Geneva, Ontario Co., N. York, Capt. George DERR, formerly a resident of Frederick Co., after a painful illness of two years.

Died on 7th ult. at the same place, Henry LAMBRECHT, late of this town, after an illness of 8 days with the quinsy.

George BAER forewarns persons from stealing from his garden of watermelons, cantaloupes, cucumbers and other vegetables.

Philip PYFER, Jr. has removed from his late stand, Market St., and has taken the house recently occupied by Joseph LARKIN - Boots and Shoes, Hats.

Lancaster and German School of Liberty-town will have a large and commodious room ready for the reception of scholars around 1 Sep. Thos. SAPPINGTON, Sec'ry to the board of trustees.

Christian SMITH of Woodsboro' has taken up a stray gelding. Certified by J.P. Eli TOWNE.

Thomas NEWENS, Frederick Town, offers reward for James BALLARD, apprentice to the chair making and house painting trades, age about 20 years, 5 feet, 4-5 inches, fair complexion, dark hair, grey eyes, stoop shouldered, down look.

John NELSON withdraws from election.

38. 11 Aug 1819
Samuel BARNES recommended to the General Assembly in the place of John NELSON, by the Republican General Committee.

Board of Directors of the Frederick Town Branch Bank for the ensuing year: John TYLER, President, John M'PHERSON, Wm. E. WILLIAMS, Casper MANTZ, William ROSS, Joseph SMITH, Richard POTTS, John BRIEN and Henry KEMP - Thomas SHAW, Cashier.

Married in this city on Sunday morning last by Rev. ARMSTRONG, Henry BROOKS, of Loudoun Co., VA, to Miss Mary LEAPLEY, of the same place.

Died in Baltimore on Monday evening, 2d inst. after a lingering illness, Thomas WOOD, leaving widow and several children

Died at his brother's residence in Baltimore on Thursday morning, after a few days illness, age the age of 19 years, George Washington SWIFT, son of Jonathan SWIFT, Esq. of Alexandria.

Public sale at the dwelling of Arthur SHAAFF, dec'd., household and kitchen furniture. Mary SHAAFF, Wm. MARBURY, R. B. TANEY, extrs. of Jno. T. SHAAF.

The commissioners appointed by the law for incorporating a water company in the town of Emmitsburg, will open a subscription book for the sale of stock at the house of Henry WATERS in Emmitsburg. Daniel W. MOORE, Sec'ry.

J. SCHREINER & HALLER have commenced a weaving business at the upper end of Patrick St. a few doors above Mr. Mayberry's Hotel.

Sale of household and kitchen furniture at Bentz-town. Hugh GREFFIN.

Lots of the late William RITCHIE, Esq., are still for sale. Apply to R. RITCHIE, E. MANTZ, or to Wm. RITCHIE.

39. 18 Aug 1819
Died in Baltimore, on Sunday morning last of an apoplexy, the Rev. Dr. James INGLIS, Pastor of the First Presbyterian Church in that city.

Died on the same day, Peter WIRGMAN, Esq., after an illness of 14 days.
Chancery sale of land of Samuel GAVER, dec'd., 7 acres, between New Town, Trap, and Sharpsburg. John NELSON, trustee.
John RIGNEY, saddler, has removed his shop from Market to Patrick St.
Wm. R. CHUNN, Lower Catoctin, about to remove from Frederick Co., wishes persons having claims against him to call on him for settlement. You may meet with him at Jacob MARTIN's tavern in New Town, Trap, on 11 Sep next.
Chancery sale at the house of Henry BOTELER, in New Town, Trap, of land of Andrew YOUNG, dec'd, 50 1/8 acres, 1 mile from New Town, Trap. It will be shewn by Christian REMSBURG.

40. 25 Aug 1819

Persons indebted to the estate of Leonard STORM may call at Jacob BRUNER & Son's store. Jacob GETZENDANNER, extr.
Sale of horses, cows & sheep, furniture - Wm. BALLINGER.
Sheriff's sale of the estate of Daniel COVER, two lots of land adjoining Union Town, taken at the suit of William GRIMES, jr.
Sheriff's sale of estate of Thomas HARRIS and Thomas LIVERS, a lot near Union Town, taken at the suit of William GRIMES, jr.
Races will be run near Emmitsburg. Jacob BOHN, Henry McHENRY.
Jacob BAYER cautions persons against trespassing on his lot in Fredericktown.
Teacher wanted by undersigned gentlemen, residing on the lower end of Carroll's Manor. Thomas C. SCOTT, Clement T. HILLEARY, Joseph HERBERT, Ignatius JAMISON.
Sale at Rocky Fountain, of horses, hogs, sheep, milch cows, waggon, sleigh and gig. John JAMISON.

41. 1 Sep 1819

Died Thursday morning, after a short but severe illness, William BAER, in his 60th year. *Star.*
B. S. PIGMAN, Attorney at Law, has opened his office in the house of Mr. DILL, next door to his tavern.
Four black boys for sale. Jesse CLOUD, Bruceville.
Sale of real estate of Richard BROOKE, dec'd., furniture, law books, other personal property - at Middleburg, Frederick Co. John Thompson BROOKE, admr.
Sale of Negroes, property of Henry STRAUSE, dec'd., two miles from Montgomery Court House. Christiana STRAUSE and Matthew MURRAY, extrs. Also Tavern stand in Hager's Town.
Journeyman blacksmith wanted. George WISINGER, 1 1/4 miles from New Town, Trap.
Jacob LEATHERMAN, admr. of Daniel SWIGART.
Geo. TROXELL, New Market, offers reward for apprentice to the hatting business, names John MARTIN, about 19 years of age, 5 feet, 8-9 inches.

42. 8 Sep 1819
Married Thursday evening last, by Rev. P. DAVIDSON, Basil NORRIS, merchant of this town, to Miss Elizabeth CHARLTON, of this co.
Died suddenly on Monday evening, in his 49th year, James CALHOUN, Esq., son of James CALHOUN; previously appeared to be in excellent health, as he was walking homewards was observed to fall suddenly on the pavement where he expired. Served as Brigade Major of the Baltimore troops. *Balt. Pat.*
William LUCKETT offers reward for Negro man named DEMBO, 26 years of age, 6 feet high.
Chancery case: George DUDDERIR and Mary his wife, vs. Peter ERB, admr. of Peter SHUTS, and others.
Mills, houses, lands, tavern stand and distillery for sale by decree of high court of chancery, at the tavern now occupied by George UMBAUGH, Harper's Ferry; property of John ECARD, dec'd. of Frederick Co. Property will be shewn by Jonah BUFFINGTON.
Equity case: Sebastian RAMSBURG vs. Andrew YOUNG's heirs.
Equity case: John FINK and others vs. Mary GAVER and others.

43. 15 Sep 1819
Joseph SWEARINGEN and Robison EASTBURN, appointed commissioners to open a road to begin at or near William M'FARLAND's factory on the road leading from Frederick Town to HUGHES's Coaling ground in Washington Co. to Middletown to intersect the turnpike between the buildings of Adam HERRING and Aaron SUMAN in said town, running from the aforesaid William M'FARLAND'S factory through part of his land to Peter SCHLOSSER's land and through his land to the widow CRAFT's land and to her merchant mill, still through her land, to intersect the old bed of the said mill road, between Adam ROUTZANG'S and Samuel BRANDENBURG's plantation ...
William PERRY has taken and fitted up the large and commodious 3-story brick house in Patrick St., formerly occupied as a store by Mr. LEVY and opened a House of Accommodation.
Sale of farm adjoining Middle Town, late the property of Leonard STORM, dec'd., called the Resurvey of Turkey Range, 180 acres. Land will be shewn by Philip WISE. John D. GROVE, John L. LEVY, trustees.
Statement by Richard HOGGINS, relating to an incident involving Robert DEAN owner of a tavern.
Benjn. HERSH offers for rent a brick dwelling house and 50 acres of land at the Monocacy Bridge known as Gombirg Ferry.
J. KEMP has commenced the fulling, dying and dressing of cloth at his Factory, 3 miles north of Frederick-town. Cloth for fulling, dying and dressing will be received at Jacob SHRIVER's store, Frederick-town and Daniel CREAGER's near Mr. WINEBRENNER's mill.

44. 22 Sep 1819
Editor (Samuel BARNES) states he was born in Queen Anne's Co., MD where his father and grandfather were born and raised.

Peter RHODES, near New Town, Trap, offers reward for stray mare.

Barton PHILPOTT offers to rent 200 and 300 acres of land where he now lives, and also to sell 20 Negroes.

W. H. GUNNEL, near the Great Falls of Potomac, Fairfax Co. VA, offers reward for yellow man who calls himself William LEE; has a wife, property of J. H. CASSADAY, near Waterford. He has gone off with a black man of Thomas SWANN, Esq., from his farm near Leesburg.

Wm. LONG, Saml. OGLE, John McKALEB, appointed commissioners to open a road from the point on the public road near which a gate has been put up a David HOFFMAN to run upon the bed of the road recently shut up to Dr. ANNAN's Mill and thence to intersect the public road from Hagers-town to Emmitsburg.

45. 29 Sep 1819

That the editor, Samuel BARNES, when he lived in Baltimore, had nothing to do with the mobs in Baltimore in 1812: Thomas MURPHY, Edward PRIESTLEY, John WILSON, John & Thos. VANCE. Further confirmation by: Edward MULLIKIN of Baltimore who was an apprentice with Messrs. IRVINE & BARNES, Sam'l. SANDS who resided with Samuel BARNES, and Thomas ROGERS.

Conrad SHERMAN, Manheim Township, York Co., PA, 6 miles from Hanover, offers reward for indented German boy, Frederick TROGLER, born in Schorndoff, in the kingdom of Wertemberg, arrived last winter in Baltimore. He left his country in the spring of 1817 and suffered shipwreck on the coast of Norwegia. He is about 18 years old, 5 feet high, dark brown hair, much addicted to swearing.

46. 6 Oct 1819

Dissolution of partnership of Basil NORRIS and Stuart GAITHER. Stuart GAITHER continues the business at the old stand.

Sale of 155 acres, 1 mile from Middle Town, adjoining lands of John BOWLUS, Henry SCHLUSSER, Philip DERR and Nicholas HOUCK. It will be shown by Samuel BUZZARD who lives on the premises or Aaron SUMAN who lives near Middle Town.

Fulling, dying and dressing of blankets, clothers and flannels, done at Christian COST's new fulling mill, 1 mile of New-town, Trap. Cloths may be left at Mr. NICHOLL's store, Carroll's Manor; Messrs. O'NEAL & Co. store, Middle town; Mr. WARFIELD's store, New Town, Trap; Mr. McGILL's store, Petersville; and at Mr. LATE's mill.

47. 13 Oct 1819

"I certify, that about the tie of the declaration of war, being then employed in building Doctor Belt BRASHAER's house, the report of cannon discharged in Frederick was heard in New-Market. Enquiry was made by Dr. BRASHAER ... he replied "if war is declared, I will give my vote for every democrat to be hung." Richard CLARK.

William McFARLAND has commenced fulling and dying at his factory on the new road from Frederick town to Green Castle. Cloth will be received at John

GETZENDANNER's, widow's SMITH's tavern, James SHAWEN's tavern in Washington co., and Mr. HARLEY's store.

Twill'd bags for sale. Benjn. WINTER.

Sheriff's sale at John DILL's tavern in Frederick-town of land of Jacob ZUCK, at the suit of Henry BUSSARD and Nathaniel HYLAND, use of John and William LAWE. Benj. HAGAN for Wm. M. BEALL, sheriff.

Sheriff's sale of estate of Greenbury KNOUFF, house and lot in Market St., being the same lot conveyed to his father, Jacob KNOUFF by John PHILLIPS, taken at the suit of Frederick OTT, surviving partner of George SMITH.

Thomas BURROWS & Co. have commenced the book-binding business. Orders to be left with James F. HOUSTON, postmaster.

Wants to hire a Negro woman. Rev. Wm. WESTERMAN, Rector of St. Mark's, Merryland Tract.

The copartnership heretofore existing under the firm of THOMAS, EMMITT & Co. is dissolved. The business will hereafter be conducted under the firm of EMMIT & PORTER who will settle all claims against the said firm of THOMAS, EMMIT & Co. John THOMAS, William C. EMMIT, John N. PORTER, Valentine THOMAS. Murfressboro', Tennessee. Dec 26, 1818.

E. DILL and A. JACOBS offer reward for apprentice to the house carpenter business named James DAY, about 19 years of age, 5 feet, 5-6 inches high.

48. 20 Oct 1819

Jacob WEIST, Frederick town, offers reward for two stray steers.

Peter SCHLOSSER admr. of Henry SCHLOSSER.

Oliver CALAME, clock and watch maker continues the business on Market St.

Sheriff's sale of estate of Michel KOLB, one moiety of lot with buildings in Frederick town, at the suits of Christian EASTERDAY and Christian SCHOLL, use of Frederick BAKER.

Sheriff's sale of Negro woman, waggons, 10 draft horses, other, of Willoughby MAYBERRY, and Catoctin Furnace - taken at the suits of Thomas DRAPER, use of Nicholas HOLTS, Samuel DOUGLASS, Charles BALTZELL, Michael HEFFNER, William E. WILLIAMS, William MULLEN, use of Cornelius McANULTY, Samuel GRIMES, use of Jacob PLAINE and Samuel JOHNSON, use of Cornelius McANULTY.

Hugh McMULLAN to open a school in 2nd St.

The will of William HOUSE of Frederick Co. is published here. Mentions housekeeper, Delilah TURNER, granddaus, children of dau Leah who married James PHILLIPS and named Mely, Maria and Rachael. Mely who married one COVENTRY is now living in State of Ohio. Maria married one GREEN now living in Ohio. Rachael married to William TUCKER and lives in Virginia. Mentions five grandchildren, children of son Daniel HOUSE who is now dead; these children are by Daniel's second wife: Nelson HOUSE, Anna HOUSE, Sarah HOUSE, Rebeckah HOUSE and Marandah HOUSE. Oldest son, George HOUSE of Frederick Co., 100 acres. To son Caleb HOUSE, 100 acres. Mentions dau Mary HARVEY relict of David HARVEY, late of Zanesville, OH and dau Elizabeth WILES wife of Thomas WILES. Whereas Christian NUSEWANGER of Loudoun married dau Ruth... Mentions dau Sarah who married Thomas HARRISON and some years ago moved to Kentucky where

"I am told she has lately died." Extrs.: John S. FRAZIER and Thomas MARLOW. Witnesses: John SHAFER, William JACOBS, James FRAZIER, Jacob COLEMAN. Henry STEINER, Reg'r.

Wm. BROWN & Co. are prepared to receive at Fleecy Dale Woollen Factory, merino or country wool.

49. 27 Oct 1819

Died yesterday morning, Thomas JOHNSON, Esq., the first governor of Maryland, aged 88 years.

William M. BEALL, Jr. offers reward for stolen horse.

Dissolution of partnership under the firm of HUGHES and BIGHAM. Persons indebted to it or the former firm of SMITH and BIGHAM are requested to settle their accounts. Those indebted to James HUGHES are particularly requested to settle theirs on or before Dec next. Charles W. BIGHAM, acting for both firms. Emmittsburg.

Sale at late residence of Theodore MITCHELL, late of Frederick Co., dec'd, 11 slaves, horses, cattle, sheep, hogs, furniture. Patrick McGILL, admr.

John RIGNY, candidate for sheriff.

James A. MITCHELL, 3 miles from Newville, Cumberland Co., PA, offers reward for stolen horse.

Brick house for rent on Patrick St. Michael HAUSER.

Proposals will be received for supplying the troops with rations at this post. Peter WILSON, Lieut., Corps of Artillery Com. Rendezvous.

50. 3 Nov 1819

Died yesterday morning between one and two o'clock, Miss Rebecca KOLB, dau of George KOLB, Esq. of this place, in her 19th year, after a painful illness of 4 weeks.

Married last evening, by Rev. SCHAEFFER, Mr. G. M. CONRADT, jun. to Miss Margaret FESSLER.

S. GAITHER, at old stand of NORRIS & GAITHER, has received an additional supply of Goods.

The Frederick-town, Georgetown and Washington Post Coach will commence running on 4 Nov. James E. JONES, agent for the proprietor, Middlebrook Mill.

Domestic Store. G. M. & T. CONRADT, at the turn of Patrick St., Fredericktown.

Meeting of stockholders of Union Bank of Maryland. Henry PAYSON, President.

Sale pursuant to the will of Thomas O. WILLIAMS, late of Prince George's Co., 1200 acres in Montgomery Co., 2 miles from Seneca mills and adjoining lands of Thomas PETER and Mr. SCHNEBLY. William B. WILLIAMS, extr.

Close stoves - HAUER & MANTZ.

51. 10 Nov 1819

Lewis BIRELY and Peter MARTIN, candidates for sheriff.

Hugh HUGHES cautions that his wife Elizabeth has left his bed and board and he will not pay her debts.

J. A. RETZER, Professor of French and German languages (lately from Europe) will give lessons at the Frederick Academy.

Vachel HAMMOND of O., 5 miles from Frederick-town, offers reward for stolen mares.

William CAMPBELL forewarns persons from purchasing anything from his Negroes, except old CHARLES, his manager, commonly called Charles BOWEN.

52. 17 Nov 1819

Married Tuesday, 26th ult., by Rev. BUCHANAN, Lewis A. BEATTY, of this co., to Miss Sarah B. MARSHALL, of Franklin Co., PA

Married Sunday evening last by Rev. P. DAVIDSON, Vachel HAMMOND to Mrs. Priscilla HAFF, both of this co.

Married Tuesday morning, 9th inst. at Needwood, in Frederick Co., Thomas Sim LEE, Esq., in his 75th year, second governor of Maryland; interred in family burial ground in Prince George's Co.

Reward for three Negro men who broke jail: Freeborn GARRETSON, 5 feet, 8 inches high, 24 years of age, blind of the left eye; Joseph M'CORMICK, 25 years of age; ROBERT, a mulatto, about 25 years of age, formerly the property of William PERRY and now the property of Justinian MAYBERRY.

John HAMILTON, Frederick Co., VA, offers reward for Negro boy named COLEMAN, 18-20 years of age.

Abednego BAKER, living near Cook's mill, Bennett's creek, offers reward for lost pocket book.

Richard POTTS will sell house where he now lives in Market St. Apply at his office near the court house.

Reward for Joseph FRANCIS, aged about 11 years, apprentice to the printing business who ran away from this newspaper office.

David HINES, George W. GIST, John RIGNEY, Lewis BIRELEY, Peter MARTIN and Peter BRENGLE, candidates for sheriff.

53. 24 Nov 1819

Died at his residence in Northumberland Co. Tuesday last, of typhus fever, Simon SNYDER, Esq., late Governor of PA.

Sheriff's sale at the house of Jonathan WOOD, of 9 Negroes, late the property of Jonathan WOOD, taken at the suit of Abdiel UNKEFER.

Sheriff's sale at the house of Dr. John W. DORSEY, of Liberty Town, black girl named HENNY, piano forte, mare, desk and book case, tables and two looking glasses, late the property of Doctor John W. DORSEY, taken at the suit of James SMITH.

Joseph TALBOTT, has repaired and furnished his Washington Hotel and continues to run his elegant hack and horses for his customers.

Sheriff's sale of moiety of a lot with buildings, of Michael KOLB, taken at the suits of Christian EASTERDAY and Christian SCHOLL, use of Frederick BAKER.

Sheriff's sale of lots of Daniel COVER, adjoining Union Town, 33 1/2 acres, taken at the suit of William GRIMES, jr.

54. 8 Dec 1819
Died 28th ult. at the residence of Beal RANDALL, near Baltimore, Nicholas RANDALL, of Frederick Co., in his 61st year. *Herald.*

55. 15 Dec 1819
Died Wednesday last in his 75th year, John HOUC, sen., long a respectable inhabitant of this co.

Sheriff's sale at the house of John STIERS, Middletown, estate of Philip CLONINGER, tract called Handsome Wife, 10 1/2 acres, taken at the suit of Nicholas HOUPT.

Reward for following deserters: John MILLIGAN, private, 2nd Battalion, U.S. Artillery, born in PA, aged 25, 5 feet, 8 inches, fair complexion, blue eyes, light hair, previously tailor and farmer; Joshua BARTON, same battalion, born in Baltimore Co. aged 24 years, 5 feet, 6 inches, fair complexion, blue eyes, sandy hair, previously a chair maker; Joseph POTTS of the same battalion, born in Dauphin co., PA, aged 25 years, 5 feet, 7 inches, fair complexion, brown eyes, brown hair, previously a potter. Peter WILSON, Lieut., Corps of U.S. Artillery, commanding rendezvous at Frederick-town.

Michael NULL, extr. of Michael NULL.

Semi-annual examination of the Academy. Robert ELLIOTT.

Dissolution of copartnership existing under the firm of H. G. O'NEALL & Co. Levi CAIN will collect debts. H. G. O'NEAL, F. RICHMOND, J. REMSBURGH, Middle-town.

John FREEMAN, Culpepper, to sell his farm, Independence, 400 acres on Mill Run, between Warrenton and Fairfax, with saw and grist mill.

Equity case: Joseph S. NELSON vs. Robert HOOD, John SHARER and others. John SHARER lives out of the state of Maryland.

Isaac LYON, insolvent debtor, discharged from jail, seeks relief from debts.

Sheriff's sale of Negro man named ISAAC of John COOK and 56 acres, part of Addition to Grimmitt's Prospect on Bennett's Creek, set apart to the said John COOK in severalty, by a deed of partition made between Ann BRASHAER, Thomas COOK and John COOK. Taken at the suits of Joseph JOHNSON, Andrew AGNEW, John BAER and Samuel BAILY, Thomas TEUSY use Francis MANTZ and Richard ROBERTS and John TALBOTT, extrs. Evan PLUMMER.

56. 22 Dec 1819
Jacob GROVE, sen. will sell 36 town lots adjoining Middle-town. David BOWLUS has been authorized to sell same.

Chancery sale of real estate of Henry BLACK, dec'd., tract, The Mansion Place, 105 acres on west bank of Tom's Creek, adjoining lands of Casper WELTY, John PICKING and others. Also 32 acres of woodland on South Mountain; John BLACK will show, living at the first described tract. Geo. M. EICHELBERGER, trustee.

John FIREY, Sen'r., 3 miles from Hagers Town, offers reward for Negro ABRAHAM, age about 36, and his wife, ESTHER, about 30. He generally calls himself Abraham BAILY.

57. 29 Dec 1819

Married Tuesday evening, 14th inst. by Rev. PHINNEY, David SCHLEY of this town, to Miss Anna Mary, dau of Peter HOKE, of Hartford Co.
Negro HARRY, property of William ROSS, has taken up a stray gelding.
Geo. HARDMAN, on Monocacy, 2 miles from Woodsborough, has taken up a stray steer.
Brick house in Liberty for rent, formerly the property of Abraham CRAPSTER, dec'd. Apply to John JONES, Linganore or John CRAPSTER, Taney town.

STAR OF FEDERALISM

58. 5 April 1817

Otho SPRIGG answers letter from R. B. TANEY published in the *Herald*.
New mill in operation, 2 1/2 miles from Pipe Creek. Jos. W. OWINGS, Baltimore Co.
James WHITE, Montgomery Co., offers reward for mulatto man, WILLIAM, about 22 years old; and mulatto man, HARRY. They have brothers living in Washington Co., one near Hager's Town, property of Mr. PETRE.
Sale of plantation, 60 acres, in Baltimore Co. John SCHRIVER.
The horse, Red Bird, will stand to cover mares at Michael SMELSER'S mill on Little Pipe Creek, and other locations (indicated). Upton NORRIS.
Matthias F. ERNST will sell a farm near Sam's Creek, 1 mile from Alexander WARFIELD Mills, 24 acres.
Mulatto man who calls himself JOHN, committed to gaol of Frederick Co. as a runaway; says he belongs to George JOHNSON of St. Mary's Co., about 20 years of age.
Sheriff's sale at the residence of Norman WEST, Negro man, late property of West, taken at the suit of Thos. P. WILLSON, and at the suit of Ann Maria LINSTEAD, admx. of Thos. LINSTEAD. Arnold T. WINSOR, sheriff, Montgomery Co.
Sheriff's sale in Montgomery Co. at residence of Zachariah DAWDEN, tract called part of the Pines, 70 acres, another tract of 1 acres, Part of the resurvey on Brandy Hall - taken at the suit of Martia B. DAWDEN by her next friend Christian T. HEMPTON.
Constable's sale of Negro man at residence of Norman WEST, taken by distress for tenement - rent due Joseph CLAGGETT. William BOSWELL, Constable.
Washington and scouring - Hezekiah TAYLOR.
New Cash Store - at Barnesville, William DOUGHERTY.
Silas HIBBERD, about to decline business, requests settlement of accounts.

Subscribers to St. Lucas Reformed Church at Union Town are requested to pay their subscriptions. By order of the Building Committee, Jacob APPLER, Sen, treasurer.

Henry THOMAS has opened an assortment of goods at the sign of the Golden Plough.

Joseph M. PALMER, Attorney at Law, has rented the office lately occupied by B. S. PIGMAN.

Luther MARTIN, Attorney at law. Apply at the office of John A. T. KILGOUR.

59. 5 Apr 1817

Nathan ZIMMERMAN, admr. of John STEM.

Chancery case in Montgomery Co., part of addition to Brookgrove, part of Fairhill or the resurvey on Brook Park and part of Brook Piney Grove, late the property of John HOUSE, dec'd., 391 acres. Also the sale right of John HOUSE to 1/2 of a tract of land called Rays Adventure, 95 acres. Edward HOUSE.

Joshua METCALF had taken Factory formerly carried on by Silas HIBBERD, near New Windsor.

Persons having books belonging to the library of J. H. THOMAS, dec'd, are requested to deliver them to John A. T. KILGOUR.

Journeymen taylors wanted - Jacob GLEIM, Uniontown.

Andrew HULL and Peter HULL admrs. of Andrew HULL.

Mordecai L. HAMMOND has established a chair factory, in Patrick St., near the Bridge.

Jacob ANGEL will sell farm, 55 acres, a tan yard, on road from Liberty to Baltimore.

Sale of 115 acres adjoining lands of Isaac ALLEN(?) and Jacob APPLER. Mary SENSENEY.

Sale of 500 acres whereon he lives at $60 per acre; also 5217 3/4 acres, in Hampshire Co., VA. John SCOTT.

Sale at the late residence of William WATERS, dec'd, in Montgomery Co., 4 miles south of Clarksburgh, several Negroes, horses, cattle, furniture. Nathaniel WATERS, Horace WATERS.

Jacob JANNEY, Occoquan, 16 miles from Alexandria, to sell a tanyard.

George WINTER and Jacob LANDES, admrs. of John WINTER.

House and lot for sale in Uniontown, part of which is occupied by Wm. HODGKISS, as a store. John KURTZ.

Groceries: HARRIS & LIVERS, Queensware, hardware and Japanned ware.

Lot for sale in Uniontown, adjoining lots of Abm. CLEMMENS and Nathan STEM. Apply to John HYDER, Postmaster, Uniontown or subscriber, Charles SOWER.

60. 19 Apr 1817

Negroes for sale. Gerrard H. SNOWDEN, Anne Arundel Co.

Three tracts for sale in St. Mary's Co, 5 miles from Leonard Town. Joseph MILLS.
Sale of 60 acres in Baltimore Co. John SHRIVER.
Daniel HARTSOCK offers for sale a tract of 320 acres in Little Pipe Creek settlement, 1 mile from Friend's meeting house. Apply to Abraham CLEMMENS opposite the Post Office at Union Town.
The horse, Eclipse Herrod will stand this season. Nicholas LEMON.
George GAITHER, Montgomery Co., near Triadelphia Factory, offers reward for Negro man, named BEN, 5 feet, 7-8 inches high.
Sheriff's sale at Andrew GRAFF's in Unity, tract of Zachariah MUSGROVE, called bare garden forrest enlarged, 280 acres.
Black smith shop for rent. Robert DARNALL, Bennet's Creek.
Tavern stand for sale, sign of the Fountain Inn, Market St. Conrad SHAFER.
John MILLER, Sen., and David LEISTER, admrs. of Elizabeth MILLER.

61. 26 April 1817
Died on Wednesday, 9th inst., after a long and painful illness, Mrs. Dorothy TANEY, wife of Joseph TANEY, Esq. of this co. *Herald.*
Died 17th inst., Mrs. Elizabeth HOWARD, consort of Joshua HOWARD, Esq. of Frederick Co., aged 70 years, after a painful illness of 4 weeks.
House and lot for sale near Crabb's mill, Henry STOLTER, living thereon.
Being in the possession of the bonds given by Thomas N. BINNS to the amount of near $9000 which bonds were secured by a mortgage from Binns to Benedict DARNALL, and by Darnall assigned to us. We caution the public against purchasing said land sold by Benedict DARNALL to Binns until the bonds are liquidated. John COOK, Levy PHILIPS.

62. 29 August 1817
Committed to the gaol of Frederick Co. as a runaway, a mulatto man who calls himself, JOHN alias TOM; says he belongs to George ASH, about 9 miles from Winchester, VA.
The partnership of FARQUHAR and GRIFFITH is dissolved. Moses B. FARQUHAR, Philip GRIFFITH, Union Bridge.
Plank for sale - George LEAPLEY, near the mouth of Monocacy.
John ROWLINGTON, having become a sober and attentive man, has opened a shop where he may be found ready to shave and dress hair.
Sale of 225 acres, south of Clarksburgh. Elisha HOWARD.
William RATRIE from George-town, has taken a house in Church St. - House and Sign Painting, Glazing.
Washington Hotel, Frederick-town. Joseph TALBOTT.
Married yesterday by Rev. Curtis WILLIAMS, Jacob CHRIST of Uniontown, in Miss Elizabeth APPLER, dau of Jacob APPLER, all of this co.
On Tuesday last, Abraham CRUMBACKER, respectable inhabitant of this co. was drowned in Little Pipe Creek, near his own dwelling. It is supposed that he slipped from a log which lay across the creek.

63. 29 Aug 1817

Races to run near Uniontown. John GIBBONY and Moses SHAWEN.

Negroes for sale. Leonard SMITH, on Carroll's Manor, near STONEBRAKER's mill.

THOMAS & EMMIT have received an elegant assortment of fresh goods.

Sheriff's sale of house of Horatio HOBBS in town of Unity, 1 acre, taken at the suits of Henry BUSSARD, admr. of Daniel BUSSARD.

Persons indebted to John HARRIS or the subscriber for the *Engine of Liberty*, are requested to make payment to subscriber or Charles SOWER, Editor of the *Star of Federalism*. Wm. HODGKISS, New Market.

A petition will be presented for the laying out and opening a public road from New Windsor by Michael SMELSER'S mill to intersect the Hagers Town turnpike road near John LEISTER's.

Persons indebted to Charles W. PEARRE, New Windsor, will call at Lemuel PEARRE'S store, for settlement.

A teacher wanted - a gentleman that will take charge of 20-25 children near Petersville, on the Merryland Tract; a man with a family would be preferred, well recommended. Levin WEST.

Sale of land on which I lately resided, 3 1/2 miles from Woodsbury on Israels Creek, 15 acres, two story log dwelling house. Thomas COE, joining the property will show it. Joseph LANSTON.

Merino Factory, formerly carried on by Silas HIBBERD, near New Windsor had been taken by Joshua METCALFE.

Dry Goods and Groceries. John L. LEVY.

Persons indebted to Doctor Charles HUBBS are requested to make settlement. Clement HUBBS, Valley Farm, near Uniontown.

100 acres for sell adjoining village of Unity, Montgomery Co., framed dwelling house. Francis SIMPSON.

William SMITHERS has commenced the tayloring business in New Market in the house formerly occupied by Jacob R. THOMAS.

Eagle and Review Tavern, North Market St., Frederick-town. M. E. BARTGIS.

64. 5 Dec 1817

Committed to gaol as a runaway, a black man who calls himself John GREEN, 5 feet, 10 inches, about 35 years of age; says he belongs to a Mr. GARDNER in Kentucky.

Committed to gaol as a runaway, a mulatto man who calls himself Allen KELLY, 5 feet, 8 inches, plays well on the violin; says he is free born; about 24 years of age.

John BURRIER offers reward for horse missing from stable of Solomon MANCHA, near the Monocacy stone Bridge. Deliver to Jacob BURRIER near the Dry Tavern on Liberty road, 3 miles from Liberty.

Edward M. G. WATSON, saddler, has commenced business in New Market, nearly opposite Dr. HOBBS's. Notice: Having sold out to Mr. WATSON, persons are requested to settle their accounts with Wm. S. WAY.

Sale of two horse waggon and two good horses and harness. Philip GRIFFITH, Union Bridge.
Elected to the Westminster, Taney-Town and Emmitsburg Turnpike Company: Jno. MCKALEB, Prest.; Henry SPALDING, Sec'ry & Treasr.; Managers, Robert L. ANNAN, Geo. M. EICHELBERGER, Jno. SHORB, Joseph TANEY, Jacob CLABAUGH, John GRABILL, Patrick LOWE, Wm. PATTERSON(?).
E. H. MAYNARD has taken Wm. HODGKISS into partnership under the firm of Maynard & Co. New Market.
Jonas CRUMBACKER & Isaac HITESHEW admrs. of Abraham CRUMBACKER.
Sale of 320 acres at Camel's Tavern, Montgomery Court House, farm on road leading from mouth of Monocacy to Georgetown, 2 miles from Darnes Town. Charles OFFUTT.
Union Barber Shop - Charles GALEZIO has removed from the Court House square to ? where he intends to shave and dress hair.
Jacob CLABAUGH has lost a silver watch between M.E. BARTGIS'S tavern and Mr. WILLIAMS' Ferry on Monocacy.
Committed to gaol, black boy who calls himself Benjamin TRUSTY, 5 feet, 8 inches high, around 20 years old; says he belongs to Nathan LEVERING, in the city of Baltimore.
Committed to gaol, mulatto man who calls himself WILLIAM, 5 feet, 10 inches high; says he is free, manumitted by Philip LOVE in Reisterstown.

65. 5 Dec 1817
Married Thursday, 20 ult. by Rev. C. WILLIAMS, Philip GRIFFITH, to Miss Sarah STONER, all of this co.
Sale at the residence of Mordecai CLEMSON, dec'd., 3 miles from Liberty Town, two Negro men, horses, cows, hogs, sheep, wheat an rye in the straw, and other. John CLEMSON, jr., admr.
Fountain Inn again opened, for many years occupied by Capt. Conrad SHAFER. Thomas CARLTON.
Sheriff's sale postponed - estate of Philip STRIDER, 150 acres, whereon Philip STRIDER now resides, being part of resurvey on Maryland Tract, taken at the suit of Mary B. HACKNEY and Barton HACKNEY, at the suit of Joel WARD, at the suit of Josiah BUFFINGTON, at the suit of Samuel W. LACKLAND, and at the suit of United States of America. Also 2 stills, 16 still tubs and 1 Negro woman of Philip STRIDER, at the suit of Christian STONEBRAKER. Peter MARTIN, for the sheriff.
Sheriff's sale postponed - property of Doctor John W. DORSEY - house and lot.
Sale of land, 807 acres, farm 5 miles east of Liberty-town; also Negroes, stock and farming utensils. Ely DORSEY of Ely.
Committed to gaol, Negro man who calls himself, JASON; says he belongs to Samuel AGER of Alexandria, VA.
John B. STIMMEL has taken the Swan Tavern on road from Frederick Town to Lancaster, lately occupied by Wm. H. GRIMES.

Henry THOMAS has removed his store to store room lately occupied by Messrs. Michael HAUSER & Sons.

66. 26 June 1818
Sale of farm adjoining Hyatts-town, 470 acres. William HYATT.
Peter TOOLE and Patrick M'QUAID, having learned the cloth manufacturing business in Europe, have rented the Union Factory, 1 1/2 miles from Middletown from Mr. REMSBURG. Cloth and wool will be received at Mr. GRIFFIN'S store opposite Maybury's tavern, Mr. BOERSTLER'S store, New Town (Trap) and at the store of Messrs. ONEAL & Co. in Middletown.
Thomas GILBREATH offers reward for two negro men: JOHN about 35 years old, 6 feet high; WAT about 30 years old. Thomas GILBREATH.
The fees of Tobias BUTLER, late clerk of Frederick Co., payable in 1816, not having been made out in time to go into the hands of the Sheriff, are put into the hands of the different Constables for collection. J.F. HOUSTON, Ad'tor.
Line of Mail Stages, Fredericktown-Winchester-Staunton - S. B. LEATHERWOOD.
Henry BERGER has removed his tinning business next door to Mr. CONRADT'S blue dying and weaving shop and 2 door's west of Jacob LEAB's (butcher), Patrick St.
John GIBBONEY, insolvent debtor, confined in jail, now discharged; applies for relief from debt.

67. 26 June 1818
Jacob F...? admr. of Leonard ZEPP.
Sheriff's sale at the house of Nicholas TURBUTT, Negro woman named AILSEY with male child about 5 years old, Negro woman named CEILY with 2 small children, Negro man named JIM, late the property of Philip STRIDER, taken at the suits of Elizabeth GARROTT, admx. of John P. GARROTT, at the suit of U.S., at the suit of Joel WARD, and at the suit of Charles K. LOVE.
HUGHES & POGUE, Groceries, have removed to the Warehouse lately (and for many years past) occupied by Andrew AGNEW, No. 30 North Howard St., Baltimore.
Married Tuesday, 16th inst. by Rev. MATHIS, John JAMISON, Esq. of Frederick co., to Miss Mary Ann QUEEN of the District of Columbia.
Married at Columbia, PA, on Thursday, 18th inst., Mr. I. EICHOLTZ, celebrated self-taught limner, of Lancaster, to Miss Catherine TRISSLER, of the same place.
Christopher OWINGS, 3 miles from Libertytown, offers reward for black woman named HENNY, about 5 feet, 6-7 inches high, 25 years old.
David ROHR, living near the mouth of Monocacy, offers reward for bound girl, Mary Ann OPPOLOW, 15-16 years of age.
The horse, Young Nebuchadnezzer, for sale. John CRAPSTER, Taney Town.
Isaac ATLEE, Sulphur Springs, offers reward for missing steer.
Peter NICHOLS, taylor.
Dr. Wm. S. M'PHERSON offers his professional services, in the house lately occupied by Col. John M'PHERSON, south Market St.

Harriot BRISH continues to keep well known public house, formerly kept by Henry BRISH, dec'd. on South West corner of Market and 3rd sts.
Wm. P. FARQUHAR admr. of Henry STOUFFER.
John JAMISON admr. of Aquilla LUCAS and admr. de bonis non of Wm. WINNULL.

68. 3 July 1818
Daniel ARTHUR, William M. BEALL, George CREAGER, Upton WAGERS candidates for sheriff.
Mr. ROCHE, from Trinity College, Dublin, to establish in this town a Classical Seminary.
PEARRE & ROHR have dissolved their partnership.
Chancery sale at John CRAPSTER's tavern, of farm whereon Elijah BALDWIN formerly lived, near Taney Town, 198 acres. B. S. PIGMAN, trustee.
Chancery sale of real estate of Mordica B. OFFUTT, dec'd., 4 miles from Rockville, 400-500 acres. John A. T. KILGOUR, trustee.
Abraham JONES, 1 mile from mouth of Monocacy, Montgomery Co., offers reward for stolen colt.
Subscriptions due to Frederick Co. Bible Society. David F. SCHAEFFER, R.S.

Henry SCHOLL, living back of the Roman chapel, Frederick-town, offers reward for stolen horse.
Eli P. BENTLEY, has removed his store to Market St. next door to Judge SHRIVER, where he has opened an assortment of Spring Goods.

69. 10 July 1818
Thomas GIST, Westminster, having declined business, requests settlement of accounts.
William P. BURGESS has taken up a stray gelding.
Geo. GOWENS, insolvent debtor, applies for relief from debt.

70. 17 July 1818
No new items.

71. 24 July 1818
Jacob CHRIST, cabinet maker, has removed from his old stand to centre of Uniontown next door to Peter SENSENY'S store.
William SIMMONS, William WINN, Jacob STICKER, insolvent debtors, confined in jail, seek relief from debt.
William COOKERLY, living between Frederick-town and Liberty, has taken up stray steers.
Dr. H. STALEY offers his services opposite store of George TRISLER.
H. HALE, has just arrived from England with a large assortment of English watches.

72. 31 July 1818

Horace WATERS, near Clarksburg, Montgomery Co., offers reward for Negro man, BASIL, 5 feet, 10-11 inches, 22 years old.

Petition to be presented for opening and straightening a road leading from the house of Christopher NEAT on the Liberty road, by John BURGESS's mill, to intersect the Baltimore and Frederick-town turnpike road.

Plasterers wanted immediately. James HENDERSON, near Taney Town.

Sale of farm on Sams Creek, adjoining land of John STONER, William HAINES and other, 119 acres. Philip CULP.

William COOKERLY has taken up stray steers.

73. 7 Aug 1818

Dr. Jacob BAER, having returned to Frederick, offers his services, residing opposite Francis MANTZ's store, Market St.

Lynchburg, VA. Murder of Major Nathaniel GREENSHAW, shot as he was to leave to visit his plantation, apparently killed by his own Negroes.

Fleecy Dale Woolen Factory, near Buckey's Town. William BROWN, C. MORSE.

Dissolution of partnership of Peter SWINEHART and George GRUMBINE, Union-town.

John CARRINGTON offers reward for Negro SAM, about 5 feet, 8-9 inches, 40-50 years of age.

74. 14 Aug 1818

Dissolution of partnership of Thos. HARRIS and Thos. LIVERS.

Dissolution of partnership of Wm. H. HAMPSTON and Joseph JOHNSTON.

75. 21 Aug 1818

Died Tuesday evening last, after a long and severe illness, Mrs. LEVY, of this town.

Died on Friday evening last, Augustus, aged about 4 years, only son of Roger B. TANEY, Esq. of this town.

John B. WEBER, commonly the New Auctioneer, is prepared to attend their sales as a public crier on moderate terms.

Robert BENSON, having removed from his old establishment, No. 92 to No. 82, Market St., has assortment of seasonable and fashionable goods.

Hacks - Each of the subscribers has a good hack and horses. David ALBAUGH and Samuel ICKES.

76. 28 Aug 1818

Married Tuesday evening, 11th inst by Rev. KENNEDY, Charles WORTHINGTON, of Montgomery Co., Maryland, to Miss Mary Ann THOMAS, dau of Samuel THOMAS, of Cumberland.

Lot of ground for sale, 8 acres, near WINEMILLER'S mill (formerly DONSON'S). Christopher NEAT.

Robert BOONE to sell 11 head of fat cattle, 4 milch cows, 45 hogs, a colt and 25 acres of corn.

Jacob DEVELSBERGER and G. HAMILTON have applied to the Judge of the court of common pleas of Adams Co. for benefit of the insolvent act.

Sale by order of the Orphans' Court of Montgomery Co., at the residence of Edward DIGGES, several Negroes, stock and furniture, property of the late Bernard O'NEILL, dec'd. Mary O'NEILL, extx.

77. 4 Sep 1818

Married Tuesday evening last by Rev. P. DAVIDSON, Alexander ROBERTSON, to Miss Mary MANTZ, all of this town.

Married yesterday, by Rev. Joseph LANSTON, Conrad HITCHEW, to Miss Elizabeth ZIMMERMAN, all of Frederick Co.

Married Tuesday evening, 18th ult. by Rev. REID, Arnold T. WINSOR, Esq., Sheriff of Montgomery Co., to Mrs. Mary RILEY, of the same co.

Married Thursday evening, 20th ult. by Rev. CLINGAN, Wm. PRINCE, Esq. of the state of Kentucky, to Miss Evelina DORSEY, of Montgomery Co.

House and lot for sale in conformity with the will of Augustus LARNED, lot whereon the dec'd. formerly lived, in the central part of New Town, with two story farm house. Sarah LARNED, extx.

Sale by virtue of a Montgomery Co. court, at the plantation of Johannah LODGE, called addition to Dear Stones and part of Bedfordshire Corner, 188 acres, subject to the dower. Also a tract called Part of Magruder and Bealls Honesty and part of Grubby Thicket, 117 1/2 acres - plus other parcels of land. Lloyd MAGRUDER, William WILLSON, Charles WALLACE, Commissioners.

"During the month of July last I purchased a Negro woman of Mr. Joseph WALLING. ... I afterwards lodged the Negro woman in the Leesburg gaol for self keeping; immediately after the Negro woman was thus lodge in gaol, the Rev. David MARTIN, of Frederick-town, very improperly interfered with my business, and in consequence of such interference, the Negro woman escaped. ..." B. HOFF. This is followed by statement by Meridith RICHARDSON of Frederick Co. who states that Rev. David MARTIN of Frederick-town brought to Davis RICHARDSON'S (his brother) house a Negro woman named SALLY and later had her delivered up to her grandmother FEBY.

John BEAM will sell the property where he lives, house and 11 acres, on Long Cabin Branch, 2 miles from KEPHART'S mills.

Journeymen blacksmith wanted. Michael CLAPSADDLE, Middleburg.

Monthly meeting at Union Tavern of Independent Hosemen. David STEINER, sec.

Henry R. WARFIELD, candidate for Congress.

78. 11 Sep 1818

Middletown Races. William PERRY.

Jacob WOLF will do all kinds of clock and watch making business.

Sheriff's sale at the tavern of Christopher ECKER, New Windsor, right of John MITTEN of house and lots in New Windsor taken at the suit of David BROWER, at the suit of Lawrence MAGERS.

Sheriff's sale of house and lots of Daniel BALL in Lewis Town, taken at suit of Thomas CARLTON, for use of Christian SCHOLL.

Died Tuesday evening last, after a lingering illness, Miss Mary THOMAS, aged about 42 years, dau of Mrs. --- THOMAS.

79. 18 Sep 1818

Sheriff's sale of a lot of Daniel COVER, in Union-town; also horse and gig, at suit of Godfrey SCISS. Patrick REED of Alex. for Joseph CROMWELL, Sh'ff.

80. 25 Sep 1818

Sale at his residence on the Maryland Tract, 1 mile from Petersville, all his stock. John F. GITTINGS.

Washington, PA, Aug 24 - On Tuesday evening last, about dark, a girl of Samuel SMITH, about 3 years old, was killed by having its hand entangled in a cow's tail and dragged to death.

Jacob YINGLING, admr. of John YINGLING.

Sale of 52 acres on Sams Creek, adjoining land of Ulrick SWITZER, Daniel HAINES, Israel RINEHART and Jehu MOORE. Nathan ZIMMERMAN.

Sheriff's sale at the suit of U.S., at the suit of John SLIFER, jun., at the suit of Samuel W. LACKLAND, a tract of Philip STRIDER, 150 acres.

Sale of 2 acres, near Union Bridge, adjoining lands of Solomon SHEPPARD, Silas HIBBERD and others. Horatio STEVENS.

81. 2 Oct 1818. No new items.

82. 9 Oct 1818

Sheriff's sale of tract of Jacob SMELTZER, called Between two Barrens, at suit of Mottelena SEUCABACH.

Sheriff's sale of 75 acres of Francis GREEN, at the suit of Lewis WEAVER use of Martin RIDENOUR.

Sheriff's sale of house and lot of George J. CONRADT, in Mechanics Town, at the suit of Jacob HARBAUGH, Jun, at the suit of John STANLEY, at the suit of Christian HARMAN, use of John CREAGER of Law.

Sheriff's sale of one-sixth part of house and lot in Emmitsburg, of Abraham HABLING and Lewis WEAVER, at the suit of George BIERLY and wife.

Sheriff's sale of tract on Bennett's Creek, adjoining the property of Cornelius HOWARD, belonging to Abednego BAKER and John COOK, at the suits of John PITTS.

Sheriff's sale of the furniture and black boy named PERRY, aged 11-12 years of age.

Married on Friday, 25th ult., by Rev. MARTIN, John BROWN, to Miss Elizabeth CLABAUGH, all of this co. [In the following issue this item was corrected to read, John BROWER.]

Persons having public arms in their possession in Frederick, Washington and Alleghany Counties are requested to deliver them to the Officers of their Regiments. Henry WAYMAN, agent.

83. 16 Oct 1818
Peter NICHOLAS, woolen draper mens's mercer and taylor.
Reomer KOLB offers reward for 14-15 missing sheep.

84. 23 Oct 1818
Married yesterday by Rev. HELFENSTEIN, Henry BROWNE to Miss Catherine MICHAEL, all of this co.
Sheriff's sale of house and lot in town of Berlin wherein John HYMES now lives, property of Adam BAUGHMAN, at the suit of Elizabeth GARROTT, admx. of John P. GARROTT.
Sheriff's sale at the house of John REID's, in Berlin, of a Negro man named HENRY, late the property of Barton HACKNEY, at the suit of Elizabeth GARROTT, admx. of John P. GARROTT.
Benj. HAGAN has the accounts of MAYNARD & Co. In his absence accounts can be paid to William COAL.
Frederick Town Races. Thomas CARLTON and M. K. HAMMET.

85. 30 Oct 1818
Joseph SNOHLE has applied to the Judges of the Court of Common Pleas of Adams Co. for the benefit of the Insolvent Act.
Married last evening by Rev. Curtis WILLIAMS, Isaac DUNHAM to Miss Catherine BOOSER, all of this co.
Died Wednesday night, in this town, Mrs. Elenor TURNER, dau of Thomas TURNER of George-Town, D.C.
Teacher wanted. Apply to Otho SPRIGG or Davis RICHARDSON.
Otho SPRIGG, admr. of Captain Thomas SPRIGG.
Sale of 500 acres, 1 mile from Seneca Mills, country mill, still-house and still, and 200 acres adjoining above tract. Charles GASSAWAY, Montgomery Co.
Sheriff's sale of 35 acres, of Francis GREEN, at the suit of Lewis WEAVER and Martin RIDENOUR.
Sheriff's sale of tract on waters of Liganore, adjoining lands of James ROBERTSON, at the suits of Samuel CLARK and Dennis SOLLARS.

86. 6 Nov 1818
Married Thursday, 29th ult. by Rev. ARMSTRONG, Daniel M. PERKINS, of Montgomery Co. to Miss Lucretia WHEELER, of Frederick Co.
Married the same evening by Rev. Burges NELSON, John ROOP (of Joseph) to Miss Mary, dau of the late Samuel STONER, all of this co.
Equity sale at Moses SHAW's tavern, Union-town, the farm of John STEM, dec'd., 90 acres and 46 1/2 perches, 2 miles above Union-town. Jacob STEM, trustee.

John WINEMILLER, proprietor of Snow Hill Hotel, 13 miles from Frederick.
Nathan HAMMOND, near Frederick-town, offers reward for Negro HARRY, about 30 years of age, purchased from heirs of Mr. BENTZ, near Frederick-town, about 3 years ago; has a brother in Frederick-town with William HANE.
Ignatius P. WARD has taken up a stray horse.
St. Lucas Church lottery to e abandoned. Produce claims to Doctor Thomas BOYER for payment. Nicholas SNIDER, sec'y.
Looking glasses for sale at store of Mr. HAUSER. Jos. HOW.
Wheat wanted - James ROBERTSON.
Sheriff's sale of Negro man NATHAN, Negro boy HENRY, Negro boy SHERMAN, late the property of Barton PHILPOTT, at the suit of Henry JARBOE, at the suit of George HUMPHREYS, and at the suit of Leonard JAMISON.
Sheriff's sale of land of David SHAWM, agreeable to his purchase from Richard TEMPLIN, at suit of Frederick and John STEMBLE.
Sheriff's sale of waggon and five horses of Henry CURFMAN, at the suit of Valantine BRUNER.
The notes give to Jacob PFOUTZ for property purchased at his sale have become due and are in the hands of the subscriber for collection. Wm. P. FARQUHAR.

87. 13 Nov 1818
Clement WHEELER, admr. of William B. RADFORD.
W. R. ELVINS & Co., clock & watch makers have commenced business in North Market St.
Notice is given to the heirs and representatives of Helena FENWICK late of Frederick Co., dec'd., that the subscriber is ready to pay over their distributive shares. Henry JENKINS, extr.

88. 20 Nov 1818
Married Tuesday evening last, by Rev. Joseph LANSTON, Israel BENTLEY, to Miss Mary HARBAUGH, all of Union Town.

89. 27 Nov 1818
Married Tuesday evening last by Rev. Curtis WILLIAMS, Johnsey HAMMOND of New Windsor, to Miss Elizabeth SHROEDER of Anne Arundel Co.
Married last evening by Rev. HIGGINS, Evan HOPKINS of this town, to Miss Mary VANFOSSEN of New-Market.
William GUNTON, druggist, has just received from Philadelphia and Baltimore, a large assortment of genuine drugs and medicines and fancy articles.
Tobacco & Snuff Manufactory. J. S. EICKELBERGER, & Co.
The undersigned have been appointed Commissioners by the Corporation of Frederick, to hear appeals and make transfers of property. Stephen STEINER, Frederick NUSZ, John CROMWELL.
Abraham CAYLAR, near Union town, offers reward for apprentice to the blacksmith's trade named Joseph COMBS, about 10 years of age, freckled face, large eyes.

90. 4 Dec 1818
Married at Hagers-town, on 24th ult. by Rev. LIND, William D. BELL, Editor of the *Torch Light*, to Miss Susanna HARRY, both of that place.
Jacob LEAB offers reward for missing steers.
Sale pursuant to the will of Benjamin BENNETT, dec'd., at the late residence of dec'd., near Charles FRANKLIN's tavern, 7 young Negroes. Elisha BENNETT, Robert BENNETT, extrs.

91. 11 Dec 1818
Married 24th ult. by Rev. W. HOOD, Odel WHEELER of Montgomery Co., to Miss Caroline DORSEY, of Anne Arundel Co.
Married Monday evening 30th ult. by Rev. ARMSTRONG, Capt. Clement T. HILLERY, of this co., to Miss Henrietta B. MULLIKEN of Prince George's.
Married Sunday evening last, by Rev. Jonathan HELFENSTEIN, Thomas DEAN to Miss Catharine WEAVER.
Married Thuesday evening last, by the same, John BALDERSTONE, to Mrs. Mary EARLY.
Married on the same evening by the Rev. F. W. HATCH, Alexander McPHERSON to Miss Matilda C. JOHNSON.
Married same evening by Rev. SCHAEFFER, Theoliphus F. CONRADT, to Miss Euenice MORGAN.
Married last evening, Dr. H. STALEY to Miss Margaret, dau of Henry KUHN, Esq., Mayor of this city.
Married in Hampstead, Job EATON to Miss Ruth SAWYER, after an undisturbed courtship of 6 years - Michael SHUTE to Miss Olive JOHNSON, after a courtship of only 8 years, 7 months and 6 days.
Joshua HALLER has a house and lot to let where he now lives at the lower end of Church St.

92. 18 Dec 1818
Joseph TALBOTT has taken up a horse left at his house.
Francis MATHIAS extr. of Catharine MATHIAS.
John REIFSCHNEIDER (hatter) offers reward for an apprentice boy named John SHARRER, about 16 years of age; has 5 years to serve, stout made, light complexion and hair, about 5 feet high.

93. 25 Dec 1818
Equity sale at the farm of John BOWER, dec'd., on road leading from Taney Town to York, adjoining land of George PETER, tavern keeper, 160 acres, mill seat. David REIFSNEIDER, trustee.
A. McILHENNY warns persons from trespassing on his premises.

94. 1 Jan 1819
Alexander Washington REEDER has commenced business as an Attorney and Counselor at Law at his office in Patrick St.

95. 8 Jan 1819

Daniel COVER to sell a farm between Middleburg and Union-town, 103 1/2 acres.

Sale of a two story frame house. Jonas CRUMBACKER will show the property. Clement HUBBS, Jesse SLINGLUFF.

96. 15 Jan 1819. No new items

97. 22 Jan 1819

Married Thursday evening, 14th inst. by Rev. Curtis WILLIAMS, Job HAINES to Miss Elizabeth HAINES.

Married Saturday evening last by Rev. SCHAEFFER, Isaac WYSONG, to Miss Elizabeth BAER, all of this city.

Catharine KIMBOLL will rent her house in Patrick St., now in the occupation of Mr. ARMSTRONG, together with the store attached. Apply to Thomas SHAW at the Frederick-town Branch Bank or to Catharine KIMBOLL.

Sheriff's sale of estate of Adam SMITH, lot no. 38 in Woodsborough take at the suit of Abraham FLENNER.

John C. GRAFF, Attorney and Counsellor at Law.

John INGELS, Sams Creek, has lost a pocket book between Taney-town and Piney Run - with a small quantity of money, Lottery Tickets and writings in it.

98. 29 Jan 1819

Married 23 Jan by Rev. MALOVA, Capt. John R. CORBALEY of the 7th regiment of infantry, to Miss Emerentienne VENCIENDIER.

John PANCOAST, New Market, has lost a note of hand for $1000, payable to Henry SMITH, by J. PANCOAST and Joseph HIBBIRD, endorses by Henry SMITH, and a payment of $400 credited thereon by Richard ROBERTS.

Sale, late the property of Michael HAINES, dec'd, a farm, near the old road leading from Liberty-town to Baltimore, 2 miles from New Windsor, adjoining lands of Hannah URNER, Jacob SNEEDER, Thomas BOND and other, 266 acres. Apply to John LUSCALLEED, living on the premises. David HAINES, George TEENER, extrs.

99. 5 Feb 1819

Died Tuesday last, Conrad ENGELBRECHT, long a respectable inhabitant of this town.

Died Tuesday morning last, David STONER, and on Wednesday interred in the Presbyterian Burial ground in this city.

Sheriff's sale of 3 Negro men, late the property of Henry R. WARFIELD, at the suit of Caleb DORSEY for Joseph M. CROMWELL and at the suit of the Bank of Westminster.

Sheriff's sale of 4 Negro men, 2 women and 2 children, late the property of Jonathan WOOD, taken at the suit of Peter BECRAFT, David WAGNER & William MUMFORD, use of William LEEKINS and wife.

Singleton DUVAL, Attorney at Law.

100. 19 Feb 1819

Married Tuesday evening late by Rev. WESTERMAN, Joseph JOHNSON, to Miss Eleanor HILLERAY, all of this co.

Married Thursday evening last by same, Fayette JOHNSON of Baltimore co., to Miss Catharine, dau of the late John JOHNSON of Frederick Co.

Died on 10th inst., Ed THOMAS, Sen. of this co., in his 80th year.

Jacob SCHAUB, desirous of moving to the Western Country, will sell two story brick house in Middleburg.

Chancery sale of real estate of Jacob DELAUTER, dec'd., in the neighborhood of Godrey LEATHERMAN and Mr. GROSNECKLE in the northern part of Middletown Valley, one tract of 100 acres and the other a mill, plus other parcels of land. Land will be shown by George DALAUTER, living on the premises.

John B. BELL, book binder, has commenced the business.

Commissioners of Tax for Frederick Co. will convene. Wm. RITCHIE, clerk.

Evan HOPKINS, hair dresser & barber, 3 door from Mr. TALBOTT's hotel.

101. 26 Feb 1819

Sheriff's sale of tract of William HYATT, adjoining Hyatt's town, taken at the suits of Jacob PRETZMAN and Robert CHANEY.

John KLINE offers reward for horse stolen from his waggon at John LOGSDON's tavern at Westminster.

102. 5 March 1819

Married Thursday evening, 25th of Feb, by Rev. Rezin HAMMOND, Henry NELSON Jr., to Miss Sarah, dau of John CLEMSON, Esq., all of this co.

Died Friday last, John BRUNER, of this co.

103. 12 March 1819

Died Saturday morning March 6, 1819, at his residence in Washington Co., Col. John CARR, rev. hero and patriot.

Chancery sale of land, 162 acres, and mills, 1 1/2 miles from Middleburg, on Beaver Dams, formerly the property of David ROOP, dec'd, adjoining land of John DEAL and Hammond RAITT. John KINZER lives near the same. Surratt D. WARFIELD, trustee.

Sale in accordance with the last will of Thomas BEATTY, dec'd., of lands adjoining Cregerstown, 215 acres. Samuel GRIMES who resides in Creagerstown will shew the property. John RITCHIE, extr.

Two pair of 5 feet French Burrs for sale. Joshua W. OWINGS, near Westminster.

Wm. HODGKISS, now confined for debt, has applied for relief under the insolvency act.

House and lot for sale. Apply to subscriber a few doors west of Mr. TALBOTT's hotel. HENRY BAER.

Partnership of Joshua C. GIST and Geo. W. GIST dissolved.

Sale of lot in Frederick-town near the court house. Jno. BRIEN.

104. 19 March 1819. No new items.

105. 2 April 1819
Isaac LINN extr. of Henry LINN.
Auction and commissioner store. HOUSTON & RUSSELL.
The horse, Young Dragon, will cover mares this season. Isaac LANDIS.

106. 9 Apr 1819
Died Sunday last, Charles HAMMOND, a respectable farmer of this co. Michael HAUSER, president of the Common Council; Wm. ROSS, president of the board of Aldermen; Henry KUHN, Mayor. Appointed by the corporation of Frederick as Town Constable: Richard HOGGINS. Bound are Richard HOGGINS and Thomas CONNOR.
Sheriff's sale of all the house and lot of Jacob GIBBONS contiguous to west end of Frederick-town on the north side of the turnpike road leading to Boonsborough, heretofore conveyed to Stephen STEINER by(?) Stephen KLINE - at the suit of Stephen STEINER.

107. 23 April 1819
Married Tuesday, 13th inst. by Rev. BLAKE, Jacob HARBAUGH, to Miss Mary HARBAUGH, dau of Christian HARBAUGH of Harbaugh's Valley.
John SMELSER and Jacob YON, admrs. of Jacob CLABAUGH.
Abraham SIMMONS admr. of Elizabeth SIMMONS.
R. G. McPHERSON gives notice not to hunt or fish on his premises.
Sale of 154 3/4 acres, 4 miles from Taney town. Michael STOVER.
The horse, Snap, will cover mares this season. Thomas BURGEE, Bennett's Creek.
Philip BARNHARD, near Little Pipe Creek, offers reward for apprentice named Daniel CLARK, taking with him my great coat.

108. 21 May 1819
David FOUTZ has his carding machines in good order at the old stand on Meadow Branch.
Commissioners (Peter SHRINER, David KEPHART, Jacob YON), appointed to open a road beginning at New Windsor (Sulphur Springs) to run from thence by Michael SMELSER's mill to intersect the turnpike road on the west side of and near to John LEISTER's dwelling house. This is to give notice to Isaac ATLEE, Allen HEBBERD, Michael SMELSER, Josiah PEARCE, Geo. LAMBERT, Catharine WINTERS (widow of the late John WINTERS, dec'd.), Adam SWIGARD, sen., John WAGGONER, Dr. Thomas BOYER and John LEISTER.
Sale near CLEMSON'S Mills, personal property of John ETZLER, dec'd., including 6 young Negroes, horses, cows, sheep. Magdalena ETZLER, George RODKEY, admrs.

Dissolution of partnership of Wm. E. HEMPSTONE, Daniel DUVALL.

109. 11 June 1819
Charles YAGER offers reward for apprentice to the cabinet making business, William HINTEN, about 16 years of age, 4 feet, 6 inches high; says he has been to sea.
Dr. L. J. SMITH, has taken an office near Buckey's Town.
New Windsor Hotel, formerly kept by John MITTEN (at the Sulphur Springs). Isaac DUNHAM.

110. 18 June 1819
Jno. COSKERY, Middleburgh, admr. of David WILSON.
Jacob BRENGLE has taken up a stray mare.
Chancery case: Thomas I. HAMMOND and Mary his wife vs. John CRUMBAKER, Jacob CRUMBAKER, Peter CRUMBAKER, David ENGLE, Isaac HITCHEN and Hannah his wife, Lydia CRUMBAKER, Ephraim CRUMBAKER, Elizabeth CRUMBAKER. Bill states that Abraham CRUMBAKER on 3 Dec 1794 made and published his will. He bequeathed to Abraham CRUMBAKER, John CRUMBAKER, Peter CRUMBAKER and Jacob CRUMBAKER (his sons), the real estate of which he should died possessed; he died without revoking said will. That Mary HAMMOND wife of Thomas I. HAMMOND is the dau of said Abraham CRUMBAKER, dec'd.; that Jonas CRUMBAKER and Mary CRUMBAKER the son and dau of the said Abraham CRUMBAKER, dec'd., were to have an equal share of the estate. That Abraham CRUMBAKER one of the devisees aforesaid, is dead, who died intestate, leaving Hannah HITCHEW (the wife of Isaac HITCHEW), Lydia CRUMBAKER, Ephraim CRUMBAKER, and Elizabeth CRUMBAKER, his heirs at law, who are all under the age of 21 years. That John CRUMBAKER conveyed by deed of bargain all his share of lands to David ENGLE who is now the owner and possessor thereof. That John CRUMBAKER does not reside within the state of Maryland.

111. 25 June 1819
The mangers of the German Reformed Congregation at Middletown announced the dedication of their church. The service will be performed in German and English languages. Peter COBLENTZ, Jacob EVERHART, managers.
James KEARNEY continues to manufacture merino and other wool.
New store - Dry goods, Groceries, Hardware, Glass. SIMMONS & BECKENBAUGH.

112. 2 July 1819. No new items.

113. 9 July 1819
Enos HUTTON, insolvent debtor, confined in jail; has been released and has applied for relief from debt.
Furniture for sale. Charles YEAGER, Patrick St., near KUNKLE's distillery.

114. 16 July 1819

Died on 1st inst., John M. MAGRUDER, of Calvert Co., in consequence of a stab with a dirk, given by Michael TANEY, senior, in the same day.

Elizabeth THOMAS, near Carroll's manor, offers reward for dark Mulatto man named JACK, about 20 years of age, 5 feet, 9 inches high; taken up by Samuel GALT near Taney town, brought to Frederick town when he made his escape.

115. 23 July 1819

Jacob GROSS and James McDANIEL, insolvent debtors and confined to jail, are now discharged; apply for relief from debt.

Joseph SMITH, Cumberland, offers reward for apprentice to the printing business, James BEACHEM, in his 17th year, about 5 feet, 4-5 inches.

Taney Town races. John BONER, John CRAPSTER, Jr.

116. 30 July 1819

Married Tuesday evening by Rev. HARGROVE, Dr. Godfrey WEISE, of this town to Mrs. Susanna Louis WEISE, of Baltimore.

117. 6 Aug 1819

Erasmus O'TUEL, insolvent debtor, to be released from jail; applies for relief from debt.

Commission to partition the lands of Michael ECKARD: Joseph TANEY, Joseph S. SMITH, Jacob BOMGARDNER, James MARK, George PRICE. This is to give notice to Jonah BUFFINGTON and Magdalena his wife, Solomon RENNEF and Barbara his wife, Thompson McCREA and Mary his wife, and Henry ECKARD, all of Frederick Co., Maryland, John COBLENTZ and Elizabeth his wife, and Jacob COBLENTZ and Catharine his wife, who reside out of the state of Maryland.

118. 27 Aug 1819

Robert DARNALL, Bennet's Creek, has black smith shop, dwelling house, garden &c. for rent.

119. 19 Nov 1819

John COSKERY, extr. of John KOCH, dec'd.

New watch making and silversmith business in frederick-town. Joseph WHARF.

Thomas SHAW, has received on consignment, paper hangings with borders to match.

Wanted - a schoolmaster. Daniel JAMES, Evan DORSEY, near New Market.

Married Sunday evening last by Rev. P. DAVIDSON, Vachel HAMMOND to Mrs. Priscilla HUFF, both of this co. *Examiner.*

THE REPUBLICAN GAZETTE AND GENERAL ADVERTISER

120. Saturday - 23 March 1816

PEARRE & ROHR have just received an assortment of silks, consisting of levantines, sattin, florence, virginias, &c.

M. E. BARTGIS, having taken at tavern in Market St., lately occupied by John DERTZBACH, The Eagle & Review Tavern.

John BAER & Co. have removed their store to the house lately occupied by Lewis J. DUGAS, one door above George BAER's store. Hardware, cutlery, saddlery & brassware.

Dennis HAGAN, Attorney at Law.

Stoves - William BAER & Co.

Highest price for clean flax seed at his house in Frederick-town. David MARKEY.

William STANSBURG, Baltzer FOGLE, insolvent debtors, discharged from jail; apply for relief from debt.

Spring and Fall Goods - BAYLY & JOHNSON.

Sale pursuant to the last will of Daniel SWIGER, dec'd., mills and farm, about 5 miles from Middletown on Catoctin creek. Joseph MILLER, extr.

Conrad OILER, near Woodsborough, offers for sale 3 Negroes.

Peter DUTROW offers for sale 150 acres, 1 mile from Henry DONSTON's mill. Thomas POWELL, extr. of Samuel TEMLIN.

Buried Wednesday, 20th inst. in the Lutheran Church-yard, Mrs. Maria Catharine MITZGER, aged 52 years.

Died Wednesday morning last, William THOMAS, at the early age of 37 years; buried at the German Presbyterian Church-yard; leaving widow and children.

Chancery sale of house and lot at the tavern of John HUSTON, the real estate of Frederick BAKER.

BASIL, NORRIS, & Co. - Groceries, Patrick St.

Chancery sale of the real estate of Simon SNOOK, dec'd., two farms adjoining each other, one containing 109 acres, the other 123 acres, on Monocacy, near the road from Frederick town to Creager's town. B. S. PIGMAN, trustee.

William BAER & Co., No. 26 Pratt St., Baltimore, offer for sale, flat, square and round iron.

The President and Directors of the Farms' Bank of Maryland have declared a Dividend of 4%. Jona. PINKNEY, Cashier.

Jacob NUSZ wishes to employ 2-3 journeymen masons.

Philip T. POTTS has just received from Philadelphia and Baltimore markets, an assortment of Goods.

Tavern to rent in Woodsborough. Joseph HEDGES.

Thomas SHAW requests the return of borrowed books.

Henry THOMAS has received from Baltimore numerous articles (listed) at his store in Patrick St.

BARTGIS'S REPUBLICAN GAZETTE AND GENERAL ADVERTISER.

121. 26 Oct 1816

RUSSELL & GRAFF have commenced the retail dry goods business at the house formerly occupied by Mr. MEDTART.

Joel MARSH has commenced the wool carding business at the Tuscarora Fulling Mill.

Mr. F. DURANG to open a Dancing Academy.

Isaac LYON requests indebted persons to settle their accounts.

John ENGELBRECHT, taylor, has commenced the tailoring business in Church St.

Frederick LINTHICUM and Adam HAUER, insolvent debtors, discharged from jail, have applied for relief for debt.

George TRISLER, has just received his Fall & Winter Goods.

A tract for sale about half a mile from Charlestown, Jefferson Co., VA. R. O. GRAYSON.

Sale of farm, 120 acres, on Monocacy, 5 miles from Frederick-town. Philip SWARTZWALDER.

Tench RINGGOLD, City of Washington, will give the highest market prices for upper leather and sole leather at his leather factory and currrying shop, between Pennsylvania Ave. and the upper Bridge.

Robert EASTBURN has taken up a stray mare.

Dying and weaving - James WALTERROTH.

Frederick STEMBEL, jun., John H. BURGESS, Adam YOUNG, insolvent debtors, discharged from jail, have applied for relief from debt.

Ewes wanted - Matthew BROWN, Montevino, near Frederick-town.

John W. THOMPSON, Morgantown, VA, offers reward for apprentice boy to the Potters business, William BURCHINAL, about 18 years of age, 5 feet, 4-5 inches, short black hair somewhat curley.

John COOK, offers reward for bright mulatto woman, about 24 years of age, named JUDE, about 5 feet, 4-5 inches high with her female child.

Henry THOMAS has received supply of castings, &c.: kettles, pots, skillets, small Dutch ovens, etc.

Charles MANN proposes a circulating library if adequate encouragement be offered him.

122. 14 Dec 1816

Charles GALEZIO has removed to the Courthouse Square where he carries on the hair-dressing and shaving business.

Sale of 67 acres 4 miles from Newtown (Trap). George RICHARDS.

John CRUSHAN offers reward for mulatto woman named MARIAH, age about 26, who took with her two children, WILLIAM, and MARY.

Grafted fruit for sale. Haines DIXON, on Turnpike road between Frederick-town and Monocacy Bridge.

John FESSLER, jun., having removed to his father's house in Patrick St. and entered into partnership with in the Watch and Clock-making business which will be conducted under the firm of John FESSLER & Son.

Leonard MILLER has taken up a stray gelding.

John BAKER having declined brewing and rented his brewery, hereby requests persons indebted to him to settle their accounts.

Frederick OTT, near Creager's town has taken up two stray cows.

Dying, Fulling & Dressing departments of Fleecy Dale Factory. M. BROWN & Brother.

Equity sale made and reported by Roger B. TANEY, trustee for the sale of the real estate of Roger NELSON be ratified.

Chancery case: Margaret KEMP, extr. of Frederick KEMP vs. Jacob STALEY and John McPHERSON and Gilbert KEMP. Object of the bill is for the complainant to be relieved against a bond executed by Frederick KEMP and Gilbert KEMP his security of Jacob STALEY, and assigned to John MCPHERSON. Jacob STALEY resides out of the state of Maryland.

Jacob SHOUP, complainant against Henry HITCHEW, Philip HITCHEW, Jacob HITECHEW, sen., Christopher HITECHEW, and Barbara his wife, Jacob HITCHEW, William HITCHEW, John HITECHEW, Abraham FLANNER and Hannah his wife, Joseph CROUSE and Elizabeth his wife, David HITECHEW, Gideon HITECHEW, Elizabeth HITECHEW, Bernard HITECHEW, Israel HITECHEW, Susanna HITECHEW and Eliza HITECHEW, defendants. Object of bill is to obtain a decree for the sale of the real estate of William HITCHEW, dec'd., for the payment of $500 payable on 1 Apr 1817 and like sum on 1 Apr 1818 for which the complainant holds the note of said William HITCHEW. William HITCHEW died intestate and did not leave personal assets sufficient to pay his debts and that he died seized of a tract called Bedford, 78 1/2 acres and a tract called Buck Lodge, 25 acres. Henry HITECHEW resides out of the state of Maryland.

123. 8 March 1817

James BERRY, insolvent debtor, applies for relief from debt.

Dying, fulling & dressing. Matthew BROWN & Brother.

House and lot for sale in Woodsborough. Charles ARTUR.

Claimants are requested to make their claims on the estate of Wm. DERN, John RITCHIE, Benjamin BIGGS, extrs.

Boot & Shoe Manufactory. David BENNET has removed to the house formerly occupied by John FESSLER, clock and watch maker, Patrick St., two doors east of George KOLB.

Conrad KELLER, admr. of Molly JOHNSON.

Married Thursday evening last, by Rev. P. DAVIDSON, Samuel WEBSTER to Mrs. Sarah SCOTT, all of this town.

Middletown Church Lottery. Richard TEMPLIN, Henry SHOEMAKER, Michael MOTTER, Henry CULLER, Adam LORENTZ.

Farm for sale, 1 1/2 mile from Frederick-town, commonly called the Winter House Tavern, 250 acres. Ashton ALEXANDER, Baltimore.

Ezra MANTZ, Holly Buch tanyard, 2 miles east of New Market, offers reward for Negro man Charles ODEN, about 28 years of age, 5 feet, 11 inches high.

Matthias BARTGIS will sell the house and lot in Frederick-town opposite to Christopher HALLER's, occupied several years as a tavern.

New Cheap Cash Store. Jacob HOUCK, New Market.

Chancery case: Joel PUSEY, Daniel SLAYMAKER, vs. Enoch TAYLOR. Object of the bill is to obtain an order ont he trustee appointed to sell the real estate of Daniel ROOT, dec'd., to pay over to the petitioners, out of the Defendants share, in right of his wife, of said estate, $367.62, it being the amount of their claim against the defendants. That defendant was indebted to certain Andrew ETZLER who obtained a judgment against him.

Daniel HAUER, jun. and Cyrus MANTZ, have formed a partnership at the house lately occupied as a saddler's shop by William MICHAEL, two doors below Francis MANTZ. Dry Goods, Groceries and Queensware.

Grain, wheat, rye, corn and flax seed, wanted. Frederick FEAGA.

124. 6 April 1817. [Date should read 5 April. Ed.]
Wood lots for sale near Bartgis's paper mill, 157 acres; also 6 lots of Linganore woodland between the woodland of John BRENGLE and James ROBERTSON, nos. 3, 4, 5, 7 And 8, each 50 acres and no. 2 of 45 acres. Eleanor POTTS, extrx. of R. POTTS. Attendance will be given by Richard POTTS.

Michael BUCKEY, admr. of Jacob BUCKEY.

Married Tuesday evening lat by Rev. SHAEFFER, Joseph EBBERT, to Miss Elizabeth RANDALL, all of this place.

Boot and Shoe Manufactory, had removed his shop next door to Doctor SMITH. Jacob SPONSELLER.

The residuary legatees of Elijah BALDWIN, who employed me to file a bill in chancery against Obadiah SMITH and Peter MILLER, are hereby informed that I have obtained a decree - that the sale and deed for the land from SMITH to MILLER has been vacated and I have been appointed trustee to make another sale. Smith and Miller have appealed to the court of Appeals for delay and as I apprehend, to enable them to buy up the claims of the legatees at a great sacrifice I therefor advise the legatees not to sell their claims. B. S. PIGMAN.

The horse, Virginia Gray, will stand the ensuing season at Andrew ETZLER's, Frederick BOYD's and at the subscribers stable, 1 mile from Creagers' town. John WILHIDE, Lawrence SHINDLE, Keeper.

The horse, Farmer, will stand the ensuing season at the subscriber's (William MORSEL) stable on Bennet's Creek.

Absolom BARTON warns all persons against trusting his wife Charlotte BARTON, on his account, as she has left his bed and board.

Sale of several Negroes at the late residence of William WATERS, dec'd., in Montgomery Co., 4 miles south of Clarksburgh. Nathaniel M. WATERS, Horace WATERS.

Chancery sale of real estate of Simon SNOOK, dec'd., on Monocacy, 123 acres. Solomon SNOOK will shew the premises.

Chancery case: Thomas C. WORTHINGTON, extr. of Thomas CONTEE, vs. Edward BURGESS, jun., Ninion CLAGGETT and wife, and others. Object of bill is to obtain decree for sale of lands in Montgomery and Frederick counties and sold to Edward BURGESS, sen., dec'd., by Thomas CONTEE, dec'd., for the purpose of paying money due for said land, by the heirs of said Edward BURGESS, sen. The bill states that Thomas CONTEE sold to Edward BURGESS, sen., several tracts of land for the sum of 2000 pounds; that all purchase money is due and unpaid. Ephraim BURGESS does not reside in this state.

The horse, Saratoga, will stand the ensuing season at Thomas CARLTON's tavern, James RICE's, David EATOR's smith shop. Adam WINRICH.

Philip GOODMAN has tract for sale within 3 miles of Frederick-town, 17 acres.

125. 12 April 1817

Married Saturday last by Rev. William DAVAU, Isaac ROBERTS, of Frederick Co., to Miss Jane Maria MATTHEWS, of Elk Ridge.

Baltimore and Winchester Line of Stages, by way of Frederick. HALLER & LEATHERWOOD.

Benedict L. ADAMS, 4 miles from Montgomery Court House, offers reward for dark mulatto man, JACOB, about 6 feet high, about 20 years of age.

Chancery case: Adam SNOOK vs. Joab WATERS, Henry G. WATERS and Thomas OWINGS. Object of bill is to obtain a decree for the specific performance of a certain article of agreement made by Henry G. WATERS as attorney, in fact for Joab WATERS with the complainant for the conveyance of a tract of land in Frederick Co. Bill states that Joab WATERS of the Missouri Territory, being seized and possessed of a tract of land in Frederick Co., containing 238 acres, by his letter of attorney, appointed Henry G. WATERS, his attorney; that by virtue of the power of attorney Henry G. WATERS sold the land to the complainant for $6000, to be paid upon making a good title. Afterward Henry G. WATERS sold said tract to Thomas OWINGS.

George DERTZBAUGH, Frederick-town, offers 6 cents reward and a wax-end for apprentice to the Boot and Shoe-making business, named James TURNER, 17 years of age, 5 feet, 7 inches high.

Matthias BARTGIS offers reward for apprentice lad, bound to the book-binding business, by name of John ATKINS, who ran away from the subscriber's Printing Office.

Michael BUCKEY offers 6 cents reward for apprentice to the tanning business, named John Alfred PORTER, about 5 feet, 6-7 inches, 20 years of age.

Joseph SMITH, Staunton, VA, offers reward for Negro man, named ANDERSON, age 25-30.

Adam FLUCK who formerly kept the White Swan tavern, Race St., Philadelphia, has taken the noted house, No. 140, North 2nd St., Sign of the Camel, formerly kept by Joseph CARR.

126. 31 May 1817

I am prepared to pay over on demand to the heirs of Philip Jacob MILHOFF, dec'd. Adam HOFFMAN, extr.

Union Tavern, Market St., formerly kept by Captain SCHLEY. Nicholas TURBUTT.

Daniel BOYCE offers reward for Negro slaves, HARRY, about 22 years of age, and black girl, ESTHER, about 17 years of age, both raised in Morgantown, Monongali co. VA, by Col. EVANS and Rolly SCOTT.

146 acres for sale, 14 miles from Frederick-town, joining lands of Peter STALEY and William HOBBS. Jacob FARE.

Thomas H(?). BOWIE, Annapolis, offers reward for Negro lad named CHARLES, about 17 years of age, purchased from Henry WARRING, of Prince George's Co., who still owns his mother. When owned by Mr. WARRING, his name was NACE or NACEY.

Jacob HARTMAN has opened a house of Public Entertainment in Charlestown, Jefferson Co. at that house and stand, formerly kept by Henry HAINES on main St.

Land for sale on the drains of Sleep Creek, Berkeley co., 438 aces. Apply to John ROBINSON, Bath, or to subscribers in York, PA: Zachariah SPANGLER, Charles WEISER.

Levy Court stands adjourned. John SCHLEY, clerk.

Shad & herrings by the barrel - John HANE.

Apprentices wanted 14-16 years of age, to the tayloring business. William BARR, Middletown, MD.

Lawrence EVERHART offers reward for horse which strayed away at Middletown.

Thos. WILES has taken up a stray mare.

Tin Factory, Middletown. Peter HOSE, Enoch GREENWELL.

S. MAGILL has rented tavern house in Cumberland, MD.

127. 7 June 1817

Frederick-town Porter Brewery. Andrew THOMSON has bottled ale and porter for delivery.

128. 14 June 1817

Woodward EVITT has taken up a stray gelding.

Christopher SWOPE cautions person against trusting his wife Catharine SWOPE, she having left his bed and board without provocation.

Chancery sale by Frederick A. SCHLEY of real estate of Michael MENSER, dec'd., to be approved. Thomas H. BOWIE.

William SUMAN offers reward for apprentice lad named Arthur SUMAN, bound to the house carpenter and cabinet business.

129. 21 June 1817

Sale of tavern stand, Market St. Conrad SHAFER.

John BAST has taken up a stray milch cow, 5 miles from Frederick-town.

Charles P. WILLIAMS, Frederick-town offers reward for 3 Negro men who broke jail: PERRY, 24-25 years of age; John DUN, was in Baltimore jail many months and was to have been hung for killing his wife but was pardoned on condition that he would be sold out of the state; BEN, purchased of Luke HOWARD, jun., Kent Co., Eastern Shore, just brought from Philadelphia as a runaway.

130. 28 June 1817
John B. BAYLES, Selby Mills, Anne Arundel Co., offers reward for German Redemptioner, named Godfried PFUND; had light hair, broad forehead, blue eyes, large nose, walks a little lame, 5 feet, 3 inches high, 24 years old, miller by profession; has the figure of a cog wheel with animals on one of his arms in red ink; native of Wirtumburg; ran away once before and changed his name to John MARTINS.
Saml. B. T. CALDWELL, Leesburg, offers reward for mare missing from pasture of Gen. A. T. MASON.
William WYATT, Frederick Co. will sell his farm adjoining Wyatts town, 470 acres.

131. 5 July 1817
Died Friday, 27th ult. after a lingering indisposition, in his 46th year, Mr. WINGER, Innkeeper of this place; buried in the German Lutheran Burying Ground.

132. 23 Aug 1817
John MILLER, John H. BURGESS, confined in jail as insolvent debtors, apply for relief from debt.
Chancery sale of house in Frederick-town, of Peter BEALL, adjoining property of John CAMPBELL.
Land and saw mill for sell, 5 miles from Frederick-town near Nicholas HOLTZES, 14 acres. Henry FEAGLER.
Peter NICHOLS takes notice of the publication of James F. HUSTON in the *Political Examiner.*
Chancery case: Nicholas HOLTZ vs. Francis MANTZ, John BOYER, Matthias BARTGIS. Object of the bill is to foreclose John BOYER from his equity of redemption in two mortgages of real estate called Boyer's Gap, executed by John BOYER and to sell the real estate. John BOYER resides in VA.
Washington Tavern, Frederick Town, upper end of Market St. Henry FOGLER.
Chancery case: William HERD vs. Aaron HERD, Nathan MAYNARD, Joseph W. LAWRENCE and Henry CREAGER. Object of bill is to obtain a conveyance of part of a tract called Middle Plantation which Aaron HERD sold to the complainant and gave his bound to convey the same.
Joseph W. LAWRENCE resides in the state of VA and Henry CREAGER resides in OH.
William KOLB, Frederick town has taken up some stray sheep.
Jacob READ, 1 mile from Frederick-town, has taken up a stray steer.
Michael STRAVER will sell his farm, 125 1/2 acres, 4 miles from Frederick-town, adjoining lands of Gilbert KEMP and Isaac HEDGES.

Marsh Mareen DUVALL, confined in jail as an insolvent debtor, to be released; applies for relief from debt.
Chancery sale of real estate of Tobias BUTLER, dec'd., approved.
Henry SHRUPP offers reward for missing horse.
Silver watch found. Peter ARTNER.
John POFFENBARGER has taken up a stray mare.
John FITTERLING has taken up a stray horse.

133. 30 Aug 1817
Chancery case: Joshua RIDGELY vs. Joshua RIDGELEY and James RIDGELEY, heirs at law of Sam. RIDGELY. That the sale of real estate of Samuel RIDGELEY, dec'd. be confirmed.

134. 6 Sep 1817
Sale by John BANTZ where he now lives.

135. 13 Sep 1817
William P. BURGESS, confined in jail as an insolvent debtor, to be discharged and applies for relief from debt.

136. 20 Sep 1817
Married Tuesday evening, 16th instant by Rev. David MARTIN, Jacob BARNES, to Miss Nancy HITON, all of this place.
Money found on the road, 5-6 miles from Frederick-town. Benjamin STEVESON.

137. 27 Sep 1817
Ordered that the sale of estate of Charles CHANEY reported by Henry WERTMAN, be confirmed.
The mill of James ROBERTSON is back in operation.

138. 4 Oct 1817
Died Friday 12th instant, in his 68th year, Major Hanson BRISCOE, clerk of the County Court. His illness confined him nearly 4 weeks. He was a native of St. Mary's Co., MD and held a commission in the militia during the Rev. war. *Allegany Freeman.*
Chancery case: Levi PHILLIPS vs. Benedict DARNAL, Thomas N. BINS, Ninian EDWARD and Elvira EDWARDS, his wife and James B. LANE. Object of bill is to obtain a decree for the conveyance of 5000 acres in Montgomery Co. which the complainant purchased of Benedict DARNAL, one of the defendants. That Thomas N. BINS purchased 600 acres in Montgomery Co. of Ninian EDWARDS and Elvira EDWARDS his wife and James B. LANE. That Thomas N. BINS has secured the payment of the purchase money. That Thomas N. BINS swopped 500 acres of said land with Benedict DARNAL for all the tract of Benedict DARNAL for a certain mill in Hargrave Co., VA.

Benedict DARNAL, Ninian EDWARDS and Elvira EDWARDS, his wife and James B. LANE, reside out of the state of MD.

139. 1 Nov 1817

James M'CONKEY, Bedford Springs, formerly of the New Theatre Tavern, Baltimore, has selected a building adjoining his farm house, for lodging.

Elected at Graceham as officers of the Hagers-town Turnpike Road Company: Joshua DELAPLANE, President; Samuel OGLE, Treasurer; Managers: John WELTY, George HAPE, Dr. Thomas BOYER, Christopher NEWCOMER, Jun., Jacob G. CONRADT, Marmaduke W. BOYD, Henry STOUFER, John CREAGER, of L.

James M'HAFFIE, extr. of Regena GRANDADAM.

Dissolution of partnership of S. B. LEATHERWOOD and Joseph HALLER, in the line of stages from Frederick To Winchester.

John HOUCK has opened Glove Inn.

James MURET has found two bags of grain near the Baptist Meeting House, one with the name of George MICHAEL on it.

George LECHLIDER has taken up a stray gelding.

140. 15 Nov 1817

This is to forewarn persons from hiring my black man, PETER. Benj. HEATHERLEY, Sen., Benj. HEATHERLEY, Jun.

The fifth drawing of the Protestant Episcopal Church Lottery will take place this day. Samuel BARNES, John P. THOMSON, Lewis GREEN at the Frederick Town Bank, Ezra MANTZ, at the office of Pay & Receipt, James F. HUSTON, William GUNTON, Richard ENGLISH, Henry BANTZ.

141. 22 Nov 1817

Elkton and Swedish Bar Iron for sale - John M'DONALD.

John BAER of Hen. has removed to the shop formerly occupied by Doctor J. BAER, in Patrick St. Earthen ware from the Hagers Town Pottery; also oats.

Joel ELLIOT, insolvent debtor, confined in jail, now released, applies for relief from debt.

Sale at the house of John RINE, 2 miles from Liberty Town, all of property of said Rine, being an insolvent debtor. West BURGESS, trustee.

142. 29 Nov 1817

Died suddenly on Saturday evening last, Mrs. Amelia BRENGLE, consort of Jacob BRENGLE.

143. 6 Dec 1817

Chancery case: John CROMWELL vs. Thomas N. BINNS, Robert DARNALL, Joseph M. CROMWELL, W. F. MERCER and Benedict DARNALL. Object of bill is to obtain a decree for sale of the lands of John DARNALL, dec'd., willed to him and to his brothers William DARNALL and Charles DARNALL which at the decease of the said John DARNALL descended to his brothers Raphael DARNALL, Benedict DARNALL and Robert DARNALL. The bill states that after the said John DARNALL took the estate in the lands of Thomas DARNALL, he became indebted to Raphael DARNALL in the sum of $460 ... that Raphael DARNALL for a consideration assigned his claim to the complainant; that the said John DARNALL hath died intestate without leaving a person estate sufficient to pay his debts; that he left a real estate to wit: all his interest in the lands willed to him and to his brothers William DARNALL, and Charles DARNALL, by Thomas DARNALL in Frederick Co., to descend to his surviving brothers, Raphael DARNALL, Benedict DARNALL and Robert Darnal, that Benedict DARNALL sold his interest in said estate to Thomas N. Binns; that the sheriff by writs of fieri facias sold all the interest of Raphael DARNALL in the estate of Thomas DARNALL to Thomas N. BINNS who sold to Charles Fenton MERCER. Charles Fenton MERCER resides in the state of VA and Benedict DARNALL resides in OH.

Sale of the personal property of Elijah BEATTY, dec'd. Sarah BEATTY, admx.

144. 13 Dec 1817

Died at a very advanced age, Mrs. Barbara BALTZELL, consort of Michael BALTZELL, on Tuesday evening; remains interred at the Presbyterian burial ground.

Tan Yard for sale in Martinsburgh, used as a tannery for nearly 30 years. Valentine AYLE.

Sale for the benefits of creditors of John MILLER, all property of John MILLER. William SPRINGER.

145. 20 Dec 1817

Meeting to from a fire company under the name of the Independent Hose Company of Frederick. John WILSON, Secretary.

Reward offers for apprentice to the Printing Business, John Harris M'KENNIE who ran away on 15 Oct last, about 5 feet, 7 inches high with 2 years and 2 months to serve when he will be 21 years of age.

John CROMWELL offers reward for David BALTZELL, apprentice to the house carpenter and joining business, about 5 feet, 9 inches high.

146. 27 Dec 1817

Meeting to suppress circulation of notes below the denomination of one dollar: George BEAR, chair; Samuel BARNES, secretary. Signers: George BAER, John NELSON, George TRISLER, Benjamin RUTHERFORD, John BAER & Co., John HOFFMAN, HAUER & MANTZ, William GUNTON, James ROBERTSON, Frederick NUSZ, Eli P. BENTLEY, John M. LOWE, Thomas CONNER, Lawrence DOYLE, David BENNETT, J. LARKIN, John DOYLE, Henry FOGLER, John P. THOMSON, William B. BURKE, Lewis BIRELY, John MARKELL, William MICHAEL, William POPE, George W. ENT, Jacob SHRIVER, George BENTZ, John RIGNEY, Philip HAUPTMAN, Nicholas TURBETT, Samuel BARNES, Joseph TALBOTT, Joseph M. CROMWEL, Henry BANTZ, Joseph SWEARINGEN, George BALTZ

Henry GETZENDANNER, Richard ENGA.., Henry FUNDENBURG, Thomas CARLTON, Mathias E. BARTGIS, George HOUCK, John HOUCK, PEARRE and ROHR, George WEBSTER, George SCHULTZ, Henry SCHULTZ, Valentine BRUNER, Samuel MITTER, David MARTIN, William R. SANDERSON, John M'PHERSON, Jacob STEINER, William & Daniel HANE, WILLIAMS & STINCHCOMB.

Chancery case: Benjamin BLACKFORD, John COOKERLY and others vs. John MESSONIER, Christian MESSONIER, John HARRIS, James HARRIS and Elizabeth his wife, Ignatius LIVERS and Catherine his wife, Samuel LINEBAUGH and Mary his wife. Object of bill is to obtain decree for sale of real estate of George MESSONIER, dec'd., for payment of his debts. Bill states that George MESSONIER died intestate and without issue, seized of real estate in Frederick co. which hath descended to the defendants. That the defendants, except Samuel LINEBAUGH and wife, do not reside in Maryland.

147. 3 Jan 1818. No new items.

148. 10 Jan 1818

James FISHER, Esq., appointed Post-Master, at Westminster, in the room of James M'HAFFIE, Esq., dec'd.

James HUNTER was hung at Gettysburg, PA, on the 3d instant. In his confession he states that he never retained any il will toward Henry HEAGY, although previously that had been at variance; states he was in a drunken state, but does not plead that for an excuse.

149. 17 Jan 1818

Died Thursday morning last, Philip POTTS, amiable young man of this town.

Robert DAVIS was robbed on Fredericktown turnpike, 5 miles from this city [Baltimore]; five villains took 3 watches, about $8 and a bundle of clothes.

Equity case: Henry GARNHART vs. John ZERRICK and Henry BRISH. Object of bill is to obtain a decree for recording a deed of bargain and sale from John ZERRICK to part of lot number 107 in Frederick-town that was devised to said John ZERRICK by his father Anthony ZERRICK which deed the complainant omitted to have recorded within the time prescribed by law. John ZERRICK made another deed of bargain and sale to Henry BRISH. John ZERRICK resides out of the state of Maryland.

Nicholas HOLTZ offers reward for Daniel FINK, apprentice to the tanning business, about 20 years of age, 5 feet, 5-6 inches, black hair.

John REMSBURG has taken up some stray sheep at his farm, 1 mile from Frederick Town.

Lewis G. APPOLOW will engraft all kinds of fruit.

150. 24 Jan 1818

Sale of 177 acres of land, about 5 miles from Frederick Town, on road to MAYBERRY's Furnace. John GESEY lives on the land. B. S. PIGMAN.

151. 31 Jan 1818
Law. BRENGLE, mayor of Frederick, cautions persons not to visit the jail at this time because of the likelihood of spreading small pox.
Henry FRALEY has taken up a stray mare.
Dry Goods, Hardware, Crockery and Genuine Drugs. Isaac LYON.

152. 7 Feb 1818
Peter GAVER admr. of Samuel GAVER.
Chancery sale of real estate of Jacob TROXALL, dec'd., 202 acres, in the neighbourhood of Emmitsburg.
Married Tuesday evening last by Rev. F. W. HATCH, John SCHROEDER to Miss Sarah BELT, dau of Capt. Jeremiah BELT, all of this co.
Died in Frederick town Friday evening, 30th ult. after a short illness in her 96th year, Mrs. Esther DIGGS.
Died 3d instant at the house of Col. John HUSTON, John CLAGHORN, aged 35 years, from the City of London.
Died same day, Jacob MIXELL, an old, respectable inhabitant of this town.
Died Saturday evening, 31st ult. after a short illness, Mrs. GETZENDANNER, wife of Jacob GETZENDANNER, respectable farmer near Frederick Town.
Notice that the Alms house will be kept fee for the preaching of the Gospel to the poor in said house, to any denomination of Christians. H. STEINER, Overseer.

153. 28 Feb 1818
Married Tuesday evening last, by Rev. David F. SCHAEFFER, John W. MILLER, Miss Ann Catherine KOLB, dau of Wm. KOLB, Esqr., all of this city.
Elected as members of the common council for Frederick: 1st Ward, Henry STEINER, jun.; 2nd ward, Col. John M'PHERSON, 3d ward, John CROMWELL; 4th ward, Michael HAUSER; 5th Ward, George A. EBERT; 6th Ward, Henry KUHN; 7th Ward, a tie of the two candidates.
Died Tuesday morning last of the Small Pox, Mrs. Elizabeth DURST.
Died Wednesday, 18th inst., George YOST, age 91 years, 8 months and 17 days; emigrated from Germany and has resided upwards of 60 years in this co.; oldest member of the Lutheran Congregation.
Chancery case: Jacob LEASE vs. Martin MILLER & Susanna MILLER his wife, George Adam EBERT & Margaret EBERT his wife, William FOUT, John Henry FOUT and Elizabeth FOUT. Object of bill is to obtain decree for sale of lands held by the complainant and George Adam EBBERT and Margaret his wife, William FOUT, John Henry FOUT, and Elizabeth FOUT as Tenants in Common. Bill states that Balzer FOUT late of Frederick Co., dec'd., died intestate, leaving Susanna MILLER, Margaret EBBERT, Ann FOUT, Christianna MOTTER, Elizabeth SEVER, his children and heirs at law. At the time of his death he was seized in fee of two tracts of land, Rockey Spring and Duvalls Forest, 150 acres. Christianna MOTTER and John MOTTER, her husband, Elizabeth SEVER and Frederick SEVER her husband sold their interest to Samuel DUVALL. Susanna MILLER and Martin MILLER her

husband, sold their interest in lands to William DUVALL and William DUVALL sold said lands to Samuel DUVALL and Samuel DUVALL sold said lands to complainant. Martin and Susanna MILLER reside out of the state of Maryland.

Chancery case: Maria Julian STALEY vs. Jacob STALEY and Dorothy KEMP. Object of bill is to obtain decree for payment of legacy left to the complainant by Joseph STALEY by his last will. Bill states that on 4 Feb 1804 Joseph STALEY made his will wherein he devised his dwelling plantation to defendant Jacob STALEY, charged with the payment of 200 pounds current money to the complainant. Jacob STALEY resides in OH in insolvent circumstances. That Jacob STALEY has since sold said land to Frederick KEMP who is now dec'd., leaving Dorothy KEMP his sole extx. and devisee of his estate.

William TOMS cautions persons from trusting his wife Polly TOMS, as she has left his bed and board, without any provocation.

Sale of lots in Lewis-town, Frederick Co. Thos. DRAPER.

Vendue notes given to John KREBS, will be due March next. Francis MANTZ.

Sale of 100 acres on Big Hunting Creek, 2 miles from Mechanics-town. Jacob WELLER.

J. JOHNSON has lost a red morocco Pocket Book between Frederick-town and Mr. MAYBERRY's toll gate. Deliver to Benjamin WINTER or to Mr. MAYBERRY at the toll gate for reward.

154. 7 March 1818

Died on 25th ult., Mrs. Elizabeth STINCHCOMB, consort of Beal C. STINCHCOMB, Esq. of this co, in her 25th year, leaving an infant 8 days old.

Sale of 500 acres adjoining Creagers-town in accordance with will of Thomas BEATTY, dec'd. Samuel GRIMES will shew the property. John RITCHIE, extr.

To receive subscriptions for the stock of Frederick Co. Bank: George BAER, Abrm. SHRIVER, John STALEY, John L. HARDING, Jno. GRAHAME, F. A. SCHLEY.

Chancery sale of tract held by Christian CHAMPER and Basil CHAMPER, 277 acres, 6 miles from Frederick town in the neighbourhood of Captain CAMPBELL's and LAURENCE's mill.

Sale of Grist mills, 24 miles from Baltimore and 1 mile from the new road from Baltimore to Liberty. Also carding machine, saw mill with 2 dwelling houses, barn and other buildings. James SMITH.

The subscriber intending to remove to the Western country, is disposed to sell at his residence 1 mile north of Frederick town, all his household and kitchen furniture, waggon. Benjamin BYERS.

Thos. C. WORTHINGTON, Attorney at Law, no longer encumbered with the business of the state, will devote his attention to civil and chancery proceedings. He will attend at his office in 2nd St. next door to the Collector and not far from the Westminster office of Pay and Receipt.

155. 14 March 1818

Married on the 1st instant, by Rev. David F. SCHAEFFER, Mr. C. J. WOL-

LENDEN [should read WOOLFENDEN], to Miss Mary LAMBERT, both of this town.

Died Wednesday, 10th instant, Josephus STEMBLE, son of John STEMBLE, merchant of this town.

Sale at his residence, 3 miles from Middle-town, waggon, milk cows, steers, plows, kitchen cupboard, 10-plate stove, farming utensils. Thos. PATTAN.

156. 28 March 1818

Married Thursday evening last by Rev. David F. SCHAEFFER, Cyrus MANTZ, merchant, to Miss Elizabeth KUHN, dau of Henry KUHN, esq. of this place.

Died on good Friday, after a short illness, .?.. Lear YOUNG.

Died Wednesday last, Mrs. Catherine RES(?), aged 88 years and on Thursday her remains were interred in the Lutheran burying ground.

Died Wednesday evening last, Henry BRISH, Inn keeper of this town; remained interred in German Lutheran burying ground.

Mary SMITH and George SMITH, extrs. of Jacob SMITH.

Samuel MAGILL continues business at Cumberland Hotel, Allegany Co.

157. 4 April 1818

We have observed a publication in the Westminster Observer of the 13th inst. stating the circumstance of the death of a certain William M'CREA, near Taney-town. We beg leave to report that the widow of the deceased is an amiable woman and has reared a numerous offspring of amiable children. William M'CREA was found hanging by the neck, not in the orchard but at the house on a pin above the back door, nor on Saturday night previous to the 13th instant, but on Monday morning the 9th instant. He was sober not intoxicated. The whole of the statement in the Westminster Observer is false. Jury of Inquest: Jos. Sim. SMITH, acting coroner; jurors: Benjamin JONES, Foreman; Samuel S. FORNEY; Nich. UMSTEAD; Joseph SHRUNK; John CRAPSTER, jun.; Jacob KUHNS; William M'CHIRGAN; Andrew WALKER; William KNOX; Joel WOOD; Samuel GALT; William WALKER.

The horse, Matchem, bred by Col. Philip M'KELFRESH, will stand for mares this season at Mr. HERRING's tavern, Middletown; Henry BUTLER's tavern, Newtown (Trap); Mr. ELDER's tavern, Buckeys-town. Joseph PURDY, Keeper.

158. 25 April 1818

Married Thursday last by Rev. David F. SCHAEFFER, John BASH, to Miss Catherine LEASE, ll of this co.

Wool Carding - Philip HEMP and Henry HEMP, jun., continue to carry on the business on Fishing Creek.

Lewis B. APPOLOW has a new method of cleaning teeth.

159. 2 May 1818

William WILLIS, boot and shoe maker, South Market St.

Died Sunday morning last, John BAER, in his 63d year, farmer in the vicinity of this town; interred in the Presbyterian burying ground.

Died Saturday, 25th ult., in Baltimore, Col. George ARMISTEAD, 39 years of age.

Married Tuesday evening last by Rev. David F. SCHAEFFER, Henry HOFFMAN, to Miss Margaret KEMP, dau of Col. Henry KEMP, all of this co.

Abraham HUMSTOTT, Montgomery Co., offers reward for apprentice to the black-smith business, Alexander PAGE, 17-18 years of age.

Lindsay SPOTSWOOD, Carlisle, warns that Thomas KERR, probably a native of Norfolk, VA, swindled him out of $10-15.

160. 9 May 1818

John FOX will sell his property, 5 miles from Frederick town, adjoining lands of Adam SIMON and John KLISE, 4 acres with two story log dwelling and stable with orchard.

F. M'CREADY, Professor of the Arts of Penmanship and Drawing, will provide instruction in these arts.

161. 16 May 1818

Married Thursday evening, 7th instant, by Rev. David MARTIN, John BAST, to Miss Catherine WINTERS, all of this co.

Died Monday, 11th instant, at Liberty, captain Enoch TAYLOR; buried with Masonic honors.

Died Tuesday morning, Mrs. Mary MANTZ, consort of Francis MANTZ of this city; buried at the German Lutheran burying ground.

Benjamin HOFF wishes to purchase a few young Negroes.

162. 30 May 1818

Married Thursday evening last, by Rev. Jonathan HELFFENSTEIN, Samuel CARMACK, to Miss Caroline SMITH, all of this co.

John GRABILL, 1 1/2 miles from Emmitsburg, offers reward of Negro man PETER, who calls himself Peter PORTER, about 26 years of ge, 5 feet, 7-8 inches high.

James TORRANCE, admr. of Andrew YOUNG.

Shadrach BURGISS, gives notice that Henrietta GUILLARD, slave of John MERRYMAN, dec'd., Baltimore Co., has left his bed and board, not being lawfully married; he will not pay any of her contracts.

163. 6 June 1818

The murder of Dr. Robert BERKLEY, Winchester, is described.

Married Tuesday evening last, by Rev. HELFFENSTEIN, John T. SPURRIER of Anne Arundel co. to Miss Mary SMITH of this city.

Married Thursday, 28th ult., by Rev. HELFFENSTEIN, Peter STALY, jun., to Miss Margaret ALBAUGH, esq., both of this co.

164. 13 June 1818
Report of mayor Lawrence BRENGLE with the following account of expenses: FOSS & BAILEY for paving public squares; Peter MYERHEIFER for whitewashing market house and lime; George BAER of Wm. for 1 set weights; John REICH for John BEALL, labourer; sundry expenses in surveying the town; Negro for wheeling weights to standard keeper and back; George BAER, Esq. for lead; John BUCKEY as Judge for ward no. 1 in 1817; Charles James WOLFENDEN as clerk; Hilleary HATLEY as clerk; John RIGNEY as Judge of ward no. 2; George SENLEY as clerk; William STEINER as clerk; George W. ENT as Judge for ward no. 3; Philip REICH as clerk; Samuel POWELL as clerk; Valentine BRUNNER as Judge for ward no. 4; William HAUSER, clerk; Leonard J. M. LITTLEJOHN as clerk; James F. HOUSTON as Judge for ward no. 7; George Jacob HOUX as clerk; Eli OGLE as Judge for ward no. 5; Joseph SCHELL as clerk; Cyrus CARY as clerk; George SCHULTZ as Judge for ward No. 6; Martin SCHULTZ as clerk; David SPRENGLE as clerk; Henry BAER, George HAUER and John L. HARDING as Judges of the Election for Mayor and Aldermen in 1817; Robert RITCHIE and John J. McCULLEY as clerks; John P. THOMPSON for printing; Samuel BARNES for printing; Christopher MYERS for carrying pole; Ezra SCHELL for carrying pole; Francis KLINEHART for repairing streets; Henry SCHOLL for flag stone; John EBBERT for work done about bridge; Peter MYERHEIFER for making sewer; John L. HARDING for furnishing pump in Market St.; William SCHLEY as clerk to the board of Aldermen; Peter SOWERS for repairing alley; John RIGNEY for furnishing stone; John L. HARDING for carts employed in filling up and compleating sewer in Market St.; Henry KOONTZ, Esq. for assessing town property; Valentine BRUNNER for paper for election books in 1817; John REICH for the use of the Commissioners of the town; Jacob BERGER for value of his hogs returned and for scales in Market House; HALL and FEABUS, masons, for making sewers &c. in bridges; Philip WERSTHERN; Tobias HALLER; Henry McCLEERY for repairing pavement in Market house; Costs of suit vs Thomas JONES for breech Market law.

165. 20 June 1818
Died Tuesday last, Richard M. STEINER, son of Henry STEINER, aged 4 years and 4 months.
Married Tuesday evening last, by Rev. Burges NELSON, Philip ENGLAR, to Miss Jane BROWN, all of this co.
Married same evening by Rev. DAY, Gideon MANTZ, of Holly Bush, to Miss Eliza SIDES of Anne Arundel Co.
Married same evening, Hon. Charles J. KILGOUR, of Rockville, Montgomery Co., to Miss Louisa M'ILHANEY, of VA.
The Vestry of the German Reformed Congregation announces that on 2 July a corner stone will be laid of their New Church. Peter COBLENTZ, John EVERHART, managers.

166. 27 June 1818
Henry HARBAUGH, extr. of Jacob HARBAUGH, Sen.
Daniel JAMES, Warrenton, Fauquier Co., VA, offers reward for John M. BRODERICK who absconded with a light grey mare belonging to him, probab-

ly on his way to the Western Country, about 28 years of age, 5 feet, 4-5 inches, fair complexion, black eyes, dark curley hair, from New York where he supposedly left a wife and children and married another in this town which he has also left.

167. 4 July 1818
Jacob S. GRIFFIN offers reward for horse missing from Wm. COOKERLY's tavern.
Sale of farm whereupon Elijah BALDWIN formerly lived, near Taney-town, 198 1/2 acres.

168. 11 July 1818
Died Friday, 3rd inst. after a short illness, Jacob LATE, long a respectable inhabitant of this co.; buried in the German Lutheran Burying ground.
BROADRUP & MORGAN, Pleasant Dale Paper Mill, 5 miles from Fredericktown, offer reward for apprentice to the paper making business, John LINTON, about 20 years of ge, 5 feet.
F.(?) B. MOORE offers reward for mulatto man named BOB, who absconded from jail of Frederick-town.

169. 18 July 1818
Married Thursday, 11th ult. at Brookville (Indiana Territory) by Rev. Lewis DEWESE, William M'CLEERY, of this town, to Miss Eleanor KNIGHT of that place.
Married Thursday, 2nd inst. by Rev. P. DAVIDSON, John DARBY, merchant, to Miss Catherine RIED, both of Taney town.
Ordered that chancery sale of Peter BEALL's estate be ratified.

170. 25 July 1818
Married Tuesday evening last by Rev. Bishop KEMP of Baltimore, John THOMAS, merchant of this town, to Miss Eliza Sophia SPURRIER, of Anne Arundel Co.
Green Tree Tavern - John BONER has removed from Emmitsburg to well known stand in Taney-town, formerly occupied by Mrs. CROUSE.
Walter BROOKES, Loudoun Co., VA, offers reward for Negro man named TRENT, about 5 feet, 8-9 inches, about 25 years old.

171. 1 Aug 1818
Samuel KEEFFER offers a reward of 1 cent and a not of mortar for apprentice to the stone-mason and brick laying business named Godfrey GROVE, 17-18 years of age.
John W. MILLER, Frederick, offers reward for red cow.

172. 8 Aug 1818
Jacob GROSS, insolvent debtor, confined at jail, now released, applies for relief from debt.

173. 15 Aug 1818
James COFFMAN offers reward for horse stolen from his waggon at Mr. GILL's Tavern.

174. 22 Aug 1818. No new items.

175. 29 Aug 1818
Elected to the Directors at Frederick Town for the Branch Bank of Farmers' Bank of Maryland: John TYLER, John M'PHERSON, Wm. E. WILLIAMS, Casper MANTZ, William ROSS, Thomas HAWKINGS, Richard POTTS, John BRIEN and John SMITH.

Hagers-town - William LIZAR of this co. was murdered on Wednesday, 19th inst. by his son George LIZAR. *Torch Light.*

Louis B. OPPELLO will let off a balloon on Cannon Hill on Tuesday next. The balloon is 12 feet long by 10 square. He will depend entirely on the generosity of spectators for remuneration.

Henry H. WARFIELD, candidate for Congress, 3rd Congressional Dist.

176. 21 Nov 1818
Sale of 850 acres of land, 1-2 miles from Mechanicks-town. J. GIST, Long Farm.

Sale of tract of land, 124 acres, on the premises of Jacob DARNER, dec'd., 3 miles from Middletown, 1 mile from Henry POWLES's mill. Frederick DARNER, extr.

The Mansion Hotel, 11th and Market St., Phila. to be let. Thomas LEIPER.

Nathaniel CRAGHILL, Jefferson Co., VA, offers reward for Negro named FA; he calls himself Billy Gardner FAY, about 28-29 years old.

Dissolution of partnership of Mary LAMBERT and Charles James WOOLFENDEN.

Jacob STOCKMAN forewarns persons not to trust his wife Betsy, as she has left him without any just cause and he does not mean to pay any of her debts.

177. 5 Dec 1818
Died Monday last, after a long and protracted illness, Jacob FOGLER, in his 33d year, leaving a widow and one child. He had labored for 2 years past under a pulmonary complaint.

Thos. Ap. C. JONES offers for sale 125 acres in Fairfax Co., VA. Dr. H. BALL lives adjoining the property.

Philip LEWIS, insolvent debtor, confined in jail, now discharged, seeks relief from debts.

178. 19 Dec 1818
Died at York, PA, William C. HARRIS, editor of the *York Gazette*, in his 26th year.

Adam W. CAMPBELL, has applied to the Court of Common Pleas of the Co. of Franklin, PA, for the benefit of the insolvent laws.

Joseph MILLER has taken up a stray mare.

THE REPUBLICAN GAZETTE & GENERAL ADVERTISER 63

179. 26 Dec 1818
Married Sunday last, by Rev. D. F. SCHAEFFER, Jacob SNYDER, to Miss Mary CARMACK.
Married Tuesday last by same, John KNOX, to Mrs. Margaret TAILS.
Married Thursday last, by the same, Wm. STOCKMAN, to Miss Elizabeth MONTGOMERY.
Married same evening by Rev. HELFENSTEIN, Nicholas LEASE, to Miss Polly STONER, all of this city.

180. 9 Jan 1819
George SHOPE, cabinet maker, carries on the business next door below Frederick NUSZ, North Market St.
Sale on the premises, about 15 miles from Frederick-town, 1 mile from Godfried LEATHERMAN's plantation on the new cut road leading to Mr. HUGHES' Gap, a tan yard with lot of 10 1/4 acres, 2 shops, a beam house, bark house, first rate patent bark mill, 14 lay-way vats and 1 1/2 story dwelling house. Christian SHOUP.
Christopher ZANCK offers reward for stolen horse.
William CHYNOWATH, digs wells; call at his dwelling opposite the Lutheran Church in Church St.
George FOX has taken up a stray mare.
Reward for George AMEY who escaped from Frederick jail, about 5 feet, 8-9 inches, 30 years of age, fair complexion, light hair, long nose and has a family in PA.
Samuel EVAN lost at Jacob HALTLERMAN's Forge, at the mouth of Yellow Breeches Creek, Cumberland Co., PA, a military land warrant, no. 568.

181. 16 Jan 1819
George RICE has lost on the Harper's Ferry Road, between Frederick Town and HIME's Tavern, a box containing two frocks, two pair of shoes, two pair of hose, a gold breast pin and sundry other articles. For reward deliver to him in Frederick Town or to Henry BOTELER, New-Town Trap.
Chancery case: Jonathan MILLER and John STOVER vs. Robert PICKENS, Margaret PICKENS & Mary PICKENS. Object of bill is to obtain a decree to cancel and destroy a certain deed for real and personal estate made by Robert PICKENS to Robert PICKENS, one of the defendants, and to George PICKENS, dec'd. Bill states that Robert PICKENS, at the same time he made the said deed, was indebted to one of the complainants, Jonathan MILLER, and also to a Philip STOVER, dec'd.. That John STOVER the other complainant is the admr. of Philip STOVER dec'd. Robert PICKENS, dec'd., with a view to defraud the complainants, pretended to convey said deed, all his estate, real and personal to his two sons, Robert and George PICKENS; that Robert PICKENS from the time of making said deed, to the time of his death, was constantly in possession of the property. George PICKENS died intestate, leaving Margaret PICKENS and Mary PICKENS, his children and heirs at law, both of whom reside in the state of KY.

Chancery case: Elizabeth RAITT vs. Andrew SWAIDNER, Nathan RAITT, Margaret RAITT, Joel PUSEY, Ann PUSEY, John REEP, Christian ROOP, Sally ROOP, Elizabeth ROOP. Object of the bill is to obtain a decree to compel defendants to convey 3 acres and 1 rod of land, part of tract, The mill rights design, to the complainant. Bill states that Andrew SWAIDNER, about Oct 1792, purchased said land from Christian SAILOR, and paid him and received possession. That said SWAIDNER sold said land to complainant and received purchase money for it. That David ROOP in Nov 1797 purchased the balance of the tract with other lands from Christian SAILOR and from the general words of the agreement the 3 acres and 1 rod of land aforesaid was inadvertently included. David ROOP died intestate. Andrew SWAIDNER resides out of the state of MD. The other defendants are the children and heirs of said ROOP, residing in Frederick Co.

Sheriff's sale of land of John WHITEHILL, 2 miles of Middleburg, the following tracts: Retirement Corrected, 7 1/4 acres; Bedford; part of Logsdon's Amendment; part of The Resurvey on Brothers' Agreement. The last three contain 200 acres - taken at the suit of Jacob STIEMMEL, use of Joseph M. CROMWELL and at the suit of John CLEMSON.

182. 30 Jan 1819
John CRUMMELL offers reward for missing horse.
New Tavern, North Market St. William KOLB.
Samuel LEAMING, has applied to the Judges of the Court of Common Pleas of Adams Co. PA, for benefit of the Insolvent act.
Kensey HARRISON, James M'ELROY, John HARGESHEIMER, and Joseph ..., Philip M'DEVITT, John QUEEN, John STAUNTON or STANTON, are notified that further information is required by the War Department, in relation to their respective applications for a pension.
Rosanna MEASEL forewarns all persons of cutting timber from her plantation, whereon the subscriber lives, or from their mountain land, near Mr. KLISES'.

183. 6 Feb 1819
Died Tuesday last, Conrad ENGELBRECHT, long a respectable inhabitant of this town.
Died Tuesday morning last, David STONER; interred in the Presbyterian Burial ground in this city.
Michael BARNDOLLAR vs. George FISHER. Object of the bill is to obtain a decree for recording a deed executed by the defendant on 12 March 1785, part of a tract of land called Resurvey on Brother's Agreement.

184. 13 Feb 1819. No new items.

185. 20 Feb 1819
Sheriff's sale at the tavern James WAGERS in New Market, the estate of James WAGERS, house and lot, now occupied by him as a tavern - taken at the suit of Dennis POOLE.

Sale of tract of George PRICE, dec'd., on Opequan Creek, Frederick Co., 6 miles east of Winchester, adjoining Duvall's Sulpher Spring, 18 acres. Apply to Michael PRINTZ, residing on part of the land. The widow holds a life estate in about 30 acres. Henry SEEVERS, extr.

186. 27 Feb 1819

Hezekiah WEBSTER forewarns persons not to trust his wife Liddy WEBSTER, as she has left him without any cause.

Fire on Sunday night last, about 9 o'clock, the town was alarmed of the cry of Fire, the barn and hay-stack on the farm occupied by Jacob REED, about 1/2 mile from town.

Died Friday morning last, John BRUNNER near this town, old respectful inhabitant of this co.; interred in the Presbyterian burying ground.

Chancery case: John GUNN, Jacob DADISMAN and Sarah DADISMAN, his wife, John MILLER and Christiana MILLER his wife, Caleb FULLER, and Margaret FULLER his wife vs. John Curry Cunningham GUNN, Solomon D. GIBSON, Stephen Decatur GIBSON and Peter BRUNNER, Junior. Object of this bill is to obtain a decree for cancellation of certain deeds. The bill states that Margaret BRUNNER being seized in fee of lot number 223 in Frederick-Town, died intestate, leaving John GUNN, Sarah DADISMAN, Christiana MILLER, Margaret FULLER and John Curry Cunningham GUNN, her heirs at law. John Curry Cunningham GUNN, son of Christopher GUNN, dec'd., who was a son of the said Margaret BRUNNER, by a former husband, that the said Christopher having died before the said Margaret BRUNNER, the said John Curry Cunningham GUNN is entitled to the undivided moiety of the said lot be descent, that his father Christopher GUNN would have been entitled to had he survived his mother; that the said lot hath descended to John GUNN, Sarah DADISMAN, Christiana MILLER, Margaret FULLER and John Curry Cunningham GUNN; that the said John Curry Cunningham GUNN conveyed his undivided interest only to Solomon D. GIBSON in trust for Stephen Decatur GIBSON; that the said lot is now held jointly by the said complainants and Solomon D. GIBSON.

187. 6 March 1819. No new items.

188. 20 March 1819

Died Saturday, 6th ult. at Woodsneck(?), VA, Jacob HAAS, old and worthy inhabitant of this co., leaving relations and friends.

Chancery sale of lot, 9 acres, adjoining town of New Market, late the property of Wm. GIBSON, dec'd. Richard ROBERTS, trustee.

Rezin M'GRUDER, near Middletown, has taken up a stray steer.

Chancery sale of tracts of land in the upper part of the Middletown Valley, adjoining lands of Levin HAYS and Jacob WOLF: Toms Safe Guard, 120 acres and John Toms Luck, 289 acres. These lands compose together the farm on which Hezekiah ROBINSON lately lived. Richard POTTS, trustee.

189. 27 March 1819. No new items.

190. 3 April 1819. No new items.

191. 10 April 1819. No new items.

192. 17 April 1819
Married 10th inst., by Rev. Thomas P. MAY, David SOWER, jr., Editor of the Norristown Herald, PA, to Miss Cecelia CHOLLET of Philadelphia.
Married Tuesday last, Solomon FORMWALT, to Miss Elizabeth ECKER, dau of George ECKER of the neighborhood of Union Town.
Died Monday, 5th inst. at his residence near Frederick, of a pulmonary disease, Charles HAMMOND, in his 38th year, leaving wife and 2 small children. Herald.
Died Tuesday, 30th ult. in Taney Town, John HUGHES, old and respectable inhabitant of that place.
Died Thursday morning, 8th inst., Jacob CLABAUGH, Esq., near Union Town.
John BEAR of Henry, opposite Dr. J. BALTZEL's in Patrick St., has just received a large assortment of earthen ware.
D. HANE & J. KINKERLY, waggon makers, New Market, carry on the business in the house formerly occupied by Casper KLINE.

193. 24 April 1819. No new items.

194. 1 May 1819
Michael MILLER, Frederick Town offers reward for apprentice boy bound to the coopering business named Absalom WILLIAMS.
The horse, Canadian, will stand the ensuing season. Isaac GRIFFITH, Samuel WADSWORTH.

195. 8 May 1819
Chancery case: Adam BAUGHMAN vs. William JENKINS and Patrick MAGILL. The bill states that William JENKINS for the use of Patrick MAGILL, sen., obtained a judgment in the Frederick co. court at the March term 1819, against Adam BAUGHMAN for the sum of $321.80 with interest; that Adam BAUGHMAN was necessarily compelled to suffer said judgment for the want of legal testimony; that William JENKINS be compelled to disclose on oath all the facts. William JENKINS resides out of the state of Maryland.

196. 15 May 1819
Married Monday evening, 3d May by Rev. Nicholas ZOCHIE, John CRAPSTER, Jun. to Miss Frances SHORB, all of Taney Town, Frederick Co.
Married Tuesday evening, 4th inst. at St. Peter's Church, Baltimore, by Rev. HENSHAW, William BRADFORD, of Frederick-town, to Miss Jane RINGGOLD, of that city.
Died at Oakland, Monday, 5 April, Miss Rachael Howard HOOD, 2nd dau of Col. Thomas HOOD, in her 15th year.

Jacob DEBIS, Frederick Co., offers reward for Negro man named TOM, about 30 years old.

197. 22 May 1819
Samuel MERITT, Liberty Town has purchased well known tavern stand in Liberty Town at the sign of the Indian King, lately occupied by William MYERS.

198. 29 May 1819
Married last evening by Rev. P. DAVIDSON, Cornelius CRAMER to Miss Amelia FULTON, of Woodsborough.
Died at Wheeling, VA, Monday, 17th instant, after a tedious illness of a pulmonary affection, John A. SHELMERDINE, of this co., in his 24th year.
Died Wednesday night, George W. MURDOCH, Esq., Attorney at Law, in his 27th year.

199. 5 June 1819
Richard NOKES, tailor, to carry on his business in the store belonging to Mrs. John STIMBELL, fronting the old Market House in Bentz-town.
Sheriff's sale at the Tavern of John CREEGER of Lawrence, in Graceham, 8-day clock, 5 10-plate stoves, desk, book-case and other, late property of said John CREEGER, taken at the suit of SCHLEY and SEWELL.
Fresh burnt lime for sale at his lime kiln, 3 miles from Frederick-town on the new cut road, leading to the High Knob. Peter SHOOK.
Commissioners appointed to locate a public road from Taney-Town to Middleburg, from thence to or near George WEBB's store and from thence to Liberty Town: Surratt D. WARFIELD, John DUDDERAR, Wm. P. FARQUHAR. This is their effort to give notice to Joseph TANEY, Edward J. WILSON, Leonard SIX, Christian SMITH, John DEAR, Henry MAYNARD and others.
Chancery sale of property in the cause of Jacob BRENGLE against Abraham B. WOODWARD, confirmed.
Sheriff's sale of house and lot in graceham, no. 11, of John CREEGER of Lawrence and house and lot no. 8 - taken at the suit of John HOFFMAN, Peter and Benjamin FAHNESTOCK, John and Thomas EDMONDSON, George SEASE(?) & BARR, KEYS & WELSH.

200. 12 June 1819
Died Tuesday last, George William HOFFMAN, aged about 26 years.
Constables appointed by the Levy Court, Jun 1819: Frederick HUNSBERRY, west Middle-town; Benjamin HAGAN, Linganore; Edward L. BOTELER, Ballinger's creek.
Wood-land for sale, 22 1/2 acres near the saw mill of Jacob HETIZ, on Fishing creek. B.S. PIGMAN.
Jeremiah JONES notifies that John IIAMS has taken up a gray gelding at his farm near Plummer IIAMS' mill.

201. 19 June 1819. No new items.

202. 26 June 1819
Died at Hagerstown 13th inst., Daniel WITMER, innkeeper, in his 60th year.
Peter STALEY, jr., has taken up a stray horse.

203. 3 July 1819
Henry THOMAS, insolvent debtor, now confined in jail, now discharged, applies for relief from debt.

204. 10 July 1819
Died Wednesday evening last, Charles SCHELL, Jr. of this town, aged 33 years, 11 months, of a lingering illness.
William M. BEALL, sheriff, offers reward for two white men who broke jail, one named Samuel BLACK, aged about 30 years, 5 feet, 6-7 inches, black hair and beard, rather a dark complexion, scar on one of his cheeks, rather talkative, has a tavern stand at Greenleaf's point, Washington City - the other named Michael CONNOLLY, native of Ireland, aged about 38 years, 5 feet, 5-6 inches, square built, sandy hair, large whiskers, ruddy complexion, somewhat fond of liquor.

205. 17 July 1819
William HAUSER, insolvent debtor, confined in jail, now released, seeks relief from debt.

206. 24 July 1819
Frederick FEAGA, insolvent debtor, confined in jail, now released, seeks relief from debt.
John B. WEBER, having no wish to be released from his debt by praying to the benefit of the act of insolvency, requests to meet with his creditors.
Chancery case: Ignatius LIVERS & Catharine LIVERS his wife, Samuel LINEBAUGH and Mary Ann LINEBAUGH his wife & John MESNER vs. Christian MESNER, Henry MATHEWS, Thomas SHUFF and Rachel SHUFF his wife, Elizabeth MATHEWS, Peter MATHEWS and Benjamin MATHEWS, Elizabeth HARRIS and James HARRIS. Object of bill is to obtain a decree for sale of tract in Frederick Co., held by the complainants and defendants as tenants in common. Bill states they are entitled to tract of land as heirs at law of George MESNOR, dec'd. and land will not admit of property partition but may be well sold and proceeds distributed. Henry MATHEWS, Thomas SHUFF and Rachel SHUFF his wife, Christian MESNOR, Elizabeth HARRIS and James HARRIS reside out of the state of Maryland.

207. 31 July 1819
Died at Abbott's town Wednesday, 14th inst., in his 90th year, Lewis ROSENMILLER, Senr., maternal grand-father of Rev. SCHAEFFER of this place.

Phileman POOL has taken up a stray gelding.

208. 7 Aug 1819
During the storm on Tuesday last, the west side of the brick livery stables belonging to John MANTZ, and now in occupancy of Joseph TALBOT, in this city, was thrown down.
Sale at his farm, 3/4 mile west of Frederick Town, horses, cows, steers and hogs and farming utensils. Israel MYERS.
Chancery case: Elizabeth BIRELY extx. of Frederick BIRELY vs. Jacob FAUBLE, William HINKS, John WERTENBAKER, William WERTENBAKER, George WERTENBARGER, Elizabeth OTT, Michael OTT, Catharine SULL and Peter SULL. Object of bill is to obtain a decree for sale of undivided seventh part of certain houses and a lot in Frederick town which is the real estate of Michael WERTENBAKER, dec'd. for the payment of his debts. Michael WERTENBAKER in his life time was indebted to Frederick BIRELY, dec'd, on a single bill for 13 pounds, 2 shilling sand 9 pence. That dec'd. left the complainant sole extx.; that whole of money is now due on bill; that Michael WERTENBAKER hath died testate without issue and without personal estate to pay his debts. That at the time of his death he was possessed of real estate in Frederick Co., to wit, an undivided seventh part of certain houses and lot which came to Jacob WERTENBAKER, John WERTENBAKER, William WERTENBAKER, George WERTENBAKER, Elizabeth OTT wife of Michael OTT, Catharine SULL wife of Peter SULL, his brothers and sisters. That Jacob WERTENBAKER since the death of said Michael WERTENBAKER hath also died intestate without issue, leaving John WERTENBAKER, William WERTENBAKER, George WERTENBAKER, Elizabeth OTT and Catharine SULL heirs at law.
Sheriff's sale at Capt. Daniel SMITH's saw mill, tract of Henry WELLER, called Hammer and part of tract called Creegers Scheme, on Owings Creek.

209. 14 Aug 1819
John REESE and Jacob REESE, extrs. of Adam REESE.

210. 21 Aug 1819
Died near Rockville, Montgomery Co., on 11th inst., William A. DOWNEY, Printer, aged 24 years and 9 months.
Chancery case: Gilbert DAVIS & Eliza his wife, Joseph DAVIS, Walter DAVIS, George GEBHART & Catharine his wife, Sarah RADCLIFFE & James DEAN. Object of bill is to obtain decree for sale of real estate not being susceptible to division. Bill states that Joseph RADCLIFFE died, seized in fee of considerable real estate, having made his last will. After bequeathing sundry legacies he directs all his real estate as follows: to Elizabeth wife of Gilbert DAVIS, 1/4 part; to grand children, the sons and daus. of Susanna DAVIS, 1/4 part; to his dau Catharine DEAN by her first marriage but by her second marriage, Catharine MANNACAY, 1/4 part and in case she shall not live to receive it to be divided among the heirs of her body and to his son Thomas RADCLIFFE. That Susanna DAVIS named in will is dead, leaving heirs at law the complainants, Joseph DAVIS and Walter DAVIS. Mary who married

Moses CANNON is now dead leaving the following children: William, Grace, Catharine, and Nace CANNON, all of whom are infants, Catharine DAVIS who married George GEBHART and George DAVIS and Denton DAVIS, minors. Thomas RADCLIFFE is also dead since the execution of will, leaving the following children, his heirs: Sarah, one of the complainants, and James, Joshua, Mary, Joseph, Elizabeth, William, Thomas and Upton, who are minors. Catharine MANNACAY was married to Barney DEAN by whom she had the following children: Sarah who married Alexander HERRY, Thomas, Joshua and James DEAN, the last of whom is one of the complainants. Said Joseph RADCLIFFE at the time of his death was seized of a tract called Rights of Man, 500 acres.

211. 28 Aug 1819

Died Tuesday morning last, 17th inst., Mrs. Frances RITCHIE, relict of the late William RITCHIE, Esq. [See also *Herald*.]

Died Thursday morning, Joseph, 2nd son of Joseph M. PALMER, esq. of this town.

212. 4 Sep 1819

A committee appointed to ascertain the state of the manufactories in this city and precincts at 3 different periods, viz: during the war in 1814, in 1816 and at the present time. Mr. DUANE and Mr. CAREY appointed to report suitable names, the following were adopted: Mark RICHARDS, Ironfounder; Jonathan LUKENS, Saddler; James RONALDSON, Type founder; William YOUNG, Wollen manufacturer; Seth CRAIGE, Cotton manufacturer; John HARRISON, Chemist; William FRY, Printer; Henry HORN, Silver plater; Patrick M'KELL, Manufacturer of hosiery; James JOSIAH, Manufacture of glass; Thomas FLETCHER, Manufacturer of screws, &c.; Franklin EYRE, Ship builder; Edward SHELMERDINE, Hatter; J. D. LANGSTROTH, Paper maker; Hugh HENRY.

Married Tuesday, 31st ult. by Rev. Jonathan FORREST, David ARMOUR, of Illinois, to Miss Maria MOORE, of this co.

Chancery case: Nimrod FRIZEL & Ann his wife, David FISHER & Eleanor FISHER, vs. Nicholas SHAFER & wife, John FISHER, David FISHER & others. Object of bill is to obtain a decree for sale of real estate of David FISHER, dec'd., and to divide the proceeds of the sale, among his children. Bill states that said David FISHER being seized of real estate in Frederick and Baltimore Counties, in Oct 1815 died intestate, leaving 14 children, all of whom are complainants and defendants in the bill. David FISHER one of the defendants at this time resides out of the state of Maryland.

213. 11 Sep 1819. No new items.

214. 18 Sep 1819

Sale of dwelling house and 50 acres on turnpike road from Frederick Town to Baltimore at the Monocacy Bridge known as Combing Ferry. Benj'n. HERSH, residing on the farm.

215. 25 Sep 1819
Jacob MALAMBRE, has removed to the house nest to the bridge in Patrick St., opposite to William SPRINGER, hatter, where he manufactures all kinds of ladies and gentlemen's boots and shoes.

216. 2 Oct 1819. No new items.

217. 9 Oct 1819
John CROMWEL, who formerly resided in Charlestown, Jefferson Co., VA, and went on to the Western country, to the state of OH or KY, will hear something to his advantage if he writes or comes to Frederick town.
Michael KOLB offer reward for persons who robbed him of a number of scales and weights.
Died Thursday morning last, Philip PYFER, esqr. an aged and respectable inhabitant of this town.

218. 16 Oct 1819
Sheriff's sale of Negroes of Jonathan WOOD, taken at the suits of Peter BECRAFT, Abdiel COKEFER and William WOOD, use Philip HINES.
Sheriff's sale of lot of ground and black smith's shop and other buildings of James WOOD, devised to him by his father Joseph WOOD, taken at the suit of Peter BECRAFT.
Sheriff's sale of a lot with buildings, of Henry M'HENRY, being in Shield's Addition to Emmitsburg, No. 3, late the property of Henry M'HENRY, taken at the suit of Thomas RADFORD and George GROVER.
Sheriff's sale of estate of Jacob SHORB to 35 acres being part of Hamilton's Recover and part of Digges lot, late the property of Jacob SHORB, taken at the suits of Farmers Bank of Maryland and the Hagerstown Turnpike Road Company use of John and Philip FISHER.

219. 23 Oct 1819
Sale of the farm of Jacob BECHT, dec'd., adjoining Woodsborough, 186 acres. George FOX, Jacob BEARD, extrs.

220. 30 Oct 1819
P. RUSSELL has an exhibition of Columbia's Heroes in Phatasmagoria which he invites ladies and gentlemen to view at Mrs. SHAFER's tavern this and every evening until further notice. Admittance 25 cents. Children half price.

221. 6 Nov 1819
Married Tuesday last by Rev. SCHAEFFER, John LINK, to Miss Lucy FILLER, both of this co.
Died 27th ult., Doctor John N. Andrew BOGEN, of Carlisle, PA, for many years a resident of Frederick Town.

Died Tuesday morning, between 1 and 2 o'clock, Miss Rebecca KOLB, dau of George KOLB, esq. of this place, in her 19th year, after a painful illness of 4 weeks.

222. 13 Nov 1819

John REIGH has taken up a stray sow and 3 pigs.
Died Thursday morning last after a short illness, Joseph HOWARD, about 24 years of age, son of widow HOWARD of the Manor.

223. 20 Nov 1819

Sheriff's sale of 150 acres of Barton HACKNEY, being part of Merry Land on which he now resides, taken at the suits of Dennis O'BYRNE, Peter MARTIN use of Joseph M. CROMWELL, Philip BLESSING, Sarah LEARNED extx. of Augustus LEARNED, Anna Maria COST extx. of George COST, United States, Alexander GRIM, Basil & Harper WILLIAMS use of Basil MULLIKEN, William DOUGHERTY use of George KOLB, Richard ENGLISH, Ann GARROTT, Patrick O'BURN, use of John ECARDS, admrs., Francis MANTZ & John C. FRACIN.
Sheriff's sale at the house of John GARROTT, Negro man named PLATO and Negro boy HENLY, late the property of said John GARROTT, taken at the suits of Benjamin DEAVER, use of Joseph M. CROMWELL and the suit of George BUTT.
Sheriff's sale of estate of Barton PHILPOT, 116 acres whereon Barton PHILPOT now lives, being part of tract called Merry Land, taken at the suits of Peter MARTIN use of Joseph M. CROMWELL, George BAER, Joseph SMITH senior, Unites States and George BAER use of Francis MANTZ.
Blacksmith seeks employment - John DRUNENBERGER, Frederick Co.

224. 27 Nov 1819. No new items.

225. 4 Dec 1819

Died Thursday night, 25th ult. in his 70th year, Henry M'CLEERY, for many years a resident of this town. *Herald.*
Independent Hosemen to meet at Union Tavern. F. A. GEPHART, Sec.
William SMITH, insolvent debtor, confined in jail, to be released; seeks relief from debt.
John B. WEBER, father of 6 children explains his plight.
Sheriff's sale of Negro man, property of Abraham KARNS, at the suits of Eve M. REED and Joseph WALLING.

226. 11 Dec 1819

Sheriff's sale of Mordecia L. HAMMONS's undivided tenth part of a tract called Polly's Inheritance, 185 1/2 acres, near Turnpike Gate, 2 miles west of New Market - at the suits of Jacob SHRIVER, John HAMMOND, Benjamin & Joshua JOHNSON, Thomas HAMMOND, John GEBHART and John SCHILLER.

Chancery sale of part of the real estate of Abraham B. WOODWARD, approved.

John HOOPER has lost a leather pocket book, with a note of hand against Jacob KUHN for 25 pounds, 9 shillings.

227. 18 Dec 1819

Died Wednesday, 8th Dec last, in his 75th year, John HOUCK, sen., long a respectable inhabitant of this co.

Dissolution of partnership of James and Joseph WALLING, Jr. James WALLING will carry on the boot and shoe making business in the same house.

FREDERICK-TOWN HERALD

228. Saturday Jan 6, 1816

Died at Creagers-town on the 31st ult., Thomas BEATTY, aged about 81 years, after a lingering indisposition of some months. He was a revolutionary patriot.

Died Saturday last in the prime of life, John EARLY. His complaint, a quinsy, which from perfect health carried him off in the short space of 50 hours.

Died Monday last in this town, Jacob FISHER, a young man between 18 and 19 years. While carelessly running along, with his hands in his pockets, he dropped and fell with his breast on the curb stone. It is supposed that in the fall he ruptured a large blood vessel. He survived the fall but a few minutes.

On the 7th of this inst. was committed to the jail in the borough of Pittsburgh, a Negro man who calls himself Henry WARNER, between 25 and 30 years of age; says he was raised by and belonged to John WASHINGTON of Maryland who died some time since. Samuel HUBLEY, jailer.

Reward offered for Negro man named MOSES, 31-32 who raw away from my farm, 4 miles of Frederick-town, raised by Richard WOOTTEN of Montgomery Co. John L. HARDING.

John ANDREWS has removed his residence from Williamsburg, Va., to Frederick-Town, Maryland, where he offers his services as a practitioner of law at Northeast corner of Market and Second sts., opposite to Col. John HUSTON's tavern.

Farm for sale where subscriber now resides, 280 acres, on Sams Creek, Frederick Co. Ann WILLIS.

Having rented John HUGHES' farm near this place I hereby forward persons from trespassing. Thomas POWELL.

S. CLAGGETT offers reward for mare missing from his pasture, 2 1/2 miles from Frederick-town, on the Harper's Ferry road. Give information to Daniel GANTT, living at Mr. ANDERSON'S, near Frederick-town.

A large black & white hog has been trespassing on me all last fall. J. GRAHAME.

229. 13 Jan 1815

Sale of farm, 250 acres, adjoining lands of Samuel REYNOLDS, late John KENEGE and others. Andrew KAUFFMAN, jun., John KAUFFMAN, heirs of late Andrew KAUFFMAN. Also 70-80 acres of mountain land adjoining STALEY's and Adam SUMAN's lands.

Sheriff's sale at the house of Conrad SHAFFER, Frederick-town, tract of Raphael's DARNELL called the Hope, taken by sundry writs of Maryland, at the suit of David EVELAND, at the suit of Samuel REYNOLDS, at the suit of Jacob SCHRIVER, at the suit of Peter SOWERS, at the suit of George PAYNE, at the suit of Benjamin RUTHERFORD and the suit of the state. Peter MARTIN for Joseph M. CROMWELL, Sheriff.

Sheriff's sale of estate of William JENKINS, 1/2 of house and lots in which said Jenkins lives in Frederick town, plat nos. 177 and 178; seized at the suit of Samuel NIXDORFF.

Sale of land formerly belonging to Nehemiah HALL, late of Baltimore Co., dec'd, 140 acres in Baltimore Co. on Pare's Falls, 1 mile from William ENSEY's tavern; also tract adjoining, 125 acres; and tract of 107 acres on Pare's Falls. Apply to Warfield HALL, living close by. Benjamin HALL.

Sale of lot of ground in New-Winsor (Sulphur Springs), Frederick Co., Maryland, 60 feet fronting on Bath St. and 150 feet fronting on High St., 2 story frame house; also furniture. John DAGEN.

Star of Federalism about to be published in Uniontown. Charles SOWER.

John BUCKIUS, Auctioneer, New-town (Trap).

Mills and land for sale in pursuance of the last will of Sebastian STONEBRAKER, Frederick Co. Grist mill, saw mill and plaister mill, 82 acres on Carroll's Manor. Sebastian STONEBRAKER, ex'r.

230. 20 Jan 1816

The four Negroes convicted of the murder of Edward OWINGS, at the late Special Court, care to be executed on Friday next, 26th inst. at 12 o'clock.

Appointments: Orphan's Court - John M'PHERSON, Ignatius DAVIS and John GRAHAME. Levy Court - Alexander WARFIELD of Charles, Benjamin BIGGS, Stephen STEINER, James MORRISON, Otho SPRIGG, William P. FARQUHAR, Joshua GIST. Magistrates - David BOWLUS, Thomas B. JONES, Frederick UNKEFER, Francis B. SAPPINGTON, Henry M'ELFRESH, Belt BRASHEAR, William GRIMES, jun., Jason PHILLIPS, Henry WILLIAMS, William EMMIT, William LONG, Jacob MATTHIAS, Joseph S. SMITH, Joseph TANEY, William B. HEAD, Jonas CRUMPACKER, William P. FARQUHAR, Henry KOONTZ, jun., Davis RICHARDSON, Ezra MANTZ, William DURBIN, jun., Jacob BAER, James MURPHY, Levin HAYS, George KOLB, Michael HAUSER, Jonathan M'DANIEL, Benjamin BIGGS, John S. FRAZIER, Jacob CLABAUGH, Vachel W. RANDALL, David BUCKEY, James SIMMONS, jun., Jacob LATE, George HOFFMAN, Dannie POOLE, John BALL, Peter ERB of Christopher, John H. SIMMONS, Richard THOMAS of Samuel, Abraham ALBAUGH, Jonathan NORRIS, Samuel P. RICHARDSON, Philemon GRIFFITH, Patrick REID, sen., Thomas C. SCOTT, Philip ROHR, William COUGHLIN, John JIAMS, Charles TALBOTT, Roger BROOKE, Andrew SMITH near Middle-Town, Andrew SMITH near Emmittsburg, Samuel OGLE, Greenbury MAGERS, Joshua JONES, Washington VANBIBBER, William POLE, George KEILER, Surratt D. WARFIELD, William HART, George PRICE, John LEATHERMAN, Singleton WOOTEN, John GLISAN, Joseph PENN, George

CREAGER, Thomas GIST, G. W. BOERSTLER, Jesse MATTHEWS, John SMITH of Daniel, Charles MANN.

231. 27 Jan 1816
Negroes JONATHAN, HARRY, NIMROD and SOLOMON who murdered Edward OWINGS early in November last, were executed yesterday at 12:00 o'clock.
Married on the 23rd inst. at Newtown (Trap) in this county by Rev. George WILLIAMS, James HOOK to Miss M'GILL, daughter of Patrick M'GILL of said place.
Meeting of the Frederick Academy Board of Visitors. John BALTZELL, Secretary.
Henry THOMAS has received various articles from Baltimore and offers for sale at reduced prices.
A young man wanted immediately with a small family to take charge of a farm and a few hands. James PEARRE, 4 miles below Liberty-town on the road to Baltimore.
Charles CUNNINGHAM, to resume the mercantile business, will rent his farm whereon he now lives, near the river Potomac, Frederick Co., 200 acres.
Examination of the several departments of the Frederick Academy will commence on Thursday. John V. WEYLIE.
Christian SCHOLL has taken up a stray bull.
Two farms for sale, 458 acres, 2 miles from Frederick-town, being part of her farm which has been improved by clover and plaister of Parish. Also a plantation of 251 acres, part of which is called Hawkin's Merry peep a day and part of Maryland Tract, situated on the Potomac river, adjoining the town of Berlin, 5 miles from Harper's ferry. V. VINCENDIERE, near Frederick-town.
Sale of 2 1/2 acres adjoining Frederick-town and belonging to William JENKINS. John GETZENDANNER, John BAYLY.
Overseer wanted - Baker JOHNSON, Auburn.
John NEIDIG will lease the grist and saw mill with 200 acres, 4 1/2 miles from Frederick-town, formerly owned by John WALKER and at present occupied by Joel FUNK.
Sale of tract o 670 acres in Frederick Co., 12 miles from Frederick-town on the head waters of Israel's creek. Capt. Philip SMITH will shew. Henry MAYNADIER, Annapolis.

232. 3 Feb 1816
Married on 30th inst. by Rev. George WILLIAMS, William TOWNSEND, to Miss Delia BELT, both of the Merryland Tract.
J. F. HUSTON having taken pains to qualify as a scrivener, &c. will draw wills, deeds, mortgages, bills of sale, releases, &c.
Ig. DAVIS offers reward for mare missing from his farm near Bucky's-town. Said mare was sold a few months ago by Leonard YOUNG, near Liberty-town.
Committed to the gaol of Frederick Co. as a runaway, a Negro man who calls himself NACE; says he belongs to Henry ANCHLING near Hancock, Maryland.

Whereas a petition was filed at March Term 1814 in Montgomery Co. court by Thomas SEDWICK of Montgomery Co., Maryland stating that William SEDWICK, his father, died in 1813 intestate, seized in fee simple of certain real estate in Montgomery Co. and that he left at his death 8 children and 2 grandchildren who were entitled to 1/9 part as the representatives of their deceased mother; that the said heirs and representatives of William SEDWICK were all of lawful age except the two grandchildren, Anna and Rebecca RILEY for whom William RILEY was appointed guardian. John DARBY, Edward BURGESS, Amon RIGGS sen., Adan DARBY and Samuel DARBY were appointed a commission to determine whether the said real estate would admit of being divided without loss. They determined that the land could not be divided without loss. Thomas SEDWICK the eldest son, at March Term 1815, refused to take the whole estate and pay to the others their just proportions and it being suggested that Frederick RILEY an infant and Ninian MOCKBEE and his wife and Elexander CARRICO and his wife are absent from Montgomery Co. and that Ninian MOCKBEE and Alexander CARRICO are the persons next entitled to elect to take the said real estate at the valuation made by the commission and are hereby notified.

Sale of Tavern stand which he now occupied in Market St., Frederick-town, known as the Fountain Inn, plus tract 3 miles from Frederick-town called "Altogether," 230 acres formerly owned by Melchior STALEY now deceased and now in the tenure of Peter and Frederick STALEY. Also a lot in Market St. adjoining the property of Mrs. Eleanor POTTS. Also a lot near Hunting Creek called "Long Point," 2 acres which will be shewn by Frederick C. HAASE in Creagerstown. Conrad SHAFER.

Sheriff's sale at Mr. MURPHY's Tavern in Barnesville, of tract called part of Conclusion, 82 2/3 acres, 2 miles of Barnesville, taken at the suits of John DOUD, use of Wm. W. AUSTIN. Arnold T. WINSOR, Sheriff of Montgomery Co.

233. 10 Feb 1816

Thomas SHAW requests that borrowed books be returned.

Notice is given by commissioners of company to pave a road from mouth of Monocacy to intersect the Frederick and Baltimore turnpike at the Poplar Springs. Nicholas CLOPPER, Joseph JOHNSON, Ely DORSEY, jun., Solomon DAVIS, CHARLES WILSON.

House and several lots for sale, lately occupied by George REMSBERG, near the west end of Patrick St. Apply to Justinian MAYBERRY near the property. SEBASTIAN REMSBERG.

Sale of land at Edward KENNEDY's tavern on the Baltimore turnpike road, about 3 miles below New-Market, called Just as You Like, 89 acres; to be sold agreeable to the decree of the Chancellor. Henry WAYMAN, trustee.

Nathan RAITT, having decline farming will sell stock of young horses.

Fresh clover seed - George TRISLER.

Teacher wanted. Apply to Ignatius JAMISON, near the mouth of Monocosy, Frederick Co.

Persons are cautioned from cutting timber or trespassing on the Hope Farm, lately the property of Thomas DARNALL, deceased. Robert DARNALL, Thomas N. BINNS.

Dennis POOLE (on adjoining property) will let blacksmith shop, at present occupied by Capt. Jacob ECKMAN. The shop, lately erected, is 20 by 24 feet with two brick furnaces.

William EARLY, Madison Co., Va., offers reward for Negro man named BILL, about 24 years old.

234. 17 Feb 1816
Chancery sale of real estate of Philip COBLENTZ, deceased, 273 acres, in Frederick Co. on Piney run, 2 miles of Gettysburg turnpike road. Property will be shewn by Jacob COBLENTZ on the premises or Peter WOLF near Emmitsburg. B.S. PIGMAN, trustee.

Chancery sale of house and lot on Market St., real estate of Frederick BAKER, dec'd.

Sale of 365 acres belonging to the heirs of William ROBERTS, dec'd., Frederick Co. in the well known settlement of Little Pipe Creek, 2 miles from New-Windsor (Sulphur Springs). Isaac ATLEE, William DURBIN, John NICODEMUS, Jacob SHRIVER, Michael BARTHOLOW, Pipe-Creek.

Sale of lot in Frederick Co. near the Tuscarora paper mills, 14 acres. Henry FEAGLER.

Dennis HAGAN, Atty at Law, has opened his office on Court St.

A blue dyer wanted. Jacob BOWLUS & Son, Middle-town Cotton Mill.

Man wanted with small family who understands all kinds of plantation work. Joseph STAUFFER, 6 miles from Frederick-town, near Israel's Creek.

Sheriff's sale of Negro man at Liberty-town, late the property of Frederick POOLE and James WAGERS, seized at the suits of Susannah PITTS and Ezra MANTZ and several issued at the suits of Isaac DAVIS, Seth CLARK, James M'DANIEL, William RYAN, Zachariah DANNER, John WAGNER, Daniel ARTHUR, David CONDON, Andrew ETZLER and David HARTSOCK. Daniel ARTHUR, Nathan ENGLAND.

235. 24 Feb 1816
Grafted apple trees, half way between Frederick-town and Monocacy Bridge. Haines DIXON.

Tavern to rent in Woodsborough which he now occupied, Joseph HEDGES.

Died Friday, 16th inst., at the seat of Mrs. NICHOLS in the neighbourhood of Baltimore, Ann Rebecca, only daughter of Major John GRAHAME of this county, aged 18 years.

Sheriff's sale at Isaac SHRIVER's tavern, Westminster, Frederick Co., all right of Lewis WEAVER to house and two lots in town aforesaid, seized at the suits of Deterick KEISER and Charles ROBINSON. Patrick REID of Alex., for J. M. CROMWELL, Sheriff.

Vachel PUMPHREY, near Jones' mill on Linganore, has taken up 4 stray sheep.

Sale at the farm lately owned by Thomas BEATTY, dec'd., adjoining Creagerstown, 13 Negro slaves, furniture, hogs, farming utensils, grain. Apply to S. GRIMES on the premises. John RITCHIE, ex'r.

Sale of estate of Margaret COOKERLY, dec'd, at her late residence adjoining William GALT's tavern on the York road, 10 miles from Taneytown, Negro woman, cattle, and the farm on which the dec'd resided, 200 acres. Jacob COOKERLY, ex'r.

236. 24 Feb 1816

Sale of farm on east side of Monocacy at Bagg's Ford, late the property of Edward OWINGS, dec'd, 180 acres. Nimrod OWINGS at the Fountain Rock Farm, adjoining the above property.

Edward COLSTON, Atty for Mary I. THOMAS, gives notice that persons who made purchases at the sale of the personal property of the late Dr. THOMAS, are requested to make payment.

Sale of property of Thomas MULLINUX, dec'd, a farm, 200 acres, 2 miles from Edward KENNADY's tavern. Charles MULLINUX, ex'r.

Books will be opened on the 18 March next for the purpose of taking subscriptions in shares of twenty dollars each to turnpike a road from the Baltimore and Frederick turnpike road, beginning at the west end of Frederick-town, then through New-town (Trap) to Harper's Ferry, under the direction of the following commissioners to wit: at the bank in Frederick-town, by Col. John M'PHERSON, George BAER, Thomas SHAW, John HOFFMAN, and Peter MANTZ; at New-town (trap) by Patrick M'GILL, James SIMMONS, jun, Jacob FISTER and Jesse MATTHEWS; at Petersville by Dr. William HILLEARY, Grafton DUVALL, John SLIFER, jun: and Benjamin WEST; at John ECKARD's tavern by John BRIEN, Thomas BOTELER, John ECKARD and Alexander GRIM and in the city of Baltimore, by William JESSOP, John E. HOWARD, James LABES, Luke TIERNAN, Henry PAYSON, James L. HAWKINS, Andrew ELLICOTT, Isaac TYSON, George HOFFMAN and Philip THOMAS.

Philip BARNHART offers reward for apprentice to the shoemaking business named Jacob BARNHART.

Sale of 418 acres, on the premises of Jacob WARENFELS, dec'd, real estate of the dec'd., on new cut road from Frederick-town to Washington Co. Apply to Jacob WARENFELS or Peter WARENFELS, living on the premises. Joseph MILLER, ex'r.

237. 2 March 1816

Thomas C. WORTHINGTON, Esq. is appointed prosecutor for the county of Frederick, in the place of Wm. T. T. MASON, esq., resigned.

Married in Philadelphia, Thursday, 22nd ult. by Rev. Dr. RODGERS, Major Robert G. M'PHERSON of this place, to Miss Maria DAVIS of that city.

Died Wednesday last, in this town, Rev. George ASKINS, for may years preacher of the Gospel in the Methodist Church.

Westminster, Taneytown & Emmitsburg turnpike company. Subscribers are requested to pay the fourth installment of two dollars. Nicholas SNIDER, Treasurer, Taneytown.

Sale of Negro girl, horses, cows, sheep and hogs. Jacob ECKMAN.

Mary EARLY, extx. of John EARLY to sell mulatto girl, about 19 years of age.

Sale at late residence of Joseph RATCLIFF, deceased, on Bush Creek, adjoining Johnson's Glass Works, 2 young Negro men, horses, cattle, sheep, hogs, farming utensils and other. Gilbert DAVIS, ex'r.

Hanson WILSON, adm'r of Hezekiah WILSON, Montgomery Co.

Sale at Col. DORSEY'S old quarter, 1 mile from William LOWE's mill on Linganore, corn by the barrel, rye, horses, cows, &c. Michael DOWNEY.

Sale by order of Orphans Curt of Montgomery Co., Negro lad, horses, cattle, etc. John POOLE, jun., ex'r. of John POOLE.

238. 9 March 1816

Died Wednesday morning 28th ult. at 4 o'clock, in Frederick-town, Rev. George ASKIN, aged 39 years, after a short and painful illness, leaving a widow. He was a native of Ireland, emigrated to America with his parents at a very early period of life; minister of Methodist Episcopal Church.

Died Monday evening last, 4th inst, after a long and severe illness, Mrs. Mary Magdalena BRUNNER, consort of Jacob BRUNNER, in her 48th year.

Sale of personal property of Morris JONES, Frederick Co., dec'd., beds, bedsteads, chair, tables, secretary, maps, looking classes, and Negro boy. Tobias NIXDORFF, one of the ex'rs.

Chancery sale of mill and 40 acres of John KENAGE, dec'd., 1/2 mile from Middle-town, on Catoctin creek. Frederick A. SCHLEY, Trustee.

David RIDGELY, offers reward for Negro man named LONDON who calls himself London TURER, late the property of George W. HIGGINS of Anne Arundel Co., 38-40 years of age.

Sale of Negro woman and Negro boy, at the late residence of John P. GARRETT, dec'd., on the Merryland Tract, cattle, horses, sheep and hogs. Elizabeth GARRETT, adm'r. Also much of the real estate of John P. GARRETT. Erasmus GARRETT, Trustee.

Sheriff's sale of lot No. 5 in Clarksburg, of James BROWNING, at the suit of Zachariah WATERS. Also lot of Jesse BROWNING in Clarksburg on High St. at the suit of Zachariah WATERS.

Sale of mill and 300 acres on Jones' Falls. Apply to manager Joshua ANDERSON on the premises or to subscriber, Richard CATON.

Caleb KNOTT, Toms Creek, to sell house and tenements in Toms Creek Hundred, Frederick Co., 1 mile from Emmitsburg.

To Plaisterers. The subscribers will receive proposals for plaistering the church in Creagers-town. Fr'dk. EICHELBERGER, Matthias SHRUP, George ZIMMERMAN.

Creditors of Peter CRABS, jun., drover (now confined in the jail of Adams co., Pa.) are notified that he has applied for relief of debt.

Basil DORSEY, ex'r of John DORSEY of John.

Jacob CRAMER, adm'r of Michael MYERS.

Michael BUCKEY and Stephen REMSBERG, admr's of Charlotte REMSBERG.

39. 9 March 1816

Jacob SERGEANT give notice that his wife Polly SERGEANT has left his bed and board and person are cautioned against trusting her on his account.

Samuel P. RICHARDSON, wishing to retire from the farming business, will offer his farm for sale, 247 acres, 6 miles of New-Market.

Stephen STEINER, adm'r of Dr. John FISCHER.

Negro boy and girl for sale. Apply to John GLISAN, Liberty-town, or Jesse WRIGHT, New Market.

Tract of land for sale in Montgomery Co., 3 miles below Clarksburg; Call on Joseph FUNK, living near said land or the subscriber living in Washington Co., 6 miles from Hagers-town. Henry NEWCOMER.

William BOYD offers reward for horse missing from his waggon at Rockville, Montgomery Co. Deliver to Jannaros S. FARROE, Rockville or to himself in Adams Co., Pa., 12 miles from Gettysburg.

240. 16 March 1816

Married at Philadelphia, 6th inst., by Rev. TURNER, John NEILL, tailor, formerly of this place to Miss Eliza BAXTER of that city.

Sale agreeable to the last will of William SMITH, house and lot no. 119 on Second St. Gideon BANTZ, ex'r.

Sale at his residence 4 1/2 miles from Frederick-town, horses, cattle, hogs, ploughs, harrow, hay ladders, wheat fan, cutting box, grain. Joel FUNK.

Sale of farm in Montgomery Co., 1 mile from river Potomac, lately in the occupancy of Capt. James WHITE, grist and saw mills; also stock of every description. Burgess B. WHITE, Addison WHITE.

Robert STEWARD, Chambersburg prison has applied for benefit of insolvency laws.

Eliza NELSON, adm'rs. request payment be made by purchasers of the estate of the late Gen. NELSON.

Persons are cautioned from cutting timber or trespassing on farm, late the property of Benjamin PITTENGER, dec'd. John PITTENGER, Daniel PITTENGER, James PITTENGER, Jeremiah PITTENGER, ex'rs.

Joseph MYERS, adm'r of Jacob MYERS.

Sarah SALMON, adm'rx. of William SALMON.

Jacob BAER & Co. have removed their store to the house lately occupied by Lewis J. DUGAS, 1 door above George BAER's store in Market St. - hardware, cutlery, saddlery and brassware.

241. 23 March 1816

Frederick BROWN cautions persons from taking assignment on notes given by him to Bartley RONEY.

242. 30 March 1816

Henry WILLIS, Wakefield, will sell waggon and saddle horses and other.

John HINCKLE, Jefferson Co., Va., adm'r of Theodore BEALL, late of Frederick Co., Md., dec'd.

Basil WOOD, Junr. to relinquish the farming business, to sell his farm in Frederick Co. on Monocacy, 1 mile from Creagers-town, 100 1/2 acres.
Chancery sale of two farms adjoining each other, one of 109 acres and the other 123 acres, real estate of Simon SNOOK, dec'd. Property will be shewn by Solomon SNOOK, living near the same.
John R. M'ATEE to sell or rent tavern which he now occupied in Montgomery Co. on main road from George-town to Frederick-town.
Charles MANN proposes a circulating library.
Chancery sale at the house of Henry BOTELAR in New-town (Trap) real estate of Ludwick HERRING, dec'd., farm called "Enough and to Spare," adjoining New-town, 169 1/2 acres, and another tract called "Fielderea," 1 mile from New-town, 105 acres, house and lot in Newtown, late the residence of Ludwick HERRING. Property will be shewn by Sebastian REMSBURG. Also farm near Boonsboro in Washington Co., part of tract called Nottingham, 91 acres. John NELSON, Trustee.
Sale of 807 acres, part of the real estate of late General CRABB in Montgomery Co.. Charles H. CRABB, residing near the property will shew it. Thomas LINSTID, Robt. P. MAGRUDER, Trustees.
Sale at late residence of Lewis HARDING, dec'd., 1 mile from Buckeys-town and same from Matthew BROWN's factory, personal property of dec'd., Negro woman with child, 3 boys, 1 girl, and other. Jacob RIDGELY, adm'r.
Sale at late residence of Christian ORNDORFF, dec'd., 4 miles from Westminster, Negro woman and child, horses, cows, hogs and sheep. Eve ORNDORFF, John EILIE, adm'rs.
Sale of lot of mountain land, 20 acres 4 1/2 miles of Frederick-town. Solomon STECKEL.
Sale of 250 acres of Loudoun land. Dade P. NOLAND.
Notice is given that Elizabeth BIRELY, Frederick-town has declined carrying on the Tanning and Currying business and the business will be carried on under the firm of Lewis BIRELY & Co.
Notice of meeting of 47th Regiment of Md. Militia. John GALT, Maj. 2d batt., 47th Reg.

243. 30 March 1816
Sale of tract on which he resides, known as the Red House, 1 mile of Martinsburgh, 620 acres. Moses T. HUNTER.
Charles CARTER, Corrottoman, Lancaster, offers for sale his landed estate near Culpepper Court house, 1000 acres.
David ARNOLD to rent a blacksmith shop, 1 mile from BURKETT's store, 5 miles from Middletown.
James M'DANIEL, Liberty-town, offers reward for black man named BILL who calls himself William BANKS, about 30 years of age.
Petitioners for the incorporation of Frederick-Town: William R. SANDERSON, George TRISLER, John HOUCK, Joseph SWEARINGEN, George BALTZELL, John L. HARDING, Richard POTTS, John S. MILLER, Valentine BRUNNER, William PEARRE, George ROHR, Frederick LOEHR, John DILL, William BAER, Abraham STONER, John TYLER, Michael

HAUSER, John C. FRITCHIE, Henry STONER, Jacob BAER, Henry THOMAS, Daniel HAUER, Jr., George HAUER, Daniel HAUER, sen., John MARKELL, Charles SCHELL, Catherine KIMBOLL, William GUNTON, John BAYLY, William JOHNSON, John GEPHART, Henry M'CLEERY, Jacob ROHR, William STEINER, Frederick BIRELY, George BAER, James ROBERTSON, Henry STEINER, jr., George BENTZ, Benjamin STALLINGS, William MICHAEL, William JENKINS, John HUGHES, Samuel WEBSTER, George KOLB, John D. SMITH, David WEBSTER, Basil NORRIS, John N. A. BOGEN, Thomas CONNER, John BALTZELL, Henry HOFFMAN, Frederick W. HOFFMAN, Benjamin RUTHERFORD, James F. HUSTON, Philip HALLAR, William DUNAVIN, Henry DOYLE, George BAER of Wm., William B. TYLER, William POTTS, George W. MURDOCH, Wm. M. BEALL Jr., Frederick HEISELY, Conrad ENGELBRECHT, J. HELFENSTEIN, John P. THOMSON, Wm. ROSS, Wm. GOLDSBOROUGH, John HUSTON, Thomas B. JONES, John P. HUSTON, Wm. EMMIT, Jos. BIGGS of John, Richard ENGLISH, George HOUCK, George RICE, Frederick NUSZ, George SHULTZ, Henry SHULTZ, Joseph M. CROMWELL, Henry BRISH, Frederick STONER, Lewis CROSS, Jacob MEDTART, David BOYD, John RIGNEY, Frederick SHAYNBOLTER, Jacob HANE, John MARTIN, Henry SMITH, Henry STEINER, Isaac MANTZ, Josiah GOMBER, Philip PYFER Jr., Joseph WALLING, John NELSON, Jacob STEINER, Leonard J. M. LITTLEJOHN, Peter NICHOLS, William POTTS Jr., Jacob BRUNER, John REITZELL, George PAYNE, Justinian MAYBERRY, Charles MANN, Jacob SHELLMAN, Henry BAER, Conrad RIGHTMYER, Benjamin WINTER, William HAUSER, Henry KOONTZ Jr., P. DAVIDSON, F. W. HATCH, David MARTIN, David F. SCHAFFER, Frederick A. SCHLEY, Thomas W. JOHNSON.

William M. BEALL, esqr., postmaster at this place for nearly 22 years, having resigned, James F. HUSTON, esqr. has been appointed his successor.

Married 17th inst. by Rev. George WILLIAMS, Patrick M'GILL to Miss Polly HOOK, niece of Col. James HOOK, of this co.

Died Wednesday, 20th inst., in his 38th year, William THOMAS, father of a rising family.

Having understood that Alexander C. HANSON declines a re-election, I will represent the citizens of the district in Congress, if they thing proper to elect me.

Hill DORSEY, Dorsey's Manor, about to remove to Virginia, to sell 500 acres, 7 miles from Baltimore.

244. 6 April 1816

Married Sunday last by Rev. David F. SCHAEFFER, Jacob KELLER to Miss Catharine HEISELY, dau. of Frederick HEISELY, all of this town.

Died Sunday evening last, Mrs. Eleanor HARDING, consort of John L. HARDING of this town.

Died Tuesday last, Mrs. Susannah REISNER, in her 78th year.

Died Wednesday last, John SHELLMAN, in his 93rd year. He was among the earliest settlers in Frederick-town and at the time of his death, its oldest inhabitant.

Died Saturday last in her 28th year, Mrs. Sarah BEATTY, wife of Lewis A. BEATTY and dau. of Col. Joshua GIST, afflicted for several years, leaving husband and two small children and parents.

Persons owning property on Market or Patrick Sts., are notified that trees and posts are to be removed and paving of the footways be extended to the curb stones where said streets have been paved. John MARKELL, clk.

Sale by order of Orphans court of Montgomery Co. of personal property of Joseph BIRNSIDE, dec'd., 2 miles from Clarksburg - horses, cattle, sheep, hogs, furniture. Ann BIRNSIDE, Aquilla BIRNSIDE, Henry BIRNSIDE, adm'rs.

John RHODES, adm'r of Joshua M'CLANE.

245. 13 Apr 1816

Evan BELT to sell farm adjoining the road below Hyatt's town, 140 acres.

Of the 1st Regiment, drafted Maryland militia, under the command of Col. Stephen STEINER, are requested to make out their accounts and present them with their discharges to me at Newtown, Trap, before 20th inst., that I may make estimates and draw for the amount. G. W. BOERSTLER, Paymaster, 1st Regt., M.M.

Carding of merino and country wool has commenced by the subscribers at the Woollen Factory on Never Fear Branch, 1 1/2 miles of the main road from Middletown to Trap. Joseph A. HUGHES, carder; Christian REMSBERG.

J. GRAHAME near Frederick Town will sell 1000 acres on the east side of Monocacy, 5 miles from Frederick Town.

Tract for sale whereon Elizabeth DORSEY formerly resided, 1 mile from Liberty-town on the south side, 165-170 acres. Ely C. DORSEY, Otho DORSEY, Mary DORSEY.

Eli ELLIOTT, near New-Market, offers reward for apprentice boy, Daniel MURRAY, about 18 years of age.

Died Sunday last about 3 o'clock at his plantation, near Frederick-town, in his 67th year, after a long and painful disease, Edward ANDERSON; buried at the family burying yard, on his plantation.

Sale at the late dwelling of Wm. THOMAS, dec'd., 1 1/2 miles east of Frederick-town, of young Negro woman and child, horses, cows, sheep, etc. Catharine THOMAS, adm'rx.

Hiel PECK has lately removed from Middlebrook Mills in Montgomery Co to Montgomery Court House and occupies tavern, the White House, lately occupied by Jannaro S. FARRE.

L. FUNDENBURG will rent part of the house presently occupied by Mr. ELLIS, near Catoctin Furnace.

Sheriff's sale of estate of John M'DANIEL of land on main road from Frederick-town to Liberty, known as Stoney Spring, 73 acres, seized at the suit of Dennis SOLLERS. Daniel ARTHUR, for sheriff.

246. 20 April 1816

Philip T. POTT's store, about to remove to Baltimore - Bargains - Dry goods, groceries, crockery ware, cutlery, hardware, saddlery.

Sheriff's sale of estate of Philip STRIDER, 150 acres, at the suits of Christian HEMP, John SAFER(?), Adam WEVER, John WHITENECK, Richard and John JOHNSON, Ephraim HOLLOWAY, Elisha EATON, Mathew R. ALLEN.

247. 27 Apr 1816
Sale by order of Orphan's court, Negro woman and her children, property of Mary HARTSOCK, dec'd. John HARTSOCK, Adm'r.
William G. PENN, Damascus, Montgomery Co., offers reward for mare missing from Major William COOKERLY's waggon yard, in New Market.
John W. B. GRAYSON, near Snicker's Gap, Loudoun Co., VA, offers reward for Negro man named SAM, owned by James MAHONEY of Loudoun Co., hired to subscriber for present year, 19- 20 years of age
Samuel and Allen BANKS to sell land of 694 acres, called Bunkers Hill Fortified, in Anne Arundel Co..
Sheriff's sale of 60 acres, lands of George MARKER, at the suit of George BECKENBAUGH.
John STIER has commenced waggon and plough making business in New-Market, opposite Henry SMITH's blacksmith shop.
Persons who gave their notes for property purchased at sale of personal estate of Jacob BENTZ, dec'd., are requested to make payment. George BENTZ, Stephen REMSBURG, John BRENGLE, adm'rs.
Jacob COOKERLY, adm'r. of Margaret COOKERLY, Frederick Co.
Chancery sale of real estate of Col. Henry GAITHER, 827 1/4 acres in Montgomery Co., seat of the late Col. GAITHER, 1 mile from Tiggints Tavern. Benjamin GAITHER, Trustee.
Monocacy lands for sale where I reside on west side of Monocacy, 12 miles from Frederick-town. Lawrence BRENGLE, surveyor, will provide information. Nicholas CLOPPER, Greenfield, Frederick Co.
Corn, oats and rye for sale at Montmerinoe farm, formerly Major DARNALLS quarter. Henry JUDY, manager.
We the undersigned, proprietors of wool carding machines in Middletown Valley have associated ourselves to agree on prices: John KEAFAUVER, Jacob GROVER, Christian REMSBERG, Christian COST, William M'FARLAND.
Chancery sale of property of Joseph HINCKS, dec'd., house and back buildings with 9-10 acres in New Lisbon. A. L. LEMONNIER.

248. 4 May 1816
Charles WATERS, Anne Arundel Co., offers reward for two Negro men, JACK and PETER, purchased a few months past of Robert LOWE of Calvert Co., which said Negroes have lived at Johnson's Furnace in Frederick Co. for last 3 years. JACK is about 28 years of age and Peter is about 28 years of age.
Married 16th ult. by Rev. COBELER, Rev. M. MEYERHEFFER to Miss Lucy CRIGLER, dau. of late Major CRIGLER of VA.
Nicholas HALL, sen., offers reward for Negro NICK or NICHOLAS, about 28 years of age.

Chancery sale of property of Benjamin STODDERT, dec'd, 200 acres, 2-3 miles from the Capitol. Thomas T. GANTT, Trustee.

Abraham JONES adm'r. of Tabitha DORSEY.

Abraham JONES adm'r. of Basil WOOD.

Daniel STONER, living on Little Pipe Creek, 2 miles from Middleburg, offers reward for Negro named JACOB, formerly the property of Mr. SHELMERDINE near Fredericktown and since owned by Joshua DELAPLANE, 32 years of age.

Edward T. IGLEHART, near Carroll's Manor, Anne Arundel Co, Maryland, offers reward for Negro DEB, from Samuel BEALL'S in Montgomery Co.

249. 11 May 1816

Died Sat last at an advanced age, William MARKELL of this town.

Died Wednesday in his 27th year, Thomas W. SCOTT of a pulmonary complaint, under which he has long suffered.

Died Thursday in childbed, Mrs. Sophia MARKELL, consort of Jacob MARKELL, in her 24th year of her age.

Died Saturday, the 4th inst. at his residence in Hagerstown in his 35th year, Col. John RAGAN.

Attention Riflemen. Ordered that the first Washingtonian Rifle Green meet for the purpose of joining the second Battalion at William DEAN's old fields, completely equipt. Jacob GETZENDANNER, Capt.

G. M. CONRADT offers reward for apprentice to the weaver business named William CURFMAN, about 20 years of age, 5 feet, 6 inches high.

Special Committee for Frederick Academy reports that there are not about 120 students at the academy; Mr. WEYLIE, principal; Mr. DAVIDSON, professor of mathematics; Mr. MARKELL, teach of the introductory English school. Roger B. TANEY, John BALTZELL, Fred'k A. SCHLEY.

Persons indebted to Mrs. Mary I. THOMAS for purchased made at the different sales are informed that their notes are now due. Persons having claims against the estates of Dr. THOMAS or John H. THOMAS are requested to bring them in. Edward COLSTON, Atty for Mary I. THOMAS.

Wanted - 5-6 good potters at the Hampshire Furnace. James DAILEY, Romney, VA.

Persons who made purchased at the sale of the property of John DERTZBACH, dec'd. are informed their notes are due and should call on Frederick NUSZ. J. GRAHAME, ex'r.

John HUGHES gives notices to purchasers who gave notes at his sale that payment is due.

Absalom KALB (living on the premises) offers house and lot for sale near east end of Patrick St.

250. 18 May 1816

Artillerists attention - Members of Frederick-town Artillery company will meet in compleat uniform with side arms in good order, at the Eagle and Review Tavern, for the purpose of joining the 1st Battalion. John BUCKEY, 1st Sergt., by order of the Captain.

Married Sunday evening last by Rev. HELFENSTEIN, Richard NOKES to Miss Margaret METZGER, all of this town.
House and lot for sale in Patrick St. Henry BAER.
New store - Dry goods, groceries, queensware and hardware. STEINER and GRAHAME, Patrick St.
Wm. E. WILLIAMS offers reward for missing colt.
By virtue of power of attorney from Maj. Josias T. BEALL, of Prince George's Co., the subscribers will sell land, Layhill and Beall's Reserve on North West Branch, and Cowper on Paint Branch, all in Montgomery Co. James A. BEALL, Robert A. BEALL.
Eli ELLIOTT, adm'r. of Frederick COLLINS.
Joshua JOHNSON has taken up a stray gelding.
Sale of furniture. Jesse LEATHERWOOD.
Otho SPRIGG offers reward for missing mule.
Thomas NEWENS, Frederick-town, offers reward for apprentice to chairmaking and house-painting business named Thomas MAYBURY, about 18 years of age, dark complexion, straight black hair and a down look.
Negro woman committed to gaol of Frederick Co. who calls herself ELLEN, about 24 years of age; says she belongs to James PORTER in Baltimore Co.
John RITCHIE ex'r of Thomas BEATTY.

251. 25 May 1816
Constables appointed by the Levy Court, May 1816:
Frederick-town: Thomas YOUNG, Ormand BUTLER, Lewis CROSS, John BUCKY
Upper Monococy: Cornelius RIDGE
North Manor: William H. GRIMES
South Manor: Caleb FLEMING
East Toms Creek: Joachim ELDER
West Toms Creek: Michael KEEPERS
Piney Creek: Frederick YINGLING
Taney-town: Moses GALT
Pipe Creek: John CLABAUGH
Westminster: Basil HAYDEN
Burnt House Woods: Christopher ECKER
Union: Amos ENGLAND
Linganore: Joel ELLIOT
Sugar Loaf: E. H. HARDIN
Middle Monococy: Peter STICHER
Lower Monococy: John STEPHENS
Bennett's Creek: William HYATT
Upper Catoctin: Henry COMBS
West Lower Catoctin: Jacob KOONTZ
Lower Catoctin: William R. CHUNN

West Middle Town: Christian NICEWANGER
Switzerland: Daniel TOMS
Berlin: Maryland FRAZIER
Israel's Creek: Christian NEAT
Ballinger's Creek: William WADSWORTH
West Union: Nathan ENGLAND
Middle-town: Joseph JOHNSON
Died Monday last, after a short illness, Miss Mary RITCHIE.
The Convention of the Protestant Episcopal Church will meet at Annapolis on 12 June. Henry L. DAVIS, Sec'y.
Patrick M'GILL, Prin. Assessor, 7th Dist. of Md., Newtown (Trap) will receive information on any changed which may have taken place in the assessable property of individuals.
Joseph TALBOTT has removed to the Washington Hotel, Frederick-town, on Patrick St., lately occupied by Jesse LEATHERWOOD.
Tract for sale, 600 acres, in Loudoun VA. Richard H. LEE, near Leesburg (intending to remove from Loudoun Co.).
Sale at the late dwelling of Samuel STONER, dec'd., about 5 miles east of Libertytown, near Mr. CLEMSON's mill, person property of said dec'd., horses, cattle, hogs, sheep, 10 steers, wheat, rye and oats by the bushel. Rachel STONER, Upton STONER, Sams Creek, adm'rs.
Levy Court stand adjourned until 10 June. John SCHLEY, clerk.
Charles HAMMOND warns persons from cutting wood and taking locust posts already cut, from his farm.
Sheriff's sale at the residence of Evan BELT, Negro man, Negro girl, wagon and 2 horses, late the property of said BELT, taken at the suits of Thomas PETER and James CLINGAN, use of Aaron OFFUTT.
Persons having claims against the estate of Martha HOWARD, late of Frederick Co., dec'd., are warned to exhibit the same. Richard HOWARD, Ex'r.
Wm. JOHNSON (of Jeremiah), living near Late's mill and adjoining Carroll's Manor, offers reward for missing mare.
Sale of lots on the west side of the court house, now occupied by the heirs of Wm. RITCHIE, dec'd. Wm. RITCHIE.

252. 1 June 1816
Philip BLESSING cautions persons regarding a man who calls himself George HOFFMAN, accompanied by a boy of about 13, who has swindled several persons, misrepresenting himself as a minister.
Married Tuesday evening last by Rev. J. HELFENSTEIN, Henry THOMAS, merchant, to Miss Catharine BALTZELL, all of this town.
Married at Boston, on the 18th ult., Lieut. David GEISINGER of the U.S. Navy, of this town, to Miss Catharine Russell PEARCE of the former place.
Thomas GASSAWAY will sell a farm in Montgomery Co., about 9 miles from the Court House, 1 mile from Thomas HILLERY's mill now erecting on Seneca. The farm will be shewn by Gradison CATLETT who resides near it.

Persons who own property with the following limits, from William MICHAEL's at the corner of Market and South sts.; to John HOUCK's at the corner of market and Third sts.; and from Justinian MAYBERRY's to Jacob HOFFMAN's in Patrick sts., are notified that the foot pavements on both sides of said streets are ordered to be completed by 1 August. John MARKELL, by order of the Commissioners of Frederick-town.

Nicholas HALL, jun., New Market offers reward for puppy.

150 barrels herrings. William BAER & Co., No. 26 Pratt St., Baltimore.

Dying, fulling and dressing at Fleecy Dale Factory. M. [Matthew] BROWN & Brother.

William HILLEARY, 3 miles from New-town (Trap), offers reward for missing gelding.

Ezra HYATT, Turnpike road near New Market, has taken up a stray gelding.

John A. T. KILGOUR, Attorney at Law, now occupies the office formerly owned by John H. THOMAS.

Sheriff's sale of two lots in Market St., Frederick-town, estate of Mary O'FERRELL, seized at the suit of the State of Maryland, use of Ezra MANTZ, Tobias NIXDORFF and George BALTZELL, ex'rs. of J. JONES, dec'd.

253. 8 June 1816

Appointments by the Governor and Council: Lewis GREEN, Notary Public, to reside at Frederick-town; John WOLFE, Justice of the Peace for Frederick Co.; Frederick BARRICK, Major of a Battalion, 29th Regiment, Frederick Co.; George W. BOERSTLER, Adjt. to 28th Regt., Frederick; Jacob NICHOLS, Capt. of a company, 28th Regt.; Henry CUBLER, Capt., Jacob FEASTER, jr., Lieut and Thos. RIDGELY, Ensign, of a company, 28th Regt., Frederick; Otho WEAKLY, Ensign of Capt. Easterday's company.

Died Saturday evening last [1 June], Dennis HAGAN, Esq., Attorney at Law, in his 23rd year.

Flaxseed wanted. Frederick FEAGA.

RUSSELL & GRAFF have commenced the retail dry goods business in the house formerly occupied by Mr. MEDTART.

Fresh supply of Spring Goods. BAYLY & JOHNSON, Patrick St.

Hugh SHAW, John M'KALEB, adm'rs. of Benjamin JAMISON.

254. 15 June 1816

Died 28th ult. in Lancaster Co., PA, Capt. Jacob C. ELLMAKER, in his 28th year.

Sale at the residence of Mrs. Mary RITCHIE, near the Market House, sundry beds, and other furniture. John RITCHIE, William RITCHIE and Robert M'CLEERY, for Mrs. RITCHIE.

Miller wanted. Jacob LATE, 3 miles from Buckey's-town.

Wool carding. Joel MARSH.

Sarah ELLIOTT, adm'rx. of Thomas ELLIOTT.

Peter HOFFMAN, New-town, Trap, offers reward for Negro man who left his house, named JOHN; calls himself John JOHNSON, about 26 years of age. He has a father living in Calvert Co.

Sheriff's sale at John AGNEW's tavern in Emmitsburg, 10-acre lot, estate of Francis SLOTHOW; also house and lot - at the suits of Jacob OYSTER and Jacob DANNER.

Sheriff's sale of Stoney Spring, taken by virtue of suits of George C. GELWICKS, John BIVEN, Nathan BAKER, Paul CLAPSADDLE, Zachariah and Benjamin M'CLARY, Joel FUNK, Ellis HART, Archibald M'ATEE, Daniel CREAGER and Nathan ENGLAND.

Sheriff's sale of Negroes, property of Jonathan WOOD, seized by virtue of suits of John and Mary WAGNER, Elizabeth RICHARDS, Robert HENDERSON, Ephraim GAITHER, Dennis POOLE, esq., Henry BAKER for Daniel ROOT, John CAMPBELL, jr., Upton HAMMOND and Henry BRISH.

Sheriff's sale of 1 1/2 lots in Liberty-town, of John W. DORSEY, by virtue of suit of Abraham JONES.

255. 22 June 1816

Died 20th inst. in her 32nd year, Mrs. HILLEARY, consort of Capt. Clement T. HILLEARY of this co., leaving 5 young daughters.

Adam BAER, corner of Pratt and Charles sts., Baltimore, has hardware, queens and glassware, groceries and liquors.

Dr. A. FRAZIER, informs inhabitants of Middletown Valley that he has opened a shop at John S. FRAZIER's, 4 miles from Middletown and 2 from Newtown (Trap).

John KAUFFMAN, Frederick-town, offers reward for missing horse.

Sophia RIFE and George SMITH, exr's of Jacob RIFE.

Jacob TROXEL, adm'r. of Peter TROXEL.

Land for sale in Frederick Co. on Monocacy river, 173 acres known as Miss GHISELIN's Quarter, contiguous to lands of Arthur SHAAFF and Ignatius DAVIS. Henry WARING, Montgomery Co., near Clarksburg.

Sheriff's sale of two Negro men, late the property of Henry R. WARFIELD, at the suits of Cornelius M'ANULTY, George BAER, Samuel DIFFENDALL, John BROWN and James MATTHEWS.

Sheriff's sale of estate of Philip STRIDER, tract called Maryland, 150 acres, to satisfy claims due Adam WEAVER, Ephraim HALLOWAY, John WHITENECK, John SLIFER, jun. and John and Richard JOHNSON.

256. 29 June 1816

Ervine M'LAUGHLIN has taken Union Tavern & Hotel, at Ellicott's Mills, lately kept by Mrs. S. AISQUITH and formerly by Hiel PECK.

Silas HARRY, Franklin Co., PA, offers reward for capture of thief, William MILLER, a Frenchman, about 5 feet 5 inches, dark hair, dark eyes and says he deserted from the British army. He stole articles of clothing.

Sale at their new store, variety of groceries, fish, salt, tar, &c. William E. WILLIAMS, Beal C. STINCHCOMB.

Lees' anti-bilious pills, Lee's elixir, tooth ache drops, damask lip salve, genuine eye water, &c. Noah RIDGELY (late Michael LEE & Co.)

The *American Eagle*, published at Shepherd's-Town. John N. SNYDER, editor.

Sale of two-story stone house, late the property of John SHELLMAN, dec'd. John BRUNNER, acting ex'r.

John REEDY, 1 mile of Woodstock, Shanandoah Co., VA, offers reward for yellow man named WEEDON, about 26 years of age.

John T. VEATCH, adm'r. of Nehemiah STONE, Montgomery Co.

William HICHU, 2 miles above Creagerstown, has taken up a stray Mare.

James PHILIPS forewarns persons from trusting his wife Charlotte on his account.

257. 6 July 1816

Married Tuesday, 25th ult. at Philadelphia, by Rev. Dr. HELMUTH, Lewis BIRELY of this place to Miss Catharine KREPS of that city.

David ARNOLD, sen., gives notice that notes are due from those persons who purchased at the sale of David ARNOLD, jun., dec'd.

Report of Union Lancasterian School, Frederick Co., near Frederick-town. 201 have been admitted; 125 have left school for various employments; 76 remain at present. [A summary of achievement is given; no student names are given.] Elihu H. ROCKWELL.

Sale of 3 tracts in St. Clair Township, Bedford Co., PA, 100 acres, 167 acres, 155 acres, respectively. Isaac CUPPET, Philip ALBAUGH.

Sheriff's sale of 140 acres of Evan BELT, plus Negroes, at the suit of Thomas PETER, James CLINGAN, use of Aaron OFFUTT, Henry B. HORRELL and Peregrine WARFIELD.

Sheriff's sale of 150 acres called Rich Land and resurvey on Rich Land, near Winemiller's tavern, belonging to Richard ANDREW, at the suit of Elisha R. HYATT and John H. RIGGS.

Merino rams for sale, Jacob POE, near Woodsborough.

Sale of a small lot of corn by Joseph RIDOUT, whose wife Polly has left his bed and board - sale at his residence, living on the land of Eli ELLIOTT, 2 miles from New Market.

Joseph J. W. JONES, ex'r of Sarah JONES, Montgomery Co.

Catharine GILLMEYER, ex'rx of Francis GILLMEYER, Frederick Co.

Philip BARNHART, near Little Pipe Creek Bridge, Frederick Co., offers reward for apprentice to the shoemaking business named John SMALLWOOD.

Committed to Frederick Co. gaol, Negro man who calls himself James Hall BROOKS; says he belongs to Francis RIED of Allegany Co, in this state, about 23 years of age.

258. 13 July 1816

John B. WEBER has opened a porter cellar and mead house opposite the mile stone, Patrick St.

Horatio HOBBS & Co. have just received a handsome assortment of dry goods, groceries, etc., Creagers-town.

Chancery sale of house and lot in Emmitsburgh, property of William A. LLOYD. Jacob BAER, Trustee.

Lewis MICHAEL to apply for relief of debts under the insolvency act.

Sale of 1394 acres on the road from Frederick-town to York and Lancaster. Upton REID, near Taney-town.

John COOK, Liberty, offers reward for mulatto woman [named JUDE] and child, about 24 years of age.

Peter BOWIC, Montgomery Co., near the Sugarlands, offers reward for mulatto man named JACOB; calls himself Jack HILRY, about 24 years of age.

Committed to gaol of Frederick Co., Negro woman who calls herself SARAH; says she is free; that she was manumitted by Joseph BROWN of Baltimore; about 20 years of age.

Robert NELSON has taken up a stray mare.

Ulrich ECKLER, adm'r. of John ECKLER.

259. 20 July 1816

Died at New Market, 6th of this month, in his 19th year, William BRASHEAR, son of Dr. BRASHEAR. His disease was pulmonary.

Farm for sale in Montgomery Co., 700 acres. Joshua WRIGHT living on the premises will show the land. Charles WARFIELD.

Land for sale in Liberty-town, 200 acres called Forest Farm, formerly owned by Upton SHEREDINE, 2 miles from Liberty-town. Also 2 lots in Liberty-town, one lately occupied by Mrs. Tabitha DORSEY. Thomas CAZIER.

Chancery sale of land, in the suit of Giles FITZHUGH against A. J. SCHOFIELD, 1616 acres in Fairfax Co., VA. Richard H. HENDERSON, R. I. TAYLOR, Commissioners.

Chancery sale of farm, 97 acres, 1 mile of Woodsborough, adjoining the lands of Eli PHILIPS and John SMITH. Frederick A. SCHLEY.

Persons indebted to subscriber either for the Frederick Town Plain Dealer or the German paper, for advertising or handbills, are notified that their accounts have been put in the hands of George KOLB, Esq., Frederick-town and Thomas GIST in Westminster. C. T. MELSHEIMER.

Sale of houses and lots in Frederick-town, late the property of George SCHNERTZELL, senr., dec'd. Richard BROOKE, Trustee.

Tavern stand for sale, formerly occupied by Nathan BROWNING, near the center of the town of Clarksburg, Montgomery Co. Mary GRIFFITH.

Sale in Bruceville, of grist mill, formerly known as Bruce's Mill, on Big Pipe Creek. Geo. PRICE.

Frederick Berger, near New-town, Trap, Maryland, offers reward for Negro man named Samuel CHASE, 30-40 years of age.

260. 27 July 1816

Died on the 4th inst. and in her 33rd year, of a pulmonary affection, Mrs. Mary M'KALEB, consort of Maj. John M'KALEB of Taney-town. She was the dau. of Revd. CLINGAN of the Baptist persuasion. Some time previous to her last illness she was baptized into the Presbyterian church.

Died Thursday, 18th inst. in her 25th year, Mrs. Phebe RIDGELY, consort of Thomas RIDGELY of this co.

Miller wanted. Benjamin RICE, 3 miles from the Trap.

Jacob CRONISE gives notice that persons who send grain to the Fredericktown mill should have their names in full on their bags.

Sheriff's sale at the house of Conrad SHAFER, Frederick-town, estate of Philip STRIDER.

Sale of 400-500 acres near Parrs, at the foot of Ashby's Gap on road to Fauquier Courthouse. Charles L. CARTER.

John NORRIS, near Middleburg, Frederick Co., has taken up a stray mare.

261. 3 Aug 1816

Died on the morning of 22nd ult., Sarah Ann, wife of Andrew DILL, in her 22nd year, leaving husband and two infant children.

Sale of personal estate of Adam KOHLENBERG, dec'd., Negro woman and 4 children, set of old glasswork tools, set of blacksmith tools and other. Justus KOHLENBERG, Adm'r.

KIPHART & PETERS have commenced the tayloring business in Fredericktown in the house lately occupied by Thomas W. SCOTT.

The woollen cloth manufactory erected by G. J. CONRADT in Mechanicstown, Frederick Co.

Arthur SHAAFF offers reward for horses missing from his pasture, 3 miles from Frederick-town.

William BROWN, Fleecy Dale Factory, offers reward for missing cow.

Sheriff's sale of 2 Negro men, late the property of Joseph GARRETT, at the suit of John M. BEATTY.

Walter SIMPSON, has taken up at his Mount Airy farm, 1 mile from Fredericktown, seven stray sheep.

262. 10 Aug 1816

Married Thursday last, by Rev. F. W. HATCH, Sebastian GRAFF to Mrs. --- JOHNSON, both of this Co.

Chancery sale of the real estate of William HOLLAND of Capol, late of Montgomery Co., dec'd., 200 acres, 3/4 miles from Clarksburg. Nathan HOLLAND, living on the premises. Augustus TANEY, Trustee.

John BISER has taken up a stray mare.

Sheriff's sale of tract of Raphael DARNALL, near Matthew BROWN's Factory called Right and Good Reason, 307 acres, at the suit of James WHITE use of Thomas PETER.

Henry POOL, near William LOWE's mill, 4 miles east of Liberty-town, offers reward for Negro SAM.

Sale of Tavern stand in the publick square of the Town of Cumberland, Maryland. Walter SLICER, on the premises.

263. 17 Aug 1816

John Rezin MAGRUDER cautions persons from trespassing on his lands.

James M'ATEE, for the heirs, cautions against trespassing on the lands of the heirs of Samuel C. MAGRUDER.

Wm. WILSON of John, Clarksburgh, Montgomery Co., offers reward for missing cow; deliver to Mr. MOTTER, Daniel HAUER, jun., Frederick-town or to himself.

Sale of cow, colt, stove, house and lot, by William LEWIS, occupied by him, near the east end of Patrick St.

Notice to stockholders in the Boonsborough turnpike road of election to be held at the house of John KNODE in Sharpsburg. John MILLER, Treas'r.

Committed to the jail of Frederick Co., Negro woman who calls herself JULIET, about 25 years of age; says she was sold by John DARBY of Anne Arundel Co. to some Georgia trader, and that she left them near Richmond.

Adam BURRIER, living near Jones Mill, has taken up a stray mare.

264. 24 Aug 1816

Eagle and Review Tavern, north end of Market, Frederick-town. M. E. BARTGIS.

Sale of brewery & dwelling house in Frederick-town, formerly occupied by Frederick DIEHL. John BAKER.

Christian SNIDER, adm'r. of Sarah MILLER.

James ROSS has taken up a stray mare.

265. 31 Aug 1816

Camp meeting under the direction of the ministers of the Methodist Episcopal church on the lands of Rev. James L. HIGGINS, 2 miles northeast of New Market.

George CARTER, living in Trap, offers reward for apprentice to the blacksmith's business named John PARSONS, about 18 years of age, 5 feet, 6-8 inches high.

Basil OFFUTT, near Darnes-town, Montgomery Co., offers reward for Negro man named MORGAN, about 22 years of age.

George BENTZ gives notice to person who gave their notes for property purchased at the sale of the estate of Jacob BENTZ, dec'd., that these notes due.

Bennett WOOD, Linganore, requests persons with claims, exhibit them for payment without delay.

John PITTS seeks young man with small family to work on a farm.

Chancery case in Montgomery Co. - Daniel LEE vs. Samuel B. BEALL, Robert B. BEALL, Walter B. BEALL, Asa BEALL, Isaac BEALL, Thomas BEALL, Gustavus BEALL, Mary BEALL and Sarah B. BENNETT. The object is to obtain a decree for conveyance in fee simple certain land given by Thomas B. BEALL to said Daniel LEE, on 21 May 1794, as parcel of land then made use of by Richard, James and Benjamin GITTINGS for pasture, it being all the land then unsold of the land allowed to the said Thomas B. BEALL in a division between him and his brothers; that this was a part of the land left by Richard BEALL of Samuel to be divided among his children; that the said children of Richard BEALL of Samuel agreed to divide all the real estate of their dec'd father among them. That the parcel in question was assigned with other land to Thomas B. BEALL who sold this parcel to Daniel LEE. All the children of Richard BEALL of Samuel who are living, and the heirs of those who are dead are made defendants in this bill.

266. 7 Sep 1816
Baltzer FOUT cautions person from trespassing on his farm.
Charles D. WARFIELD informs persons indebted to the estate of the late Doct. Philip THOMAS that he will attend at Talbott's Tavern to receive payment.
Joseph SEAMERS gives notice that his wife Betsey having left his bed and board, he will pay no debts of her contracting.

267. 14 Sep 1816
William GAITHER has taken up a stray horse.
Matthew MURRAY will sell waggon, plough making and blacksmith stand in Middle-town.
Jaser GARRETSON wishing to remove to the western country, to sell tanyard, tools and some bark - New Market.
Joseph MILLER, near Middle-town offers reward for Negro man named LARRY; calls himself Larry GRAHAM.
Charles F. HARDIN, at Cook's Mill on Bennetts creek, 7 miles from New Market, offers reward for missing horse.
Luke FRAZIER offers reward for horse missing from SLAGEL's tavern on the Harper's ferry road.
Committed to jail of Montgomery Co. for breaking open a home and stealing several things, a young man who calls himself Samuel DAVIS, unknown in this county.

268. 21 Sep 1816
Died Sunday last, Frederick BIRELY, in his 19th year.
Eli TOWNE denies reports "tending to impeach my moral character...."
Overseer wanted. Ely DORSEY of Ely, near Liberty-town.
Martha GRAHAM to petition the next General assembly to divorce her husband, Augustus GRAHAM.
Sale of Hope Hill, between Major Roger JOHNSON's and my residence, 180 acres; also Sugar Loaf Plains adjoining, 120 acres; also mill on Big Bennett's creek. Matthew BROWN.
Zachariah DANNER, Liberty town, offers reward for missing mare.

269. 28 Sep 1816
Married Sunday evening last by Rev. F. W. HATCH, Rev. Hen. L. DAVIS of Annapolis, to Miss Jane WINTER of this co.
Married Tuesday last, by Rev. J. HELFENSTEIN, John AGNEW of Emittsburg, to Mrs. Margaret SCHNERTZELL of this town.
Married Thursday last by the same, David CRAMER to Miss Elizabeth BARRICK, all of this co.

Died Friday, 20th inst., after a tedious and painful illness, Emanuel MANTZ, son of Major Peter MANTZ of this town.

William M'FARLAND has left the fulling mill of Jacob GROVE and commenced business for himself on the road from Frederick-town to Green Castle, 4 miles from Middle-town and 1/4 mile from Joseph MILLER's merchant mill.

Notes given at the sales of the personal estate of the late William THOMAS, dec'd, will be due on 17 Oct. Catherine THOMAS.

Committed to jail of Frederick Co., Negro man who calls himself JOSEPH; about 24 years of age; says he is free, that he served a term of years with Guy TOKINS of Fredericksburgh, VA.

270. 5 Oct 1816

Married Sunday evening last by Rev. D. F. SCHAEFFER, Michael PETERS to Miss Ann CRABEL, all of this town.

John COVER, near Woodsborough, offers reward for missing horse.

Sale of farm, 120 acres on Monocacy. Philip WARTZWALDER.

Miller wanted - Apply to Joseph M. CROMWELL, Frederick-town or subscriber, 1 mile west of Noland's ferry. Jacob MEIXSEL.

Ann GARRETT, adm'r. of Joseph GARRETT.

271. 12 Oct 1816

The co-partnership of Basil NORRIS & Co. is dissolved. Basil NORRIS and Wm. NORRIS, jun. Basil NORRIS having taken into partnership, Stuart GAITHER of Baltimore will conduct under the firm NORRIS & GAITHER - Groceries, wines and liquors.

NORRIS & MARTIN - wholesale grocers, No. 66, market St., Baltimore.

John ENGELBRECHT, tailor in Church St.

Dissolution of partnership of Henry BURKITT and David MORGAN, under the firm of BURKITT and MORGAN.

Dr. JENNINGS Patent Bath, celebrated for the removal of pains, fevers, cholics, bowel complaints, coughs, colds, rheumatisms, &c. may be had at the store of David MARTIN, Market St.

Fuller wanted. Solomon FOUTZ, Meadow Branch.

Trustee's sale of 4 farms, mill and distillery, under a deed of trust from Joseph SPRIGG of Washington Co., 840 1/2 acres. U. LAWRENCE, Trustee, Hagerstown.

Sale of two farms on the Conococheague creek, Washington Co. John C. CROMWELL, living thereon.

Sale at the late residence of Frances TRAIL, dec'd., near Medley's Hill, Montgomery Co., 10 Negroes. James TRAIL of Wm., adm'r.

Persons indebted to Isaac LYON are requested to come forward.

Sale of draft horses. John A. DEAN, near Frederick-town.

Sale of 8 lots in the new town of Damascus, in Montgomery Co. Edward HUGHES.

John MARKELL, adm'r. of William MARKELL, to sell furniture, stoves, cow, hogs, &c. of dec'd.

272. 19 Oct 1816

Married Thursday last by Rev. Nicholas ZOCKEY, Bernard COKERY to Miss Elizabeth TANEY, dau. of Joseph TANEY, Esqr. of this co.

Died Friday last, in his 20th year, Michael FESSLER of this town.

Died Monday morning last, Mrs. Cassandra WEBSTER, consort of Samuel WEBSTER, of this town, young and amiable.

Sale of 3370 acres in Fauquier lands. Bernard M. CARTER, Woodstock, Fauquier Co., VA.

Sale at the residence of Benjamin THOMAS, dec'd., 10 Negroes, 17 horses, 60 cattle, 59 hogs, 53 sheep, 3000 bushels of wheat; 2 Manor lots, one of 224 acres and the other of 144 acres. Archibald THOMAS, Otho THOMAS, Notley THOMAS, adm'rs.

James SEATON, Fauquier Co., VA, near Middleburg, offers reward for Negro man, about 20 years of age; called John COOK; raised by Wm. HAIL, sen., purchased by me from Henry HAIL, sen. near Middleburg.

Mary O'NEILL, act. ex'rx of Bernard O'NEILL, Montgomery Co.

Teacher wanted. Wm. WILLSON of John, Clarksburgh, Montgomery Co.

273. 26 Oct 1816

Plaister grinding at the mill in Frederick-town. Jacob CRONISE.

Sheriff's sale of estate of Conrad SHAFER, 4-acre lot, part of Tasker's Chance, adjoining last of George LEASE, at suit of Morris JONES' executors, suit of Isaac MANTZ, suit of Christian RIECH and suit of John A. SHAFER use of John DILL.

Sheriff's sale of two stills, 16 still tubs, horses, Negro woman and rick of hay, property of Philip STRIDER, at the suits of Christian STONEBRAKER, Henry JARBOE, Maryland FRAZIER and Elizabeth YOUNG.

Sale of tract, 35-40 acres, and merchant and grist mill, fulling mill. Apply to subscriber, Andrew MYERS, living on the premises or to Jonathan W. DUSTIN, manager of the factory.

Jno. ZIMMERMAN, Emmitsburg, offers reward for apprentice to the tayloring business named Solomon FUNK.

274. 2 Nov 1816

Saml. M'KENNEY, south side of Bridge St., 4 doors above Jefferson St., now opening a complete assortment of Glass, China and Queensware, direct from England.

John FESSLER, Jun., has removed to his father's house in Patrick St. and entered into partnership with him, in the watch & clock making business.

Michael TROAXEL, Gettysburg, having purchased of Frederick KEEFER, the Gettysburg Hotel in Gettysburg.

House and blacksmith shop for sale at north end of Woodsborough. John LARKIN, sen.

Farm, mill and distillery for sale on Bush Creek, Frederick Co. Christopher ZIEGLER.

Hannah FLAUTT, adm'rx of Christian FLAUTT.

The following officers of Turnpike Road Company were elected, John M'KALEB, Pres.; Nicholas SNIDER, Treasurer. Managers: John SHORB, Dr. R. I. ANNAN, Samuel THOMSON, Joseph TANEY, Samuel FISHER, James DRUMMOND, Jacob CLABAUGH, Francis SPALDING.

James SIMMONS, jun., near New-town (Trap) offers reward for Negro man named ROBERT called BOB, 24-25 years of age; raised by William TILLARD, near Pig Point, Anne Arundel Co.

Sheriff's sale at late residence of John H. CUSHMAN, 4 Negroes and cattle, late the property of said CUSHMAN, by suit of Ignatius DAVIS.

Samuel PANCOAST, 1 mile from Buckey's town, has taken up a stray cow.

Barney DEAN to petition the legislature of the state to grant him a divorce from his wife Catharine DEAN, who is known and now passes by the name of Catharine MONECAY.

Schoolmaster wanted - Samuel SLIFER, near Burkitt's store.

Weaver wanted. Jacob HILDEBRACK, 5 miles below Liberty, on the old Baltimore road.

Wants a situation as an overseer; enquire of Geo. KOLB, esq.

Farm, late the property of Eli PHILLIPS, 225 acres with mill, within a mile of Woodsborough. Otho H. WILLIAMS.

Tract for sale, 12 miles from Frederick-town. George RICHARDS.

275. 9 Nov 1816

Married Tuesday evening last by Rev. HELFENSTEIN, Daniel BUCKEY to Miss Evelina KEMP, dau. of Christian KEMP, all of this co.

Another new store - Daniel HAUER, junr. and Cyrus MANTZ have formed a co-partnership under the firm of HAUER & MANTZ at the house lately occupied as a saddler's shop by William MICHAEL, two doors below Francis MANTZ's, where they have just received and offer for sale dry goods, groceries and queensware.

Andrew JOHNSON has taken the brewery, lately occupied by John BAKER where he wishes to purchase barley and rye.

About 700 acres for sale on both sides of Big Seneca Creek in Montgomery Co., 2 miles above Mr. PECK's mill; also 4000 acres of land in Knox Co., KY. Nicholas W. DORSEY.

John BAKER, having declined brewing and rented his brewery, requests persons indebted to him to settle their accounts.

Rezin SIMPSON gives notice to thos indebted to the estate of Matilda SIMPSON, to make payment.

Samuel DIEHL cautions persons from taking assignment of two notes drawn by him in favor of William DIDENHOVER of Montgomery Co.

Samuel PERRELL, adm'r of Samuel PERRELL, sen., Frederick Co.

276. 16 Nov 1816

Married Tuesday evening last by Rev. J. HELFENSTEIN, William PEARRE, to Miss Catharine SPRINGER, both of this town.

Died at Emmitsburg, in her 29th year, Miss Catharine RUNKEL, dau. of Rev. W. RUNKEL.

William DOUGHERTY informs the citizens of Barnesville and its neighborhood, that he has just received and opened an assortment of dry goods, groceries and china, glass & queensware.

B. S. PIGMAN will sell the property where he now lives in Frederick-town; also where he keeps his officer near the Court House Square adjoining Col. M'PHERSON'S large building.

Christopher BARRICKMAN will sell house and lot where he now lives; also a house and lot in New Market now occupied by Hugh LEMMON.

Sale of land at the house of Daniel ARTHUR in Liberty-town, 334 acres, adjoining the lands of Samuel DORSEY, Capt. John S. LAWRENCE and Peter SCHRINER. Property will be shewn by Joseph RUNKELS, living near the premises. John DORSEY.

Sale at the late residence of Frederick UNKEFER, dec'd. of horses, cattle, hogs, sheep, 2 Negro men. Abdiel UNKEFER, ex'r.

John M. BEATTY, wishing to remove to the western country, will sell the farm he now lives on, lying on the forks of the roads from Frederick-town to Noland's ferry on the Potomac and to the mouth of Monocacy, 465 1/4 acres. Enquire of John HUGHES near Frederick-town, Elie BEATTY, Hagers-town or the subscriber on the premises.

Equity case - Richard W. THOMAS, Mary THOMAS, Samuel H. THOMAS and others against Mary THOMAS, Elias THOMAS, Eliza, Richard and William THOMAS. Object of bill is to obtain decree for the sale of the real estate of Benjamin THOMAS, late of Frederick Co., dec'd. the bill states that Benjamin THOMAS, dec'd., owned considerable real estate which has descended from said Benjamin THOMAS to the complainants and defendants - that Mary THOMAS, Elias THOMAS, Eliza THOMAS, Richard THOMAS and William THOMAS, all the defendants, are infants residing out of the state.

Ordered that the sale made and reported by Jacob BAER, the Trustee for the sale (Chancery/equity) of the house and lot in Emmitsburg, mortgaged by Lewis WEAVER to Robert I. ANNAN, be ratified.

Sale of stout, active mulatto boy, 15 years old; purchaser must be a resident of this state. Enquire of M. HAMMETT, manager at Ceresville Farm.

Alexander SLAYMAKER, adm'r. of Sarah FREESE.

Rachel BRUCE, adm'r. of Harry BRUCE.

Abdiel UNKEFER, ex'r. of Frederick UNKEFER.

277. 23 Nov 1816

Sale at Joseph TALBOTT's tavern, farm called Hope, 986 acres; apply to George PAYNE, Frederick-town, or David TRUNDLE on the land. Thomas N. BINNS.

Sale by order of Orphans' court of Montgomery Co., at the residence of the late Levin C. BEALL, near Monococy Chapel, slaves and other. Esther BEALL, adm'rx. of Levin C. BEALL.

Personal estate of John CUMMING, dec'd., Negro girl, bedsteads and furniture. John GLISAN, adm'r.

Sale at the late residence of Edward ANDERSON, dec'd., stock of horses. Lucy ANDERSON.
Sale at residence of John H. CUSHMAN, dec'd. Negroes, horses, cattle. Augustus TANEY, adm'r with the will annexed.
Races will be run on the farm of John M. BEATTY near Noland's Ferry, purse of 40 dollars. George KEPHART, John DAVIS.
Coopers wanted. Apply to David BOYD, Frederick-town, or the subscriber, 1 miles west of Noland's Ferry. Jacob MEIXSELL, jun., Dover Mills, Frederick Co.
Blacksmith wanted. Joseph JOHNSON, 1 mile from the junction of the monocacy with the Potomac.
Dr. John ROUSH, of the borough of York, PA, cures cancer with ease and safety, even when all hopes of cure have been abandoned.

278. 30 Nov 1816
Married Monday 18th inst. by Rev. ADDISON, John NELSON, Esq. of Frederick-town, to Miss Frances Harriet BURROWS of Washington city.
Married Thursday evening last, by Rev. P. DAVIDSON, Samuel REYNALDS to Miss Catharine GETZENDANNER, dau. of John GETZENDANNER, all of this co.
Died Wednesday last, after an illness of three days, Mrs. Eliza SCHLEY, consort of F. A. SCHLEY, esqr. of this town.
Debtors and creditors to the estate of Thomas BEATTY, dec'd. are desired to settle their accounts. John RITCHIE, ex'r.
Sheriff's sale of Negro man called UPTON, property of Dade P. NOLAND, taken at the suit of John BAER. Also Negro man and horses, property of Conrad SHAFER, sold at the suit of John A. SCHAEFER, use of John DILL.
Sheriff's sale of tract of land of Francis GREEN called Part of Three mill seats, 34 1/4 acres, at the suit of George WEAVER use of Martin RIDENOUR. Patrick RIED of Alex. for J. M. CROMWELL, Sheriff.
Sale of 2 tracts of Andrew SMITH, esq., near Emmitsburg, one called addition to John's Fancy, 49 1/2 acres, the other called Ramsay's Rest, 4 1/2 acres, at the suits of Ludwick RUDISELL, Joseph HUGHES use of Cornelius M'NULTY and Michael BLESSING.
Sheriff's sale of Negro girl and a horse, property of Thomas BURGESS, at the suit of Samuel THOMAS.
Sale of land of 66 acres, 2 miles from Frederick-town, part of the farm belonging to the estate of George MURDOCH; also a tract of mountain land on Fishing creek, 1020 acres; apply to David BOWLUS in Middletown. W. Bradley TYLER.
By order of Orphan's court of Frederick Co., at the former residence of Jacob TROXEL, dec'd., 2 miles from Emmitsburg, 8 Negroes. Mary TROXEL, adm'rx.

279. 30 Nov 1816
Farm for sale, 466 acres, 3 miles from Jacob ZUCK's tavern. Apply to John

SCHROEDER at New-town (Trap), to Henry SCHROEDER, sen., on the premises.

Peter LECKLITER has taken up two stray steers.

John CRUM, 2 miles from Frederick-town, has taken up a stray shoat.

Organ for sale, contains 9 stops; the compass is from GC to F in Alt; it has a shifting movement which takes off all the stops, except the three first; built in London in 1803; has been used in St. Paul's Church in Baltimore; apply to John COLE, George HOFFMAN or Solomon BETTS.

Sale, 1 mile from Catoctin Furnace, of farming utensils and stock. Wm. JOHNSON.

Farm to rent, 11 miles from Frederick-town, 1 mile from Catoctin Furnace, 700 acres; it will be shewn by William PRICE on the premises.

Jacob MUSGROVE, jail of Westmoreland Co., PA, has applied for benefit under the acts of insolvency.

280. 7 Dec 1816. No new items.

281. 14 Dec 1816

Mordecai L. HAMMOND, has established a chair factory in Frederick-town, Patrick St.

John MARTIN adm'r. of George MARTIN.

Conrad EILER and John EILER, exr's. of Conrad EILER.

Jacob TROXELL of Jno., adm'r of Peter TROXELL.

Sale of personal estate of James LACKLAND, late of Montgomery Co., dec'd., horses, cattle, sheep, 2 waggons and gears, carts, carriage and gig. Geo. Z. LACKLAND, J. C. LACKLAND, ex'rs.

282. 21 Dec 1816

Sale of distillery apparatus, 3 large stills, 2 large boilers, each holding 1000 gallons; 2000 lbs. brass used in the powder mills. Thomas EWELL, at my mills on the canal, Georgetown.

Isaac ARMSTRONG, ex'r. of James ARMSTRONG, to sell personal estate of dec'd., at his late residence, 1 mile from Taney-town.

283. 28 Dec 1816

Sale of house and lot adjoining Maj. Peter MANTZ, opposite Mrs. KIMBOLL's tavern; lot runs 62 feet to front an ally opposite John MANTZ's tanyard; also another two-story brick house and lot where he now lives, opposite Francis MANTZ's store next door to George BENTZ. George W. MILLER.

Sale at the late dwelling of John MULLOY, Montgomery Co., dec'd., 8 Negroes. Elizabeth MULLOY, Alex'r. WARFIELD, adm'rs.

Sheriff's sale at John LODGE's tavern in Rockville, tract of William P. HOWSER, called Part of Dunghill, 150 acres, at the suit of Roger B. TANEY and Augustus TANEY.

Wm. CARNAGY, near the White Post, Frederick Co., VA, offers reward for mulatto man named ALLEN; has a wife at Captain BOWMANs on Cedar creek.

Basil DELASHMUT has taken up a stray mare.

Lieutenant KUHN, of the marines, has been killed in a duel with some foreign officer. *N.Y. Columbian.* [Lieut. Kuhn was a son of Henry KUHN of this town...]

Married Tuesday evening last by Rev. J. HELFENSTEIN, George ROHR, merchant, to Miss Catharine KOONTZ, dau. of Henry KOONTZ, esqr., all of this place.

Married the same evening, William DOUGHERTY to Miss Elizabeth KOLB, dau. of George KOLB, esq. of this town.

Persons indebted to the firm of COX & WRIGHT are requested to settle their accounts. George COX and Isaac WRIGHT.

Sheriff's sale at the residence of Zachariah DOWDEN, a lot of Dowden's called Part of the Resurvey on Brandy Mall, 11 1/4 acres, and a tract called Part of the Pines, 70 acres, and 2 copper stills - at the suit of Martia (Maria?) Beall DOWDEN by her next friend Christian T. HEMPSTON.

Chancery sale of the property of Daniel BUSSARD, dec'd, farm of 116 acres on the head of Linganore creek, 230 acres on head of Patapsco Falls, and tavern stand in village of Poplar Springs, and other land. Henry BUSSARD, Trustee.

Perry W. BEALL offers reward for missing cattle.

Francis MANTZ, Frederick-town, offers reward for Negro man named CATO, 24 years of age.

John W. LOWE has taken up a stray horse.

Emanuel BIXLER, adm'r. of Sebastian TRESLER, Montgomery Co.

Lucy SALKELD, admr'x. of John SALKELD.

Bernard WELTY, adm'r. of John WELTY jun.

William STOCKMAN, ex'r. of George STOCKMAN.

John PHILLIPS of Montgomery Co. applies for relief from debts under the insolvency acts.

Nicholas SNETHEN, near Liberty-town, has taken up 2 stray buffaloe cows.

284. 4 Jan 1817

Married Sunday evening last, by Rev. J. HELFENSTEIN, Jacob SHAFFNER to Miss Harriett SMITH, dau. of Henry SMITH, all of this town.

Frederick-town Brewery - Andrew THOMSON, Frederick-town, now has beer ready for delivery.

Sale of farm of Andrew KAUFFMAN, dec'd., 2 miles from Frederick-town. Valentine BUCKEY, adjoining the same.

Joseph HEDGES intending to decline keeping a public house, will sell his tavern stand where he now lives in Woodsborough.

D. & S. WEBSTER, Frederick-town, offer reward for two apprentice boys to the shoemaking business, Henry CARNES about 18 years old, thick set and light complexion; the other is David REYNOLDS, about 16 years old, rather small of his age, light complexion.

285. 11 Jan 1817

Sale of beds, bedding, tables, etc. by Conrad SHAFER.

Stone grist mill for sale in Lewis-town, on Fishing Creek, 8 miles from Frederick-town; also saw-mill newly built. John CRAVER.

Sheriff's sale at Benjamin WEAKLY's on the Merryland tract, 2 Negro men, at the suits of Jesse MATTHEWS and Levi DEVER.

Sheriff's sale of tract of Barton PHILPOTT, on Potomac River near Berlin, 115 acres, at the suits of Frederick STEMBELL, sen. and Morris JONES' executors.

Sheriff sale of estate of Philip STRIDER, tract called Maryland, 150 acres, 2 stills, 16 still tubs, Negro woman, horses, to satisfy judgments at the suits of Ephraim HALLOWAY, John SLIFER, Christian STONEBRAKER, Christian KEMP use of Jacob WASHEY.

Persons having claims against John P. GARRET, dec'd. are requested to exhibit them. Erasmus GARRETT, Trustee.

Elizabeth ROWE, adm'rx. of Michael ROWE.

286. 18 Jan 1817

Married Thursday evening of last week, by Rev. J. HELFENSTEIN, Michael BAER of John to Miss Charlotte KIEFER, dau. of Mr. C. KIEFER, all of this co.

Married Tuesday evening last by same, Simon CRONISE to Miss Charlotte KEPHART, dau. of John KEPHART of this town.

Died Monday morning last, Raphael JARBOE, of this co.

Died in this town, Monday last, William POTTS sen., esqr., aged 76, born near Marlboro in this state.

Hyacinth LEMOINE has Havanna Segars at B. WINTER's Tavern.

Sale pursuant to the last will of Henry DARCUS, dec'd., 50 head of cattle. William GRIMES, Jr., ex'r.

Sale of farm of 150 acres adjoining Damascus, Montgomery Co. Edward HUGHES, Damascus.

Sale at Thomas GITTINGS' tavern, Montgomery Co., tract called Clean Shaving, 103 acres, sold by Daniel LEE to Francis POWER in his lifetime. Augustus TANEY, Trustee.

John RUSSEL offers reward for mare missing from Elizabeth HUGHES's stable in New Market.

Joshua RIDGELY, adm'r. of Samuel RIDGELY.

Wm. SHOEMAKER, adm'r. of Richard FRAIM.

287. 25 Jan 1817

Sale of part of what is called Hill in the Middle, 12 3/4 acres, 6 miles from Frederick-town. Daniel BALL.

Sale of 435 acres in Anne Arundel Co., lately purchased by Leonard SHAFER from Washington Co. Allen DORSEY is a resident. Walter C. HAMMOND.

Sale of tract in Washington Co., 1 mile from Hancock town, 1/2 mile from John GRAVES Mill, property of John WATT, dec'd., 143 acres. John WATT and William WATT, Hancock, ex'rs.

Sale of 49 acres, 1 1/2 miles from town, part of the estate of George MURDOCH, dec'd. Geo. Wm. MURDOCH.

Sale of real property of Abraham HAFF, dec'd., 160 acres, grist mill and saw mill. Benjamin BIGGS, John RITCHIE, exr's.

288. 1 Feb 1817

Married Sunday last, by Rev. D. F. SCHAEFFER, George BROADRUP, to Miss Margaret BURKHART.

Married Thursday evening last by Rev. D. F. SCHAEFFER, William BENTZ, to Miss Elizabeth METZGER, all of this place.

Died at the city of Annapolis, Sunday the 26th inst., John V. WEYLIE, one of the professors of St. John's College, and formerly principal of the Fredericktown Academy.

James ROBERTSON's mill on Linganore creek, 1/2 mile above Monococy bridge is so far completed as to chop rye, grind corn, &c. - with experienced miller, Francis WARTHEN.

Episcopal Church lottery. Lewis GREEN, Henry DOYLE, secretaries.

Bank of Westminster - election of Directors. James M'HAFFIE, President.

Samuel AGNEW has applied to the Court of Common Pleas of Adams Co., PA, for benefit of insolvency laws.

Nicholas BRENGLE has taken up a stray steer.

Land for sale, 168 1/2 acres at the head of the falling Waters. William B. KING, Martinsburgh.

Land for sale, 229 acres on river Potomac, Hampshire Co. Va. Thomas OARE.

Elizabeth PEPPLE, adm'rx. of Joseph PEPPLE.

289. 8 Feb 1817

Hezekiah TRUNDLE, Montgomery Co., has taken up a stray horse.

Ordered that equity sale of interest of William B. LUPTON, dec'd. be ratified.

William ALBAUGH, Liberty-town, offers reward for apprentice boy named William GAUSNELL, about 17 years of age, 4 feet 9 inches, bound to the blacksmith's trade.

Sale of lot of 3 acres adjoining the Merryland Tract. Dennis KENNEDY.

Sale of tract, late the property of Andrew ETZLER, on Israels creek, 3-4 miles from Woodsborough, adjoining lands of William CARMACK. Apply to Jacob STITEBY on the tract or subscriber, Nathan RAITT, in Union-Town.

Sale of 12 Negroes, property of Raphael JARBOE, dec'd., on Carrolls Manor. Catharine JARBOE, Alexander JARBOE, adm'rs.

290. 15 Feb 1817

Married Tuesday 4th inst. by Rev. G. M. WILLIAMS, James ALLEN, to Miss B. A. CRAMPTON of the Merryland Tract.

Land for sale, the undivided half part of 42 acres called Timber Plenty, a mile from Monocacy bridge. Upton HAMMOND, 8 miles below Liberty.

Wood land for sale, 245 1/2 acres on east side of Catoctin mountains, adjoining lands of Richard JOHNSON and Samuel S. THOMAS. James S. HOOK.
Sale of house and lot in Buckey's-town. George KELLENBERG.
Land for sale in pursuance to the last will of Charles GASSAWAY, late of Montgomery Co., bounded by Potomac river and Broad Run, 200 acres; also tract on Seneca Creek, 400 acres. William DARNES, Charles GASSAWAY, ex'rs.
Bank of Westminster, John WALSH, cashier.
Sheriff's sale of estate of George HALLER to one-story brick house at the suit of Tobias HALLER.
John BARNES, 1 1/2 miles from Middletown, offers reward for apprentice to the blacksmith's business named Patrick HART, 18 years of age, 5 feet, 3 inches high, a sour ill-tempered fellow.

291. 22 Feb 1817
An inquest was held Thursday last on the body of Jacob GETZENDANNER of Gabriel who perished during the last severe weather but had not been found or even missed until the preceding evening. The dec'd. was a laboring man and on the 5th inst. went about 1/2 mile from the house of his employer to cut wood.

Died Wednesday, 12th inst. after a lingering illness, Jacob BUCKEY, in his 29nd year.
Died Tuesday evening last, Mrs. Elizabeth BENTZ, consort of George BENTZ of this place.
John HOLTER will sell 4 Negroes and other items.
Sale of land 184 1/2 acres, 7 miles from Frederick-town, 1 1/2 miles from Henry DONSON's mill and 2 miles from Jacob CRONISE's mill. Peter DUTRO.

292. 1 March 1817
Married Thursday evening last by Rev. P. DAVIDSON, Samuel WEBSTER to Mrs. Sarah SCOTT, all of this town.
Died Saturday last after a long and severe indisposition, captain Nicholas HALL, aged 34 years, leaving widow and 4 children; his masonic brethren are invited to attend at New-market to pay masonic honors. *Examiner.*
Margaret FOUT cautions persons not to trespass on her premises on Rock creek.
Sale at the White House farm, 2 miles from Frederick, carriage horses, cattle, hogs, furniture, Negro man, boy and woman, and other. John WHITE.

293. 8 March 1817
Wheat, corn, clover seed and hay for sale. Thos. S. LEE, Needwood.
Sale at the late residence of John ELLIOTT of Frederick Co., dec'd., 1 1/2 miles north of New Market, horses, cattle, grain, other. Richard ROBERTS, adm'r.
Sale of horses, cows and hogs. Eleanor MURDOCH.
Sale of farm, 60 acres, 3 miles of Emmitsburg. James KEEPERS, ex'r.
House and lot for sale at the north end of market St. George LEASE.

Trustee's sale at the tavern of Abraham MILLER, 3 miles above Middletown, of tract called Trail's Jaunt, 52 acres, 4 miles above Middletown, adjoining lands of Philip SHAFER and Henry BOGLY - to be sold for the benefit of the heirs of Michael MENSER, dec'd. Frederick A. SCHLEY, Trustee.

Thomas CASTLE cautions persons from buying or taking an assignment of a bond given by him in favor of Barney WHIP of Frederick Co.

294. 15 March 1817

Died Sunday, 9th inst. after a short and painful illness, Mrs. Eleanor MURPHY, wife of James MURPHY, of this co. and in a few hours after her, Miss Mary Ann MURPHY his daughter, in her 17th year.

Thomas BOGEN, Frederick-town, offers reward for apprentice to the saddling business, named Levi JONES, about 14 years of age.

Sale of land on Little Pipe Creek, formerly the property of Henry WILLIS, of Frederick Co., dec'd., called Wakefield, 650 acres. Alexander WARFIELD, Samuel STEVENSON, Daniel ZOLLIKOFFER, Trustees.

295. 22 March 1817

Died 1st inst., William WINNULL of this town. On 12th inst., Lewis MAHORNEY, brother-in-law to Mr. WINNULL. And on the day following, Mrs. Mary WINNULL, consort of Mr. WINNULL.

ABSALOM KALB, about to remove and requests persons indebted to him to settle their accounts.

Sale of farm, 500 acres where he lives in Pipe Creek; also 5217 3/4 acres in Hampshire Co. VA. John SCOTT, Pipe Creek.

296. 29 March 1817

Lloyd LUCKETT, Frederick Co, near New-town, Trap, offers reward for Negro EDWARD, aged 21 years.

Persons indebted to the estate of the late George COST are requested to settle their accounts with George WARNER who has authorization from Mrs. Amaria COST, the extx.

John ZIMMERMAN, Emmitsburg, offers reward for apprentice to the tailoring business named Thomas J. MARTIN, age about 16 years, stout.

Sale at the late residence of Jacob BUCKEY, dec'd., horse and gig. Michael BUCKEY, adm'r.

Ezra MANTZ, Holly Bush tanyard, 2 miles east of New Market, offers reward for Negro man Charles ODEN, about 28 years of age.

Boots and shoes, Patrick St. Philip HAUPTMAN.

Farm for sale, now occupied by Elias CRUTCHLEY, 205 acres(?). Richard POTTS.

George TRISLER having sold his stock, requests settlement of accounts.

George KOLB, ex'r. of Lewis MAHORNEY.

Jacob LEASE and George KOLB ex'rs. of Hezekiah JONES.

John MOTTER, ex'r of Valentine MOTTER, and adm'r of Catharine MOTTER.

Martha WEYLIE and George SHAW adm'rs of John V. WEYLIE.
John HINDS adm'r of Martin HINDS.
Jacob DERR, Frederick-town, offers reward for apprentice to the joiner's business named Henry LUTEN, 19 years of age, 5 feet, 8 inches.
John HOFFMAN, at his store in Frederick-town has just received a large assortment of dry goods.
Robert CROCKETT, Wyte Co., VA, offers reward for his servant JOHN; may use the name John SMITH.

297. 5 Apr 1817
Died 23rd ult in Liberty-town, Mrs. Mary HAMMOND, wife of captain Thomas HAMMOND and only dau. of General CUMMING, in her 31st year, leaving a husband, parents and other relatives.
Sale of two story brick house in Mechanics Town; the property will be shewn by Rev. HAASE who resides there. Jonas MATTHEWS.
To let to a blacksmith, a dwelling house with blacksmith shop. Frederick EICHELBERGER, Owing's Creek.
Farm for sale on Liberty road, 2 miles from Randal's-town. James DALL, agent for the Franklin Manufacturing Co.
George GROVER, ex'r of Thomas HUGHES of Emmittsburg.
Jacob DOLL will sell 12 1/2 acres on South St. adjoining lots of Jacob KELLER's and Mrs. BIRELY.
Absalom KALB, having removed to Virginia, would recommend to his friends and former customers, William NUSBAUM, who served his apprenticeship with him and is well acquainted with making and repairing pumps. He may be found at Jacob MEIXSEL's adjoining the market-house.
Regimental Cavalry Orders. The commanding officers of troops attached to 1st regiment of the 1st regimental Cavalry District are ordered to make their returns of the number of arms in their troops. Otho H. WILLIAMS, Lieut. Col. 1st Reg't of Cavalry.
Sale of 800 acres in Montgomery Co. in the neighborhood of Ely DORSEY's mill, 203 miles from the Potomac and Monocacy rivers, adjoining the lands of William HEMPSTEAD and John BENSON. Apply to Washington BOWIE, esq. of George-town or to subscriber in Baltimore. Hugh THOMPSON.
Chancery case - Henry MOTTER vs. Jean BROWN, William and James RANDELL, Thomas BROWN and Juliana his wife, Mary, John and William BROWN, William M'CLAIN and Eliza his wife, Jacob EVERSOLE, Catharine Magdalena EVERSOLE and Solomon and George EVERSOLE. Object of bill is for the complainant to obtain a decree for the performance of an article of agreement for the conveyance of land executed by Robert BROWN, late of York Co., PA to Jacob and George EVERSOLE, dated 15 Aug 1799, for 296 acres, 190 of which is in Frederick Co., MD. The defendants with the exception of Jacob EVERSOLE, reside out of the state of Maryland.

298. 12 April 1817
Candidates for sheriff: William M. BEALL, Junr.; Eli OGLE.
David MARTIN, Pres. of the Common Council, Frederick-town

Law. BRENGLE, Mayor of Frederick-town.
Stephen STEINER, Pres. of the Board of Aldermen, pro. tem, Frederick-town.
Aquila LUCAS, ex'r. of William L. WINNULL.
George HOLDRY, adm'r. of Joseph LYND.
Mrs. SINN will open her school at her present residence in Church St.
George PHILLIPS of the late firm of ALEXANDER & PHILLIPS, Carlisle, gives notice to the young men who during the time they went to College in this place bought on credit a number of books which that have remembered to forget to pay for.
Bela WARFIELD, wishing to remove to the western country, will sell the farm on which he now resides, 250 acres, in upper part of Anne Arundel Co.
Evan DORSEY, Frederick Co., offers reward for Negro man named PHILL, about 30 years of age.
Jos. K. STAPLETON, Brush-maker, 159, Baltimore St., offers reward for German redemptioner, who absconded from him on 6th inst., who arrived her in November last by name of Maurice SCHUMACHER, about 30 years of age, 5 feet, 8-9 inches.

299. 19 Apr 1817
Sale of land pursuant to last will of Joseph JOHNSON, lot of well timbered mountain land, 19 1/2 acres, part of tract called the Resurvey on part of the Resurvey on Stony Level, 4 miles from Middletown. Joseph JOHNSON, surviving ex'r.
Ely BENNETT, Baltimore Co, offers reward for Negro man named HARRY, about 23 years of age.
John MOUGHT, near Petersville, Merryland tract, has taken up a stray mare.
William ROSS, Pres. of the board of Alderman.
New grocery store. John HANE, Fredericktown.
Dissolution of the firm of Job GUEST and Henry BAKER, Liberty, under the firm of Guest & BAKER, the business to be continued at the same store by Henry BAKER.
ELECTED Directors of the Bank of Westminster: William DURBIN, George COLEGATE, Joshua DALAPLAINE, William TYLER, Jesse SLINGLUFF, Joshua JONES, Ludwick WAMPLER, John FISHER, Samuel STEVENSON, James M'HAFFIE. John WALSH, Cashier.
Flaxseed wanted. Jacob BRUNER & son.
Conrad SHAFER wishes to sell tavern stand, sign of the Fountain Inn, Market St.
Abraham ALBAUGH, near Liberty, offers reward for stolen horse.
Mary PENN, adm'rx. of Samuel PENN, Frederick Co.
Jacob SNYDER, Adams Co., PA, adm'r. of Peter FLICKINGER, Frederick Co.
John RUDISIL has taken up a stray mare.
Farm for sale on Deer Creek in Harford Co., 900 acres. Apply to John FORWOOD on the premises, Jno. W. STUMP, in Baltimore; John ARCHER at Stafford, ex'rs. of John STUMP.

Sale of person property of John BEALL, dec'd., at his late residence in Clarksburg, young Negro man, 2 lads and a girl, grain, furniture, and other. Margaret BEALL, admr'x.

Sale of hogs and other, at LAWRENCE's mill on Linganore. Charles COPELAND.

Jacob PROTZMAN gives notice that his wife Mary has left his bed and board without any cause; person are cautioned against trusting or harboring her as he will pay no debts of her contracting.

300. 26 Apr 1817

Dissolution of firm of George BUCKEY & son. George BUCKEY, Daniel BUCKEY.

Notice is given to Jane RICHARDS and Sarah DAVIS of payment read on legacies left them by their dec'd father Daniel ROOT, sen., Frederick Co., dec'd. George FOX, adm'r. de bonis non. of Daniel ROOT, jun. who was ex'r. of said Daniel ROOT, sen.

James PEARRE, near Liberty-town, offers reward for Negro man GEORGE, about 23 years of age.

Daniel FICK, adm'r. of John FICK.

Sale at the residence of Joshua HOWARD, the former residence of Col. Charles WARFIELD, dec'd., on Linganore, of horses, milk cows, hogs, etc. Alexander WARFIELD.

Sale by order of Orphans court on the farm of James M'CANNON, dec'd., residue of his personal estate. Ann M'CANNON, adm'rx.

Sale at late residence of Christian HERSHMAN, dec'd., Middletown, a lot of mountain land, 40 acres, along with personal property of dec'd. Jonathan HERSHMAN, Christian HERSHMAN, George WARNER, exr's.

Sale of mountain land at OATE's tavern: lot of 83 acres called The resurvey on Value In Time near Ridenour's on the Harman's Gap road; lot of 100 acres called Pumpkin Hall near Wilson HAYS, adjoining land of Henry NEWCOMER, and Forrest; and lot of 142 1/2 acres called Murdoch's Inheritance adjoining lands of David WOLF. Lots were surveyed by William MURDOCH of London. Richard POTTS.

Sale of land on Pettersons creek, in Hardy Co., also land near Moorefield, VA. James MACHER.

Sale of land in Loudoun Co., by virtue of a deed of trust from Stephen DANIEL, on Snickers's Gap Turnpike Road near the widow ROZELL'S, 115 acres. Seth SMITH, Joseph GARRETT.

Sale of 500 acres on Buffaloe creek, Monongalia Co., VA. Daniel BOYER, on Catoctin creek, 12 miles from Frederick-town.

Sale of 2-story brick house. Jonas MATTHEWS.

301. 3 May 1817

Rachel KESSLER, ex'r. of Jacob KESSLER.

Jonathan KEMP having taken the carding machine of Messrs. Henry and Philip HEMP, formerly Fundenburg's on Fishing creek, had machines put in complete order for carding.

Sale at the residence of Nicholas HALL, jun., dec'd., adjoining New Market, personal estate of dec'd., Negroes, horses, cattle, &c. Thomas C. SHIPLEY, adm'r.

Schoolmaster wanted. Evan DORSEY, near Liberty-town.

Dr. Robert L. ANNAN has taken up a stray mare.

Waggons and ploughs for sale. The subscribers have opened a black-smith shop in addition to their wheel-wright shop, nearly opposite Henry SMITH's blacksmith shop. Henry STIER, John STIER, Frederick STIER, New Market.

302. 10 May 1817

Married in Ontario Co., N. York, Thursday 24th ult. by Rev. WHITE, John N. CHAMERHORN, to Miss Amie C. MANTZ, formerly of this place.

Married Sunday last by Rev. J. HELFENSTEIN, Joseph HALLAR to Miss Catharine QUYNN, of this place.

Married the same day by Rev. F. W. HATCH, Benjamin MAULSBY to Miss Charlotte MARKELL of this place.

Town commissioners: John L. HARDING, George DOFFLER, John REICH.

Keeper of the Standard of weights and measures: John ADLUM, sen.

Keeper of the Work house: Henry STEINER of John.

Town constables: Lewis CROSS, Ormand BUTLER, Jacob MEIXSELL, Thomas YOUNG.

Market Master: Jacob MEIXSELL, sen.

Flour Inspector: Jacob MEIXSELL, sen.

A board of appeal appointed by the aldermen and common council to determine all appeals. John J. M'CULLEY, Register.

Isaac CRUM forewarns persons from trespassing on his property.

Dissolution of the partnership of William C. RUSSELL and Marcus Y. GRAFF under the firm of RUSSELL & GRAFF.

MEETING of the Medical and Chirurgical Faculty of the state of Maryland, above the Mayor's office. J. ARNEST, Sec'ry.

Sale of land at TURBUTT's Tavern, Frederick-town, 30-40 acres, late the property of Hezekiah JONES, dec'd, 5 miles from Frederick-town, 1 mile from PENNEBAKER's tavern and adjoining lands of Ormond HAMMOND and J. PANCOAST. Apply to John SHEETZ adjoining the same or to Jacob LEASE. Jacob LEASE, George KOLB, ex'rs.

Thomas H. STEPHENS, Loudoun Co., VA, near Bunden's Ferry, offers reward for missing mare.

Vachel W. DORSEY, near Liberty-town, offers reward for mulatto man named JIM who calls himself James MATTHEWS, 38-40 years old.

Edward DIGGES offers reward for Negro lad BOB who calls himself Bob SMITH, about 19 years old; has a mother at Henry WARRING's near Middlebrook mill and a sister at E. BROOKS in that neighborhood; has relations near Baltimore, in Georgetown, Prince George's Co. and the eastern shore; his father belonged to Ozburn SPRIGG and his relations live with Samuel SPRIGG, Prince George's Co.

Philip CLONINGER and Adam LORENTZ, adm'rs. of Philip CLONINGER.

Frederick EICHELBERGER, ex'r. of Matthias MORT.

303. 17 May 1817

Nicholas TURBUTT has removed from Buckey's town to Union Tavern on Market St., the establishment formerly kept by Capt. SCHLEY and is repairing it.

Sale of tavern stand on road from the Trap to Shepherds-town. Conrad FLOOK.

Ten Negroes for sale at the residence of Joseph WOOD, dec'd., on Linganore. Jonathan WOOD, Aaron WOOD, ex'rs.

Sale of half of tract called Walnut Ridge, 1 1/2 miles from Liberty-town, about 270 acres; will be shewn by Vachel W. DORSEY, living thereon. Thomas GIST.

Peter KOONS and Joseph TANEY, ex'rs. of George KOONS.

William M'DANIEL has taken up a stray mare.

Citizens of Frederick are invited to attend the funeral of Arthur SHAAF, Esq. The procession will move from his late dwelling to the burial ground of the Protestant Episcopal Church in this town.

Henry FUNDENBURG, Market St., has just received a fresh supply of dry goods, groceries, hard & queensware.

304. 24 May 1817

Died at Emmittsburgh on Friday morning, 9th inst., Michael WILSON, in his 55th year, after a short but very painful illness of only 3 days, leaving a wife and 5 small children.

Died Thursday morning 15th(?) inst. in Georgetown, in his 49th year, Arthur SHAAF, Esq. of Frederick Co., born and educated in this co. His remains were brought to Arcadia, the country seat of the dec'd. Pursued a practice of law and then removed to Annapolis.

Died 15th inst. after a short but distressing illness, Mrs. Ann HAMMOND, consort of Eden HAMMOND, and dau. of Evan DORSEY, in her 23rd year.

Died Tuesday last in his 67th year, James STEVENS, of this co.

Jacob LITTLE has opened a shop 2 doors above Mr. STORM's tavern, Patrick St. where he makes all kinds of ploughs and waggons.

Woollen cloth manufactory in Mechanicks-town in full operation. G. J. CONRADT.

Dissolution of the partnership of Henry H. MARSH, Daniel SANBURN and Patrick O'NEILL, under the firm of MARSH, SANBURN & O'NEILL.

MONOCACY Bridge Lottery. Nicholas SNIDER, Benjamin JONES, clerks.

Sale of house and lot of John SHELLMAN, dec'd., Church St. John BRUNNER, ex'r.

Land and mills for sale, 20 acres, in Montgomery Co., 1/4 mile from Hyatt's-town. Benjamin WATERS is living on the property. Frederick BAKER, Benjamin WATERS.

Sale of tract, 520(?) acres near Sugar Loaf Mountain. Edward DIGGES, Barnesville, Montgomery Co.

Chancery case: John M'KALEB vs. Rebecca CAMPBELL, Quinton ARMSTRONG, Isaac ARMSTRONG, sen., Isaac ARMSTRONG, jun. and

John ARMSTRONG. Object of bill is for the specific performance of an article of agreement given by Quinton ARMSTRONG sen. of PA, now dec'd. to his son James ARMSTRONG, late of Frederick Co., also dec'd., dated 28 March 1793, for the conveyance of 151 acres in Frederick Co. Defendants reside out of the state of Maryland.

W. MASON, near Leesburg, offers reward for Negro man named JAMES, about 21 years old, formerly the property of George RUST of Leesburg.

John HOGGINS has taken up a stray mare.

John LOGSDEN has taken up a stray horse.

305. 31 May 1817
Married Tuesday evening, 20th, at Fountain Rock, by Rev. Rezin HAMMOND, Eli TOWNE, Esq. to Miss Minerva OWINGS, dau. of the late Edward OWINGS, esq., all of this co.

Dissolution of the firm of Horatio HOBBS & Co. Horatio HOBBS, John STEWART, John PITTENGER, Creagers-town.

Wm. POTTS, Retreat Farm, Frederick Co., offers reward for missing mare.

Jacob LATE offers reward for apprentice to the milling business, named Orell MURPHY, about 20 years of age.

Sale of furniture, 2 sets of nailing machines, elderly coloured woman. George W. MILLER.

Persons indebted to E. H. MAYNARD should settle their accounts; having taken Wm. HODGKISS into partnership.

Sale of 8 Negroes at the late residence of Malachi FLANIGAN, dec'd. in the Merryland Tract, near Petersville. Thomas FLANIGAN, adm'r. Trustee's sale of farm which belonged to John SHOEMAKER, dec'd., 153 acres on road from Taney-town to Gettysburg. Abraham NULL, Trustee.

Eleanor GOTT, Montgomery co, offers reward for Negro man named James DUFFIN aged 35-40 years of age.

306. 7 June 1817
J. T. SHAAFF adm'r. of Arthur SCHAAFF.

William GRIMES, jun., adm'r. of Michael WILSON, to sell 6 Negroes at residence of dec'd., near Wilson's Ford on Monococy.

Peter NICHOLS, merchant taylor, Patrick St., has received an assortment of cloths, cassimeres and vestings.

Open letter to Joshua DELAPLANE, Esq. regarding his ungentlemanly conduct and slanders; and his brother Daniel who is a gentleman [relating to the negotiating and signing of financial notes between the parties in question]. John SCOTT, Pipe Creek.

Susannah STEVENS, James STEVENS, John STEVENS, admr's of James STEVENS.

Ely DORSEY of Ely to sell farm where he now lives, 5 miles east of Liberty-town.

Carding of country wool, at the Union Woollen Manufactory, 2 miles southwest of Middletown. - Joseph A. HUGHES.

Cornelius SHAWEN, Loudoun Co., VA, 2 miles of Waterford, has taken up a stray horse.

Rezin SIMPSON seeks to find 3 small steers which strayed from him, near Liberty.

Thomas WEAKLEY has taken up a stray horse.

307. 14 June 1817

New Woollen Factory - William GREASON, Emmittsburg.

Patrick & James KEARNEY continue the Fishing Creek Factory, 8 miles from Frederick-town, near Catoctin Furnace where they intend carrying on the woollen manufacturing business.

Blacksmith shop to rent, on the turnpike road, 2 miles west of Middletown. Henry LIGHTER.

House for sale in Taney-town on Main St. Mary CROUSE.

It is requested that accounts be settled with D. & F. HINES which has been dissolved for some time past. David HINES, Liberty-town.

Sheriff's sale of house and lot of Francis SLOTHOUR in Emmitsburg, lot No. 33, seized at the suit of George ROW.

Joseph HILTEBRAND, ex'r. of Catharine CROSS.

Elizabeth SCHVEIGART, wife of Peter SCHVEIGART has taken up a stray gelding.

308. 21 June 1817

Abraham H. COLLINS cautions persons from taking assignment on note given by Barton HACKNEY to Adam BAUGHMAN.

Chancery case in Montgomery Co.: Eden BEALL vs. Thomas PLATER, Anne KEY, Elizabeth R. KEY, Mary L. KEY, Philip B. KEY, Louisa KEY, Rebeca Ann KEY, Emily KEY, Anne Arnold KEY, Elijah BEALL, Eli BEALL, Enoch BEALL and Edward BEALL. Object of bill is to obtain decree for conveyance of 220 acres, being part of tract called Bradford's Rest, lying in Montgomery Co., purchased of George PLATER of St. Mary's Co. by Edward BEALL on 9 Oct 1784. Edward BEALL, the father of complainant, paid to George PLATER the whole of the consideration money and the said George PLATER died around 1792, without conveying to the said Edward BEALL. George PLATER in his will, devised his estate in Montgomery Co. to his son Thomas PLATER who conveyed the whole of Bradford's Rest to Philip B. KEY who has since died leaving a widow and children, all of whom are made defendants in this bill.

Equity case in Frederick Co.: John WINTER, George HISS and wife and others vs. Stephen WINCHESTER, Matthew HARSNIPT and John HAVNER. Object of bill is to obtain a decree for legal title to part of a tract called The Resurvey on Part of Bedford. Bill states that Stephen WINCHESTER, one of the defendants sold land to John HAVNER another of the defendants and bound himself by a bond to convey the same to said HAVNER and his heirs. HAVNER later assigned his right to land to Matthew HARSNIPT the other defendant who afterwards reassigned his right to said HAVNER and HAVNER on 19 March 1795 sold said land to Paul CROUSE. Said Paul Crouse has since died intestate and the complainants as his heirs are desirous to get title. WINCHESTER, HAVNER and HARSNIPT do not reside in Maryland.

Equity case: Thomas ING and Frances his wife, John CROUSE and others vs. John HAVNER. Object of bill is to obtain a decree to compel the defendant to convey title of tract. [See ABOVE.]

THOMAS & EMMIT have received assortment of staple and fancy articles, at their new cheap store lately occupied by Messrs. RUSSELL & GRAFF.

Jacob EASTERDAY at his old stand, 2 miles above the Trap, on road to Harper's Ferry, has commenced the manufacture of cut nails.

John D. SMITH has repaired his machine with two new and complete sets of the finest quality cards at the old stand, lower end of Patrick St.

Persons indebted to firm of Jacob HOUCK & Co. are requested to make immediate payment. Jesse WRIGHT, jun.

John JEMISON, of Frederick Co. applies for relief from debt under the insolvency acts.

Journeymen millwrights wanted - Michael LAMBRIGHT at the north end of Market St., or apply at Casper RAMSBURG's, 3 miles below Middle-town.

Sale of farm, late the property of John KNOX, 3 miles north of Taney-town, 300 acres. Apply to William KNOX on the premises. Robert & Jno. KNOX.

Chancery sale of mill sit on Patapsco Falls, 3 miles from Poplar Springs, 10 acres. Jacob SIDES, Trustee.

Jacob WIKE, Salsbury Township, Lancaster Co., PA, offers reward for horse which strayed from the pasture of George WEBB, 3 miles from Middleburg.

John HARRITT, Emmitsburg, offers reward for apprentice to the hatting business named James MARSHALL, aged 18 years.

309. 28 June 1817

Destructive hail storm on the 20th.

Sale of court house lots, where my father, William RITCHIE, dec'd, used to reside [described]. Wm. RITCHIE.

Andrew OFFUTT, living on Big Seneca, Montgomery Co., near Darne's-town, offers reward for mulatto man named PHIL, about 19 years of age.

Land and mills for sale, the estate of Samuel ROBERTSON 3d of Montgomery Co., dec'd, commonly called Goshen, 300 acres. Thomas DAVIS, Wm. ROBERTSON, John H. RIGGS, Trustees.

Richard Bland LEE offers reward for Negro girl who absconded from the service of Richard CUTTS, called MARGERY, 14-15 years old, well known in Alexandria, having resided several years in John ROBERTS' family.

John WALKER, near Frederick-town, offers reward for Negro man named LEN, about 26 years old.

George LECKLITER has taken up a stray mare.

Henry JENKINS, ex'r. of Helena FENWICK, Frederick Co.

310. 5 July 1817

Ezra MANTZ, adm'r. of John CRUM.

Solomon DAVIS, adm'r. to sell 14 Negroes of John O'NEALE, dec'd.

311. 14 July 1817

John STEWART, near Emmitsburg, offers reward for mulatto woman named KITTY, about 24 years old, bought from Jesse CLUDE, Pipe Creek Bridge. Captain WHITE of Montgomery Co. owns her mother who also owned and raised her. Mr. CLUDE owns some of her children.

Henry KINZEY, Pipe Creek, cautions from taking assignment on any note with his name on it assigned to Mr. WAGNER of Liberty-town by Abraham STONER.

Martha M. J. WEYLIE and George SHAW, adm'rs. of John V. WEYLIE.

Sale of tract, late the property of Ninian M'BEEL, dec'd., 248 3/4 acres, lying on Seneca, Montgomery Co., near F. C. CLOPPER's merchant mill and adjoining the farms of Henry WARRING and the late James HENDERSON. Thomas C. NICHOLLS, Middle Brook Mills.

Sale of estate of the late Col. T. L. LEE of Coton - Mill lot, 51 acres, lot of 360 acres, lot of 208 acres and other. R. H. HENDERSON, Leesburg, Loudoun, VA.

Chancery case: Margaret KEMP, ex'rx. of Frederick KEMP vs. Jacob STALEY, John M'PHERSON and Gilbert KEMP. Object of bill is for complainant to be relieved against a bond, executed by Frederick KEMP and Gilbert KEMP his security, to Jacob STALEY and assigned to John M'PHERSON, dated 11 June 1812, conditioned for the payment of 300 pounds.

312. 19 July 1817

Died in Frederick Co., 11th inst., Mrs. Susan THOMAS, consort of Henry THOMAS, after a lingering and painful illness, leaving husband and 5 children.

Reuben T. BOYD & James SIMPSON, tailors, have commenced the business in New Market.

John WAGNER, Liberty-town, offers reward for Negro man, CHARLES, who calls himself Charles WARFIELD, about 20 years old.

Adam LORENTZ and Philip GLONINGER, Junr., adm'rs. of Philip GLONINGER, sen.

John CRAPSTER, Taney-town, has taken up a stray gelding.

Sale of horses, cattle, hogs, two stills and boiler. Ezra MANTZ, adm'r. of John CRUM.

Nicholas DAWSON will sell property where he now resides, at the foot of the South Mountain, 3 1/2 miles from Boonsborough.

Land for sale at Allen DORSEY's tavern at the Poplar Springs, 2 miles above Poplar Springs, 50 acres. Thomas WHITEFOOT, jun., at Lisbon.

Sale of farm formerly owned by Thomas N. BINNS, the part of Hope Farm, which Thomas N. BINNS bought of the representatives of Thomas DARNALL, dec'd. Charles Fenton MERCER, Aldie, Loudoun Co., VA.

Benjamin BYERS gives notice to those who purchased property at his sale that their notes are due.

313. 26 July 1817

Died Sunday last in his 65th year, Capt. Peter WOLF.

Dr. John H. M'KELFRESH offers professional services to the inhabitants of Frederick-town.

Zephaniah HARRISON, offers reward for Negro man named ELY, about 23 years of age.

Samuel LUKENBEEL, 1 mile from Harley's store on road from the Trap to Sharpsburg, offers reward for missing mare.

Sale of house and lot of Peter BEALL, dec'd, adjoining John CAMPBELL, on 4th and 5th sts., Frederick-town.

Benjamin RODRICK offers reward for mare that strayed from the farm of Joseph THOMAS, near Late's mill.

Levy PHILLIPS gives notice of having good claim to 500 acres of land in Montgomery Co., which Thomas N. BINNS swapped with Benedict DARNALL and which has been sold to him by said Benedict DARNALL, will file a bill in Chancery Court. The land is part of The third resurvey on the second part of the second resurvey on Friend in Need and part of tract called Farewell.

314. 2 Aug 1817

Sale of cows, horses, hogs, furniture. Peter BUCKEY, Liberty-town.

Sale at late residence of Mary GETTINGS, dec'd., on the Merryland Tract, 1 mile from Petersville, of horses, cattle, hogs and sheep. John F. GETTINGS, adm'r.

Sale of 200 acres joining the old Annapolis road, 3 miles above William HOBBS's and adjoining lands of Basil DORSEY and others. John HAMTON.

Zephaniah HARRISON, 14 miles from Frederick on the Baltimore turnpike road, offers reward for three Negroes, CHARLES, mulatto, about 19 years old; FANNY, mulatto, about 20 years of age and NANCY, stout likely woman, about 20 years of age.

Lewis SMITH, George-town, offers reward for Negro man named JACK or John POSEY.

D. & G. MANTZ, Holly Bush, 2 miles east of New Market, offer reward for apprentice to the tanning business, about 19 years old, named Samuel POOLE.

James M'KESSON, Jun., Millers-town, Adams Co., PA, offers reward for missing filly.

Henry MICHAEL, adm'r. of George MICHAEL.

Edward KNOTT and Johnsey HAMMOND, both of Frederick Co., apply for relief through benefit of the insolvency acts.

315. 9 Aug 1817

Died Saturday last, in his 54th year, Conrad SHAFFER, Innkeeper of this place.

Died Wednesday last in his 77th year, Michael LATE, sen., citizen of Frederick Co.

Only specified notes will be received at the Gates of the Baltimore and Frederick-town Turnpike road Co. Wm. JESSOP, Presd't.

William HUNTER and Edward HUNTER offer reward for John CRAIG, of Charlestown Township, Chester Co., PA, who on 19 July 1817 shot Edward HUNTER, esq. of Newton Township, Delaware Co. He is a blacksmith by trade, about 5 feet, 9-10 inches, stoop shouldered, stout built, a little knock kneed, sun burnt, freckled, thick lips, sandy complexion, large whiskers.

Sale of woodland tract, adjoining the town of Centreville; also brick store house in Middleburg, VA. Edmond DENNY.

Land and mills for sale adjoining the town of Waterford, now occupied for a woollen manufactory. Call on James MOORE in Waterford. James FARQUHAR, George JANNEY, Loudoun Co., VA.

Merchant mills for rent, lately owned by Charles A. WARFIELD, on Western Branch of the Patapsco falls. Lewis PASCAULT, Baltimore Town.

Joseph TANEY, Jun., Liberty-town offers reward for John GOOD, apprentice to the saddling business.

316. 16 Aug 1817

To let lime kiln and quarries. John HUGHES.

John TALBOTT, Richard ROBERTS, ex'rs. of Evan PLUMMER.

Sale on the 30th mile of the Baltimore and Frederick-town turnpike road, a farm and tavern, live stock, farming utensils, tavern furniture. James WHIFFING, on the premises.

Sale of tract, 350 acres, in Berkeley Co., 5 miles from Martinsburgh, pursuant to the last will of William PENDLETON. Wm. PENDLETON, John PORTERFIELD, exr's.

Sale of a number of slaves, at the late residence of Arthur SHAAFF, dec'd., near Frederick-town.

Elizabeth HUGHES will sell the farm on which she resides, 2 miles of Montgomery Court House, 200 acres, 2000 fruit trees, apples, peaches, pears, cherry, plums, quinces.

317. 23 Aug 1817

Died Saturday, 16th inst. at Rockville, Montgomery Co., Mrs. Mary TANEY, wife of Augustus TANEY, esq. in her 29th year and on the same died their infant and only child, aged 7 weeks and 3 days.

Land for sale 35-40 acres, 1 mile of Liberty-town with mills. Adam MYERS on the premises, or apply to Jonathan W. DUSTIN, manager of the factory.

Sale at the late residence of Peter WOLF, dec'd., 2 Negro women, horses, milch cows, furniture, etc. Walter POOLE, Nicholas HOLTZ, ex'rs.

Election of the Boonsborough Turnpike Co. at the house of John KNODE. John MILLER, Secretary.

Isaac HANKY has taken up a stray gelding.

318. 30 Aug 1817

Henry WINSOR, ex'r. of Christian WALLICK, Montgomery Co.

John BANTZ, Frederick-town, about to remove to the western country, will sell feather beds & bedding, furniture, 2 milch cows, 3 hogs, 3 looms, dying kettles, locust posts, rails, shingles, ash timber, and other.

A family of Negroes for sale. Leonard SMITH, on Carroll's manor, near STONEBRAKER's mill.

Philip KISER, 6 miles from Frederick, offers reward for an apprentice to the blacksmith's business named John HURD, nearly 17 years of age, 5 feet, 7-8 inches.

John V. CROSS has applied for relief from debts under the insolvency acts.

319. 6 Sep 1817

Committed to gaol of Frederick Co., a black man who calls himself Sam HANDY, about 37 years of age; says he belongs to George YELLOTT in city of Baltimore.

Property owners are notified to have their foot pavements made from Storm's alley up to Col. Stephen STONER's dwelling or the Commissioners will have it paved at the expense of the owners.

Frederick OTT, Emmitsburg, gives notice that payments are due on notes give at his sale.

Oliver C. GOSSOM, overseer at Mr. GOLDSBOROUGH's farm, 3 miles from Frederick, for the last five years, wishes a situation.

Sale of 225 acres, late the property of Evan PLUMMER, dec'd., 1 1/2 miles southeast of New Market on the waters of Bush Creek.

Stray hogs that came to Washington Gardens. Joseph HEUISLER.

William M'SHERRY, in the jail of Adams Co., PA, gives notice to his creditors that he has applied for benefit of relief under the insolvency laws.

John BISER and John SHAFFER, junr., adm'rs. of Abraham WILLIARD.

James ROBERTSON, Linganore Mills, announces that his mill is again in complete operation.

George KELLENBERGER, about to move to the Western Country, gives notice that notes are due for goods purchased at his sale in Buckeys-town.

Benjamin RICE will sell or rent his property in Buckeystown.

Sale of 240 acres, real estate of Lewis BEALMEAR, late of Montgomery Co., dec'd., two tracts called Valentine's Garden Enlarged and Two Brothers - 2 miles from Montgomery Court House. Richard ANDERSON, William WILLSON, Baker WATERS, Commiss'rs.

Benj. & Joshua JOHNSON, at Johnson's Glass House, near Frederick-town, offer reward for 2 Negro men, JOHN, mulatto about 20 years old; and CHARLES about 24 years old.

320. 13 Sep 1817

Mrs. HOFFMAN, lately arrived from Germany, to open a school in Bentz-town in the house formerly occupied by Richard ENGLISH as a store, to teach all kinds of Needlework.

Zephaniah HARRISON gives notice that his wife Mary HARRISON has left his bed and board with any cause.

Conrad KAUFMAN, Frederick-town, to remove to the western country, will sell his dwelling where he now lives, at the upper end of Market St.

Sale at her residence on the Merryland Tract, part of the personal property of Jeremiah GITTINGS, dec'd., Negroes, cattle, furniture, etc. Jane GITTINGS, adm'rx.

Sale agreeable to the last will of Conrad SHAFER at Frederick C. Haas' tavern in Creeger's-town, 11 lots of ground; also tavern stand for many years occupied by him as the Fountain Inn Tavern, and other real and personal estate. George BALTZELL, ex'r.

Henry COLLINS has taken up a stray mare.

Charles SNURR and Matthias BRANDENBURGH retract any words to the effect that John STEMBLE did make over his property to his father to avail himself of the benefit of the act of insolvency.

Chancery case in Montgomery Co.: Jannaro S. FARRE, complainant vs. Thomas W. HOWARD, Edward O. WILLIAMS, defendants. Object of the bill is to obtain a decree for a conveyance of land in Montgomery Co. bonding on Rockville, 1 1/2 acre, which the complainant purchased of the defendant HOWARD of the defendant WILLIAMS (who resides in Virginia).

Thomas RIDGELY, Frederick Co, near New-town (Trap), offers reward for missing colt.

Robert DARNALL, Frederick Co., 5 miles from the mouth of Monocacy and near Major JOHNSON's Iron works, offers reward for Negro man named DARNEY, about 25 years old, believed to have gone off with two Negro women, one of whom is his wife, about 20, with child of 8 months.

321. 20 Sep 1817

Candidates for sheriff: Lawrence BRENGLE, William M. BEALL, jun., Daniel ARTHUR.

John BUTT still carries on the fulling, dyeing and dressing of cloth at the factory of Joel MARSH on the Tuscarora.

Sale by virtue of the last will of Daniel SHUEE, Frederick Co., sale of farm of 295 7/8 acres, in the Pipe Creek Settlement, 3/4 mile from Union-town. John GREENWOOD, John ENGLEMAN, ex'rs of Danl. SHUEE.

William GRIMES, jun., adm'r. of Michael WILSON.

322. 27 Sep 1817

Rev. Jonathan RAHAUSER, Pastor of the German Reformed Congregation in Hagers-town died on 23rd inst., in his 53rd year.

Jacob LATE, Michael LATE, John LATE, ex'rs. of Michael LATE.

William STEVENSON, ex'r. of James STEVENSON.

George HAPE, gives notice, having passed his notes to George PRICE, esq. for the payment of the mill at Bruceville, in Frederick Co., he forewarns persons from taking assignment of those notes as he will not pay them unless title is made good.

Sale of 2 houses in Emmitsburg, property of John GILDEA, dec'd. Richard BROOKE, Trustee.

Sale of tract of land pursuant to the last will of Elijah LITTLER, 300-400 acres, 5 miles north of Winchester in Frederick Co. Francis STRIBLING, Charles W. LITTLER, ex'rs.

323. 4 Oct 1817

School under the superintendence of Robert RICHIE will commence.

Money found between Frederick and Richard CROMWELL's; apply to widow LESHORN, living on Carroll's manor.

John DORSEY, Carroll's Manor, offers reward for mulatto man, Bill CROSS, about 22 years old.

324. 11 Oct 1817

Death of Capt. Thomas Gist MURRAY, on board the ship Tennessee, of consumption, on her voyage from New Orleans to Philadelphia; native of Maryland. He commanded a division at Fort Plaquemine during the memorable siege of Orleans; his detachment suffered most and was continually during 9 days and nights, exposed to incessant bombardment.

John HOFFMAN has just removed his store from Baltimore to his store in Frederick-town where he has a large assortment of merchandise.

Dissolution of partnership of John BAYLY and William JOHNSON under the firm of BAYLY & JOHNSON. The Dry good business will be carried on by John BAYLY.

JOHN WILSON and William MURDOCH, Baltimore, have formed a copartnership under the firm of William MURDOCH & Co. and have taken a warehouse in South Eutaw St. where they will purchase all kinds of country produce, particularly flour and tobacco.

Notice to William MOONEY, formerly of the second regiment of infantry, Capt. SEDGEWICK's company, Col. STRONG, commander, about the year 1802, to apply to Elizabeth MOGAHAN of Georgetown, D.C. to hear of something to his advantage.

Land and mills for sale, 2 miles from Cregers-town, formerly owned by George DEVILBISS, dec'd., on Owen's creek; also 133 acres and 64 acres adjoining. Jacob PLAINE and Alexander DEVILBISS.

325. 18 Oct 1817

Petition to be presented to the Legislature of this state to open a road from new road passing through the lands of Philemon GRIFFITH, sen., and from thence to Poplar Springs.

Waggoner wanted - Wm. WEBSTER, manager at Arcadia, late residence of Arthur SHAAF, Esq.

326. 25 Oct 1817

Died Tuesday last, George STEINER, eldest son of Col. Stephen STEINER of this place, who had nearly attained his 19th year.

Benjamin HOFF wishes to purchase a few young Negro slaves.

Partnership of Samuel B. LEATHERWOOD and Joshua HALLER, in the line of states from Frederick to Winchester has been dissolved.

John BLACK, adm'r. of Henry BLACK.

Abel RUSSELL, near New Market, offers reward for apprentice boy named John WINDLE, about 20 years old, 5 feet, 10-11 inches.

Nicholas HOY, 1 1/2 miles below Liberty-town, offers reward for missing mare.

Nicholas BRENGLE has taken up a sow and boar.

Sale of houses, farm, mills, pursuant to the last will of Edward BEESON, sen. Farm in Berkeley Co. VA; lot on Burke St and Spring alley, now occupied by William RIDDLE. Jesse BEESON, Micajah BEESON, Edward BEESON, David RIDGWAY, ex'rs.

Edmund KEY to sell the estate on which he resides in Prince George's Co., 575 acres.

Lewis NEILL of Alexandria to sell land, 9 miles north of Winchester, VA, 200 acres.

327. 1 Nov 1817
Died Tuesday night last in his 71st year, John BUCKIUS, for many years resident of this place.

James M'HAFFIE, ex'r. of Regena GRANDADAM.

Jacob KENDALL offers reward for William DRURY, apprentice to the hatting business, about 19 years and 6 months old.

John POWELL gives notice of a stray cow which came to the farm of John HUGHES, 1 mile from Frederick.

Sale of 3 Negroes at ETZLER's tavern, Liberty-town, sold by the directions of the last will of Basil SIMPSON. Curtis WILLIAMS, Thos. GRIFFITH, ex'rs.

James PEARRE, near Liberty-town, offers reward for black man named GEORGE, about 22 years old.

Benjamin HIBBERD having declined the carding and fulling business, requests debts be paid; make payment to Daniel PRICE.

Elected to the Westminster, Taney-town and Emmitsburg Turnpike Co.: John M'KALEN, Pres., Henry SPALDING, Sec'ry and Treas. and managers: Robt. L. ANNAN, Geo. M. EICHELBERGER, John SHORB, Joseph TANEY, Jacob CLABAUGH, John GRAYBILL, Patrick LOWE, Wm. PATTERSON.

Peter ZIMMERMAN, living near Emmitsburg, offers reward for apprentice boy named William BLAIR, 18 years old, bound to the plough and waggon making business.

328. 8 Nov 1817
Jno. TYLER thanks the citizens of Frederick for the prompt assistance in arresting the progress of the fire on his kitchen and granary Wednesday last.

Sale at the residence of Michael BAYER, dec'd., in Church St., of 8-day clock, and other furniture. John EBERT, Jacob BAYER, adm'rs with the will annexed.

Henry STEINER, adm'r. of Thomas Gist MURRAY, late Captain of the Artillery in the U.S. Army.

George POOLE and Ferdinand O'NEALE, Frederick Co., applying for benefit of act of insolvency.

Barbara FOUT cautions person from trespassing on her property.

Trustee's sale of farm which belonged to John SHOEMAKER, dec'd., 153 acres, on road from Taney-town to Gettysburg, 1 1/2 mile from Taney-town. Abraham NULL, Trustee.

Edward HUGHES, Damascus, will sell farm, 150 acres.

Sale of property by virtue of a deed of trust executed by Abraham LANDES for securing certain debts, on High St. in Georgetown. Daniel RENNGER, Trustee. John TRAVERS, auctioneer.

Jacob BISER and John BISER, ex'rs. of Daniel BISER.

329. 15 Nov 1817

The farm, Bellevue for sale, 1 mile from Frederick-town, 200 acres. Richard POTTS.

Oliver C. GOSSOM offers reward for horse missing from pasture of William GOLDSBOROUGH, 3 miles from Frederick-town.

Henry THOMAS has removed his store to the store room lately occupied by Messrs. Michael HAUSER and Sons.

John B. STEMMEL has taken the tavern stand in Woodsberry, lately occupied by Wm. H. GRIMES.

Highest prices for wheat, if brought to Fall's Mills at the Turnpike road between Westminster and Reister's-town - John ROSS & Co.

George WOLF, Petersville, has taken up a stray steer.

330. 22 Nov 1817

Sale of farm, 1 mile from Middletown, 150 acres. Jacob BOWLUS.

Sale of house and lot in Kerns-town, 3 miles from Winchester, VA; and a lot of 5 acres. Apply to Margaret SLEMMONS who lives on lot or to Robert SLEMMONS near Charles-town, VA, who are exr's. of estate of Thomas SLEMMONS.

331. 29 Nov 1817

Married Tuesday, 18th inst. at New Market, by Rev. Frederick W. HATCH, Singleton WOOTTEN to Miss Elizabeth BRASHEAR, dau. of Dr. Belt BRASHEAR of that place.

Married Thursday, 20th inst., at Fountain Rock, by Rev. Caleb RAYNALS, John HAMMOND, son of Vachel, to Miss Mary Govane OWINGS, dau. of the late Edward OWINGS, all of Frederick Co.

Married same evening by Rev. N. SNETHEN, Howard GRIFFITH jun., merchant of Baltimore, to Miss Ruth PLUMMER of this co.

Died suddenly on Saturday evening last, Mrs. Amelia BRENGLE, consort of Jacob BRENGLE. *Examiner.*

Persons indebted to the late firms of RUSSELL and GRAFF, and STEINER & GRAHAME, are requested to call on Jacob STEINER, in whose hands the books are left for collection. William C. RUSSELL, William STEINER.

Jesse TYSON, on the head of Hollingsworth dock, Baltimore, offers reward for horse and gig, stolen from the gate of Samuel R. SMITH, 1 mile from Baltimore.

Elizabeth GRIMES, adm'rx. of William H. GRIMES.

Land for sale, 100 acres, 1 1/2 miles from Frederick-town, adjoining lands of William M. BEALL and William FOUT and now in the possession of William FOUT. Daniel GANTE.

Farm for sale, 126 acres, 1 mile from Lewistown and adjoining John DEVILBISS's sawmill; Joseph NICKUM, tenant on the land. Apply to Jacob JACKSON, 1 mile from Middletown. Lawrence EVERHARD.

Daniel BRENGLE, 1 mile from Frederick-town, has taken up a stray bull.

332. 6 Dec 1817
Andrew THOMSON has ready for delivery, strong beer.
Jacob BAKER, near Emmitsburg, has taken up a stray heifer.
Thomas MARLOWE has taken up a stray gelding.

333. 15 Dec 1817
Henry STEINER adm'r. of Christopher HALLER.

Land for sale, pursuant to a deed of trust, executed to William NOLAND, by Amos FERGESON and Harrison SIMPSON, on which said Fergeson resides, 150 acres.

Sale of personal property of Caleb BURGESS, dec'd., at his late residence, 4 miles from Liberty-town, Negro boy, horse, waggon and other. Samuel BURGESS, ex'r.

George HOFFMAN, 1 mile from Creagers-town, has taken up a stray steer.

Henry NELSON, Frederick Co., offers a reward for Negro man named CONGO, 35-40 years old.

Jacob MYERS, adm'r. of Mary MYERS.

Equity case: Daniel ENGLAR vs. William HALLINBERGER and Elizabeth his wife, Samuel STEM, Lydia STEM, Margaret STEM, Salome STEM, the heirs and widow of John STEM, dec'd, and Nathan ZIMMERMAN, adm'r. with will annexed of John STEM, dec'd. Object of the bill is for the sale of the real estate possessed by John STEM when he died, in order to pay the debt due the complainant. Margaret STEM, the widow of said John STEM, and Solome his dau. reside in PA.

334. 20 Dec 1817
Augustus TANEY, Atty at Law, George-town, D.C.
George SPALDING has found a small sum of money in Hyatt's Town.
Henry THOMAS requests persons indebted to him to make payment.

Election at New-town (Trap) of the Harpers ferry Turnpike road co., Col. John M'PHERSON, pres.; John HOFFMAN, Jesse MATTHEWS, John ECKHARD, Doct. Grafton DUVELL and Thomas BOTELER, managers - and Patrick M'GILL, treasurer. Benjamin WEST, Sec'ry.

House and lot for sale in Patrick St., now in the tenure of Thomas W. MORGAN. Lewis KLEIN, Waterford.

Equity case: David TOMS, John TOMS, Samuel TOMS, Elias TOMS, Jonathan TOMS, and Catharine TOMS, Hezekiah ROBINSON and Hannah his wife vs. Michael KNIFE and Elizabeth his wife, Jacob WILLS and Susanna his wife, George TOMS, John TOMS and Polly TOMS, children of Solomon TOMS, William TOMS, Samuel TOMS, Abraham TOMS, Jonathan TOMS and Margaret TOMS, children of Abraham TOMS, Thomas BARNES and Catharine

his wife, Robert LANG and Hannah his wife, Samuel WILSON and Susanna his wife. Object of bill is to obtain decree for sale of two tracts, one called Tom's Safe Guard and the other called John Tom's Luck, bought in Frederick Co., in which the complainants and defendants have an estate as tenants in common and to divide the money arising from such sale. All the defendants reside out of the state of Maryland and George, John and Polly TOMS, children of Solomon TOMS, William, Samuel, Abraham, Jonathan and Margaret TOMS, children of Abraham TOMS, are infants under the age of 21, residing out of the state of Maryland.
Michael SHRINER, adm'r. of Andrew RIDINGER.

335. 27 Dec 1817
Journeymen tanners wanted. Even WEBB.
Zachariah MACCUBBIN, Montgomery Co., applies for relief of debts under the act of insolvency.

336. 3 Jan 1818
Married Thurs evening last by Rev. Henry WELCH, Ignatius GRIFFITH of Clarksburg, to Miss Ruth M'ELFRESH, dau. of Col. P. M'ELFRESH of this co.
Died Christmas morning, of a lingering pulmonary complaint, John PYFER of this place in his 25th year. He took the field in 1813 under Capt. STEINER and again in 1814.
Journeyman miller wanted. James ROBERTSON - apply to him at his store in Frederick-town or to Francis WARTHEN at ROBERTSON's mill above the Monococy Bridge.
Jacob NICKUM, 1 mile from Emmitsburg, offers reward for apprentice to the shoemaking business named James THOMPSON, aged 18 last June, about 5 feet, 7 inches high.
Christopher OWINGS, 3 miles from Liberty-town, offers reward for yellow man named ELY, 25 years of age.
Roger PERRY, near John STATTLEMEYER's Tavern, 4 miles above Middle-town, has taken up a stray mare.
Sale of property of George SMITH, jun., dec'd., on southeast corner of the public square in Emmitsburg, occupied several years as a tavern and lately as a store. Lewis MOTTER, ex'r. and Frederick OTT, surviving partner.
Sale of farm on north side of Catocton mountain between Waterford and Taylors-town, 450 acres. William GREGG, Loudoun Co.

337. 10 Jan 1818
William CLARK, near Charles-town, VA, offers reward for mare missing from John STOVER's tavern, 7 miles from Hagers-town.
Fresh garden seeds. Washington Garden, adjoining Frederick, Joseph HEUISLER.
John SCOTT applies for relief from debts under the insolvency act.
John GLISAN, ad'mr. of John CUMMING.
Sarah HENDERSON, adm'rx. of James HENDERSON, Montgomery Co.

Martha MAGRUDER, adm'rx. of Dr. Zadock MAGRUDER, Montgomery Co.

John T. ELSRODDS, adm'r. of Frederick ELSRODDS, Frederick Co.

338. 17 Jan 1818
Married on the evening of the 8th inst. by Rev. Job GIST, Doctor Alfred FRAZIER to Miss Rachel PEIRCE, all of Montgomery Co.
Died Wednesday last in the 25th year, Philip T. POTTS, youngest son of the late Richard POTTS, esq.
John W. FINK cautions persons against taking an assignment on a note given by Cornelius SHAWEN to him, the note being lost.
Persons having claims against the estate of John Philpott GARRETT, dec'd. are requested to present them. Erasmus GARRETT, Trustee.
A petition will be submitted to the Frederick County court for opening a public road from Henry GAVER's new dwelling house to intersect the Turnpike road at Middle-town, between the buildings of Valentine BOWLUS and Jacob CRITZER.
Margaret BEALL, adm'rx. of John BEALL, Montgomery Co.
John FLUHART, near Poplar Spring, will sell houses and lot on the 27th mile of the Baltimore and Frederick turnpike road.

339. 24 Jan 1818
Married on 15th inst. by Rev. Jonathan HELFENSTEIN, Frederick HAUSER to Miss Christina STONER of this place.
Died Sat last in the prime of life, in this vicinity, William DEAN, leaving wife and 4 small children.
Sale of merchant mill with two pair of burr stones in Frederick Co., VA. John CASTLEMAN, Joseph SHEPHERD, James SHEPHERD.

340. 31 Jan 1818
David WEAVER has applied to the Judges of the court of common pleas of Adams Co., PA for benefit of the insolvency law.

341. 7 Feb 1818
Died Saturday last, Mrs. Barbara TICE, in her 72nd year.
Died on Tuesday last, after a lingering illness, Jacob MEIXSELL, sen.
Dissolution of the partnership of Daniel BOYLE and John DARBY, under the firm of BOYLE & DARBY.
Sale of 3000 acres, 3 miles from Taney-town. C. BIRNIE, Bearbranch.
Sale of personal property of William DEAN, at his late residence, 3 miles from Frederick-town, Negro woman and child; 5 draught horses, cattle and other. John REYNALDS, adm'r.
Sale at the late residence of Michael LATE, sen., dec'd. on Carrolls Manor, 150 barrels of corn; also rye and oats, 11 horses, 25-30 head of cattle. Jacob LATE, Michael LATE, John LATE, exr's.
John T. POTTS, adm'r of Philip T. POTTS.

Sale of property, 5 miles from Frederick-town, tract called Rocky Fountain, 480 acres; farm called Miss Ghiselin's Quarter on the Monococy; tract called Small Gains, 189 5/8 acres; a tract called New Bremen, 85 acres, 3 miles of Buckey's-town. Lease of present tenant, Leonard JAMISON, expires. Henry WARING near Clarksburgh, Montgomery Co.

Chas. CUNNINGHAM will rent his Trammelsburgh farm where he now lives in Frederick Co.

Charles B. HITCHCOCK, manager, offers reward for Negro man named JACK, calls himself John MITCHEL, 30 years of age; ran away from farm on Elk Ridge of George HOWARD.

342. 14 Feb 1818

Died 5th inst. in Baltimore, Miss Adeline Frances MILLER, aged 13 years and 6 months, dau. of George MILLER, merchant of that city; her remains interred in the Lutheran grave yard of this place.

To let a fulling mill with a carding machine, Abraham JONES, Liberty-town.

The horse will stand at the farm of John BAER, within a mile of Frederick-town. W. SMALLEY.

343. 21 Feb 1818

Sale at the residence of Valentine EBERT, dec'd, near New Town, Trap, two tracts, one of 152 1/2 acres; the other of 35 acres. Valentine EBERT, ex'r.

344. 28 Feb 1818

Died Tuesday morning last of the Small Pox, Mrs. Elizabeth DURST, being the first that has proved fatal, of three cases of this disorder that have taken place in this town.

Presbyterian Church Lottery. John P. THOMSON, Samuel BARNES, managers.

Dennis POOLE, adm'r, d.b.n., of Luke POOLE.

North Hampton Furnace, within 9 miles of the city of Baltimore, will go in blast about 26 March next. Moulders are wanted. Allen DORSEY, Baltimore.

F. L. CRAWFORD, Kentucky Farm, Baltimore Co., will rent his tanyard, 28 miles from Baltimore, within sight of the new Liberty road.

Sale in the village of Lisbon, Anne Arundel Co., of a 2-story brick house. Joshua GROVES.

Chancery sale of tract held by Christian CHAMPER and Basil CHAMPER as tenants in common, 277 acres.

Land for sale, property of Henry WILLIS, of Little Pipe Creek, dec'd., 410 acres, Alexander WARFIELD, Samuel STEVENSON, Daniel ZOLLIKOF-FER, trustees for the sale of the real estate of Henry WILLIS.

345. 7 March 1818

David MARCKEY, auctioneer.

Joseph ELLIS, jun., near Catoctin Furnace, offers reward for apprentice to the shoemaking business, named Enos METCALF, nearly 16 years of age, 5 feet, 5-6 inches high, dark hair and eyes.

Died 7th ult, at Mount St. Mary's Seminary, near Emmittsburg, Rev. Charles DUHAMEL.

Chancery sale of tract, 50 acres, 1 1/4 mile from New Market. Richard ROBERTS.

Sale of grist mill, saw mill, patent distillery, 90 acres, on Little Antietam. Abraham MOYER.

Sale of tract of land called A part of Addison's Choice, and part of tract called Pleasant Valley, late the property of Edward SALMON, dec'd., 284 acres; part of the land is in the occupancy of George CREAGER and adjoins the property of Capt. William CAMPBELL and Nicholas BRENGLE. Elizabeth SALMON, ex'rx.

John LUGENBEEL, jun. wants to hire a miller for his mill on Linganore, 3 miles from Liberty-town.

Ben. GATTON, wants a situation as an overseer, a man with a small family.

James SMITH will sell mills and land, 24 miles from Baltimore.

Persons having claims against estate of James M'HAFFIE, dec'd., are requested to bring them in; payments should be made to John FISHER of Westminster; Thomas HILLEN, Westminster.

John CONDON, adm'r. of Zachariah CONDON.

346. 14 March 1818

Died Wednesday last, in her 66th year, Mrs. Catharine WOLFE, relict of the late Capt. Peter WOLFE of this co.

Andrew THOMSON has rye malt for sale.

Plough making business, 2 doors from Mr. STURM's Inn, Patrick St. Jacob LITTLE.

James ROBERTSON forewarns persons from trespassing on his property.

Frances MEIXSELL, adm'rx. of Jacob MEIXSELL.

Peters TOOLE and Patrick M'QUAID, having learned the cloth manufacturing business in Europe, have rented the Union factory, 1 1/2 miles from Middletown.

Negro woman for sale. Samuel B. BROOKE, about half way between Taney Town and Emmittsburg.

Dissolution of partnership of George OYSTER, John NUNNEMAKER and James STORM, under the firm of Oyster & Co., a mercantile business.

Equity case: William SHOEMAKER and others vs. John SHOEMAKER and others. Ordered that the sale made by Abraham NULL, trustee for the sale of estate of John SHOEMAKER, dec'd, be ratified.

Samuel HOWARD applies for relief of debt under the insolvency act.

347. 21 March 1818

On Thursday a woman named Sarah GLISSON was tried for the murder of an illegitimate child; acquitted.

Married Tuesday evening last by Rev. Jno. HELFENSTEIN, John BRENGLE jun. to Miss Lucinda TODD, dau. of Warfield TODD of this co.

Died Sunday night last, Miss Lindley TANEHILL, after an illness of many months.

Died very suddenly on Tuesday at Emmitsburg, Maj. William EMMITT.

E. H. HARDING, near Buckey's-town offers reward for Negro man named JACOB; calls himself Jacob HAMAN, formerly the property of Leonard SMITH.

John FLICKINGER, Berwick Township, Adams Co, PA, offers reward for stolen horse.

Committed to jail of Frederick Co., Negro man who calls himself George HILL, about 31 years old; says he belongs to GILBRETH and RUSSELL, in the Western Country.

Equity case: Peter ERB vs. Joshua PARRISH and Barbara his wife, Peter YINGLING and Elizabeth his wife and Mary TIMBLE. Object of bill is to obtain conveyance for a tract in Frederick Co. Bills state that the complainant purchased of the defendants a tract of land for which they executed an instrument purporting to be a deed of bargain and sale but deed is insufficient and Joshua PARRISH and Barbara his wife and Peter YINGLING and Elizabeth his wife do not reside in this state.

John MILLER adm'r of William GIBSON.

348. 28 March 1818

Married Thursday evening last by Rev. David F. SCHAEFFER, Cyrus MANTZ, to Miss Eliza KUHN, dau. of Henry KUHN, Esq. of this place.

Died Sunday night, 15th inst., in this town, Miss Verlender TANNEHILL, at an advanced age after a distressing illness of many months; she lived to witness in this neighborhood the death of her father, mother, brother and three sisters, mostly also at advanced ages.

Died Wednesday last, after a lingering illness, Henry BRISH, of this place.

Dissolution of partnership of John HEAD and Henry SPALDING under the firm of HEAD & SPALDING, the mercantile business to be carried on by John HEAD in Taney-town.

New plaister mill, above the Monococy Bridge. James ROBERTSON, Frederick-town.

349. 4 Apr 1818

Michael ZIMMERMAN and John WELKER, exr's of Jacob BEEKENBAUGH.

I have placed all officers fees, due following the year 1817 and payable in 1818, in the hands of Joseph WEST, to be collected according to law. Joseph M. CROMWELL, Sheriff.

Wood land for sale at Catoctin Furnace, at Catoctin Furnace, joining lands of James JOHNSON, John WELKER, Baker JOHNSON and myself on the east side of the Catoctin Mountain. Will'y MAYBURRY.

Sale of two houses and lots in Liberty-town, one occupied by Daniel ARTHUR, the other in the tenure of F. & T. SAP, as a store house. Enquire of Abraham JONES. Rachel METCALF.

Sale of Negro man, 3 boys and a girl at the house of Daniel ARTHUR, in Liberty-town. Walter BEVANS.

Jacob CULLER and Henry CULLER, exr's. of Michael CULLER.

Andrew BOSTIAN ex'r. of Anthony BOSTIAN.

350. 11 Apr 1818

Miss E. MARCILLY will open an academy for young ladies, Market St., in a room of Mr. BRUNNER's house.

Died Friday last, Mrs. Elizabeth GEBHART, consort of John GEBHART of this town, leaving a husband and children. *Examiner.*

Died Tuesday, John O. M. REMICK, aged 23, from Massachusetts, only son; leaves parents and sisters.

Stephen C. ROSZEL, near Leesburg, VA, offers reward for Negro man named DICK, 22 years old.

House and lot for sale in Patrick St. John N. A. HOGEN.

Francis W. HAWKINS, near Portobacco, MD, offers reward for Negro man named WAT, aged about 30 years.

David BOWLUS, adm'r. of Mary Magdalena CLONINGER, Frederick Co.

351. 18 Apr 1818

Married Sunday evening last by Rev. D. F. SCHAEFFER, Zephaniah HARRISON, to Miss Mary HALLER, all of this place.

Dr. Wm. S. M'PHERSON offers his professional services; his office is held in the house lately occupied by Col. John M'PHERSON, south Market St.

Doct. William POTTS died on 15th(?) inst., aged 32 years and a few days.

Persons indebted to me are requested to call on Lewis REMSBERG at the Frederick-town mill and settle their accounts. Jacob CRONISE.

All unsold tickets to Monocacy Bridge Lottery are to be returned to Daniel BOYLE, Treasurer. Nich's SNIDER, clk.

Joel FUNK and D. KENEGE to run a two-horse accommodation hack from Frederick-town to Baltimore.

Sale in Millers-town, Adams Co., PA, house and lot on which there is a tan yard. James HILL.

Jonathan KEMP has rented the fulling mill and machinery of J. CRONISE and J. MARSH, 3 miles from Frederick-town on Tuscarora creek, formerly occupied by Mr. BUTT.

Mills for rent on Bennet's Creek, grist and merchant mill, saw and plaister mills, distillery, blacksmith's shop; and for sale: 9 horses, waggons, dry goods; Negroes for hire. Jno. COOK.

Negroes for sale. Aloysius ELDER, near Emmittsburg.

352. 25 April 1818

Died Thursday morning last at Lewis-town, in this county, Richard CAMPBELL, son of Rev. John CAMPBELL, of Carlisle, PA.

Wm. E. WILLIAMS and Henry L. WILLIAMS, adm'rs. of Otho H. WILLIAMS of Baltimore Co.
Henry KEMP, adm'r. of Catherine RENN, Frederick Co.
Samuel LILLY, adm'r. of Esther DIGGS, Frederick Co.
Henry HILLEARY adm'r. of David YINGLING, Frederick Co.
John STONER, adm'r. of Abraham RENNER, Frederick Co.

353. 2 May 1818
Sheriff's sale at the store of Henry THOMAS, entire stock in trade of dry goods, hardware and queensware, at the suit of HENCK and ELIOTT use of Conrad SCHULTZ and suit of Mary J. THOMAS.
Candidate for sheriff: Alexander WINSOR.
Notice to persons wishing to contract for any part of contemplated Turnpike Road from George-town to Rockville, please apply to me. John THRELKELD, Pres't. Washington Turnpike Com.
Sale of tract in Montgomery Co, 3 miles from George-town, 755 1/4 acres. Apply to William HEMPSTONE, living adjoining or subscriber living in Baltimore. Hugh THOMPSON.
Sale at Cook's Tavern in Liberty-town, of Negro boy, taken as the property of Enoch BEALL, on a warrant judgement, at the suit of Peter STEVENSON, Abraham FLENNER use of John WAGNER, David HINES, John and William LOWE and Frederick HYE. Nathan ENGLAND.
John FUNSTUN, near Liberty-town, offers reward for German indented servant, named Joseph SWOTSCOAP, weaver by trade, about 5 feet, 10 inches, slender.
C. KIMBOLL to sell tavern, occupied by her as a tavern for last 25 years.
William COLEMAN and Charles COLEMAN, ex'rs., to sell by virtue of the last will of Col. James COLEMAN, late of Fairfax Co, VA, a mill with 100 acres.
Sale of 3000 acres, property of Charles CARROLL, of Belle-vue, the greater part situated in District of Columbia. Daniel CARROLL of Dudn. and H. CARROLL.

354. 9 May 1818
Died Tuesday evening, 28th inst., after a long and tedious indisposition, Mrs. Martha M. J. WEYLIE, eldest dau. of Mrs. M. ROBINSON of this city, and relict of the late Rev. John V. WEYLIE. *Md. Gaz.*
Sale of 170 acres, part of the real estate of Joseph GARROTT, dec'd., 5 miles of Harper's Ferry. Apply to Erasmus GARROTT, adjoining. Edward GARROTT, Trustee.
Wheelwright wanted. Joseph HARDESTY, Ellicotts Mills.
Elias BRUNNER, 1 mile from Frederick-town, offers reward for Negro man named GEORGE; calls himself George WASHINGTON, aged about 18.
Sale of Negroes. Apply to Richard POTTS, Fredericktown. E. C. POTTS, R. POTTS, ex'rs. of Doct. Wm. POTTS.
Sale of merchant mill and 87 acres on Shenandoah River in Frederick Co., VA. William CASTLEMAN, David SHEPHERD.

Sale by chancery court in Winchester, VA, of real estate of John CLARK, dec'd., 500 acres. John DAVENPORT, James CURL, Comr's.
John KNOUFF, adm'r. of John KNOUFF.

355. 16 May 1818
Wishes to purchase Negroes. Benjamin HOFF; apply at J. MAYBERRY's.
Wishes to purchase Negroes. Lee SHUTE or Philip SHUTE. Apply at J. MAYBERRY's tavern.
Catherine BASH and John BASH, adm'rs. of Michael BASH.
Robert L. ANNAN and Frederick A. SCHLEY, adm'rs. of Wm. EMMITT.
J. T. SHAAFF, George-town, offers reward for mulatto lad named ALFRED, about 18 years old.
House and lot for sale, in Patrick St., in which he now lives. John N. A. BOGEN.
Merchants and others are cautioned against crediting any person on my account. Levi HUGHES.
Sale at late residence of John BAER, Sen., dec'd., 1 mile from Frederick-town, hogs, cows, sheep, horses, etc. Ezra BAER, Michael BAER, ex'rs.
Thomas DRAPER, adm'r. of Richard C. CAMPBELL.

356. 23 May 1818
Henry KUHN, esq. elected by board of Aldermen, Mayor of Frederick, in the room of Lawrence BRENGLE, esq., resigned.
Destructive hail on Thursday evening last.
Married Thursday, 14th inst. by Rev. ARMSTRONG, Robert M'CLEERY of this town, to Miss Rebecca BEALL, dau. of Elisha BEALL of Frederick Co.
Married Tuesday evening last, by Rev. Jonathan HELFENSTEIN, Lewis KEMP, to Miss Rebecca C. BUCKEY, dau. of George BUCKEY, esq. of this co.
Recently was announced the death of Mrs. Mary Ann M'KALEB, wife of Major John M'KALEB, of Taney-town, and dau. of Rev. William CLINGAN of Montgomery Co. We now have to record the death of James CLINGAN, his only son and remaining offspring.
John NICHOLAS will sell 126 acres, 1 mile from the mouth of Monococy.
Jonathan KEMP and Jonathan W. DUSTIN have rented the fulling mill and machinery of J. CRONISE and J. MARSH, 3 miles from Frederick-town on Tuscarora creek.

357. 30 May 1818
Died 13th inst. in her 53rd year of her age, Mrs. Mariam SWAMLEY, of this co. [a kind mother].
Benjamin BIGGS and Jacob MATTHIAS will attend at HARRIS' tavern at Little Pipe for contracting to build new bridges over Little and Big Pipe Creeks.
Sale at late residence of Jacob DARNER, dec'd., 2 1/2 miles from Middle-town, 2 Negro men, waggon, ploughs, furniture and other. Frederick DARNER, adm'r.

358. 6 June 1818
Tanyard for sale in Clarksburg, Montgomery Co., 6-7 acres. A. & H. BURNSIDE & Co.
Sale in pursuance of last will of Doct. William POTTS, farm called The Retread on the east side of Monococy river, 535 1/8 acres. and several other tracts. E. C. POTTS, R. POTTS, ex'rs. of Doct. Wm. POTTS.
Sale in Middleburg, of the entire stock of goods in the store of Henry STOUFFER, dec'd. Wm. P. FARQUHAR, adm'r.
Peter WILHELM gives notice that his wife Elizabeth WILHELM, has left his bed and board without any just cause.
Jacob JACKSON, near Middle-town, offers reward for apprentice named George ECKMOND, aged about 19 years.
Thomas CASTLE, living near Middle-town, offers reward for apprentice to the joiner's business named Michael MAY, 19 years and 6 months of age, 5 feet, 5-6 inches high, sandy hair.
Thomas GIST, Westminster, owing to bad health, will sell a general assortment of goods.
Fishing Creek Woollen Factory. James KEARNEY.
Land and mills for sale, 140 acres, on west side of the Blue Ridge, Rockingham Co., VA. Thomas MAUZY.
John GRAYBILL, 1 1/2 miles from Emmittsburg, offers reward for Negro man named PETER, aged about 26 years.
Peter HOKE, Martinsburgh, VA, offers reward for apprentice boy named John BARTELSON; may change his name to PARKER, about 16 years of age, stout, heavy eye brows and light coloured hair; bound to learn the taylor trade, smart; anxious to recover this boy on account of his father.
Elizabeth C. POTTS and Richard POTTS, ex'rs. of Dr. William POTTS.

359. 13 June 1818
A red morocco pocket book found. Independent GIST, near Wilson's Ford, on the Monococy.
Samuel OGLE warns against the invasion of his patent right for an improvement on the plough.
Sale of furniture, a lot of ground in Market St., with 2 story brick dwelling house. Lawrence BRENGLE.
Sale by order of the county court of Montgomery Co., at the house of Mrs. MULLICAN, who lives on the property, estate of the heirs of William MULLICAN of John, as well as the widow's right of dower to tract called The Gift, 2 miles from Middle-brook Mills, 92 acres. Zadok MAGRUDER, Trustee, Rockville.
Daniel SHUEE, Westminster, offers reward for missing cow and a mare.
John NULL, ex'r. of Mary NULL.

360. 20 June 1818
Married Thursday, 11th inst. by Rev. George KEEDY, John SLIFER, the 3rd, to Miss Mary WOLF, the former of Frederick, the latter of Washington Co.

Sheriff's sale of Negro woman, property of James WOOD, at the suit of Nathan MAYNARD.

Harry W. DORSEY, near Clarksburg, Montgomery Co., offers reward for mulatto man named TOM; calls himself Thomas JEFFERSON, 26 years of age.

Upton HAMMOND, near Liberty-town, offers reward for mulatto man, ELIAS; calls himself Elias ROLLINGS, about 30 years old.

361. 27 June 1818

William WILLIS intends carrying on the boot and shoe making business in the house formerly occupied by Francis M'KERNEY, next door to George W. ENT in South Market St.

Sale of 2 story brick house in which he resides on north side of Patrick St.; also lot in George-town and other. Michael HAUSER.

BROADRUP & MORGAN, living at Pleasant Dale Paper Mill, 5 miles from Frederick-town, offer reward for apprentice to the paper making business named John LINTON, about 20 years of age.

Richard HUGHES adm'r. of Daniel HUGHES.

362. 4 July 1818

Married Thursday, 11th ult. at Brookeville (Indiana Ter.) by Rev. Lewis DEWESE, William M'CLEERY of this town, to Miss Eleanor KNIGHT of that place.

Ignatius O'FERRALL has opened a House of Entertainment in Bath, Berkley Co., VA.

Sale of house and lot in Woodsborough. Caleb FLEMING, living on the premises.

Petition for the opening of a road from Henry GAVER's new house on the new cut road leading from Frederick-town to Hughes' coaling ground in Washington Co. and thence in a line to intersect the Turnpike road at Middletown, between the buildings of Valentine BOWLUS and Jacob CRITZER.

363. 11 July 1818

Married Thursday, 2nd inst. by Rev. P. DAVIDSON, John DARBY, merchant to Miss Catharine RIED, both of Taney-town.

Waggon and geers for sale. Christian ALBAUGH, living at the lower end of Church St., Frederick-town.

Cash for Negroes at Jesse MAYBERRY's. Thomas B. CREAGH.

Equity case: John GLISAN, complainant vs. Barbara GOSHOUR, widow of Peter GOSHOUR, Catherine CARR, Henry GOSHOUR, Peter GOSHOUR, Barbara GOSHOUR, Susanna GOSHOUR, Mary GOSHOUR, John KELLER, Daniel KELLER, Peter KELLER, Absalom KELLER, Eleanor KELLER and Jonathan SWEADNER. Object of bill is to obtain decree of foreclosure against the defendants as heirs and representatives of Peter GOSHOUR, dec'd., of a lot in Liberty-town, which was mortgaged by said Peter GOSHOUR to secure payment of $65. John KELLER, Daniel KELLER, Absalom KELLER and Peter KELLER, Henry GOSHOUR and Jonathan

SWEADNER, defendants, reside out of the state of Maryland; Peter KELLER is under the age of 21.

364. 18 July 1818
Levin THOMAS, Carrol's Manor, offers reward for mulatto man named SANDY; calls himself Sandy WATSON, 23 years old.

365. 25 July 1818
Dr. H. STALEY offers his professional services.
Two German servants for sale, man and his wife, who have 4 1/2 years to serve, about 22 years of age, stout. John STRAUSBERGER, 5 miles below Liberty.
Tailor & habit maker, at New Market, James SIMPSON, having dissolved partnership with Mr. BOYD, at the shop formerly occupied by Doct. John SMITH as a Post Office.
Lots for sale in Baltimore Co., 300 acres, adjoining lands of Major MANRO. Dennis SOLLERS, near Liberty. James PORTER will shew the property.

366. 1 Aug 1818
Persons who gave their notes at the sale of personal property of Jeremiah GITTINGS, dec'd. are notified that those notes are due. James MORRISON, Merryland Tract.
Having purchased of Miss Elizabeth NOLAND her tract of mountain land, 4 1/2 miles west of Frederick-town, Jno. HUGHES forewarns person from trespassing.
J. T. SHAAFF, Arcadia, offers reward for missing horse; William WEBSTER, manager will pay the reward.
Independent Hosemen to meet. David STEINER, Sec'ry.
William WARNER applies for relief from debt under the insolvency act.

367. 8 Aug 1818
Evan HOPKINS, hair dresser and barber, has opened shop at Mrs. WRIGHT's Patrick St.
Farm and tavern for sale, in Jefferson Co., VA. Henry GARNHART.
Christopher OWINGS, 3 miles from Liberty-town, offers reward for black woman named HENNY, 25 years old.
Frederick ECKERSON has taken up a stray horse.
William ALBAUGH, Liberty-town, offers reward for apprentice boy named William GAUSNELL, 18-19 years of age, 4 feet, 9-10 inches high, bound to the blacksmith's trade.
Sale pursuant to the last will of Barnard RENS, dec'd., tract called the Resurvey on part of Mount Pleasant, 170-180 acres. Barnard RENN, ex'r., Henry KEMP, agent.
Peter FOOT cautions person from crediting his wife Anna on his account, as he is determined not to pay any debts of her contracting as she has left his bed and board.

368. 15 Aug 1818

Farm for sale, 70 acres, in Middle-town Valley. John HOUSE.

Mill and lands for sale, late the property of Dr. Stephen COOKE, dec'd., on Goose Creek in Loudoun Co., 508 acres. John R. COOKE, Martinsburg.

Sale of farm, late the residence of Nathan HAMMOND of Baltimore Co., dec'd., adjoining lands of Capt. Henry SNOWDEN, Elias and Wm. BROWN, and Wm. H. MARRIOTT, 1000 acres. Bazil DORSEY, adjoining the land, will shew it. David R. GIST.

Chancery sale of Prince George's Co., at the house of Isidore HARDY, in Piscataway, property of George R. LEIPER, dec'd., called Montpelier, 600 acres. Apply to the subscriber, Thomas MUNDEEL, Trustee, or Aquilla BADEN, present manager of the farm.

369. 22 Aug 1818

Married Thursday last, by Rev. Geo. CRAVER, Walter F. GILL, to Miss Elizabeth LORENTZ, both of Middle-town.

Died Wednesday last, after an indisposition of several months, Mrs. LEVY, relict of David LEVY of this place.

Wanted at the paper mill of the subscriber, 5 miles from Frederick-town, persons with a family of children. George BROADRUP, Tuscarora Mill.

Sale on the plantation where I now live, adjoining New-town (Trap), mare, cows and hoggs, furniture. Jacob TABLER.

Land for sale, 456 acres, adjacent to the estate of Robert DARNALL. Apply to Davis RICHARDSON, residing near the premises, to Col. Henry KEMP who has leased, to James SIMMONS who has purchased part of the adjacent lands or to the subscriber, Charles F. MERCER, residing at Aldie, a post town in Virginia.

370. 29 Aug 1818

Farm in Loudoun Co., VA, 4 miles from Leesburg, adjoining the lands of Major ELGIN and Stephen C. ROSSEL, 140 acres. Richard BROOKE.

Sale of farm of about 470 acres, 9 miles from George-town. Aquila BECRAFT, on the premises.

Frederick BAKER, ex'r. of Benj. SOUDER.

Jacob SINGER, ex'r. of Samuel SINGER.

371. 5 Sep 1818

Married same evening, by Rev. David F. SCHAEFFER, J. KRAUTH to Miss Susan KELLER, also of Frederick-town.

Married 18th ult. by Rev. David F. SCHAEFFER, Nelson HOFFMAN to Miss Elizabeth TEMPLING, all of this co.

Houses and lots for sale, one occupied as a tavern, in Poolesville. Joseph POOLE, junr. for the heirs of Joseph POOLE, senr., dec'd.

Henry KAUFMAN has recommenced the boot and shoe making business, at his house in Third St., next door to Thomas YOUNG.

Margaret FOUT cautions persons from trespassing on her farm.

Sale of small island, 6 7/8 acres in Potomac river near Noland's Ferry, opposite Walter BROOKES in Virginia. Thomas SANDS. Property will be shewn by Capt. Clement T. HILLEARY, living near the same.
Sale of land, 205 acres, near Fredericktown on which Mr. CRUTCHLEY resides. Richard POTTS.
Sale of the whole of the Wakefield and Long Mountain Tracts, 8300 acres in Culpepper Co., VA; also the estate where he resides in Loudoun Co., called Clifton, 530 acres. Joseph LEWIS, Jun.

372. 12 Sep 1818
Sale on the premises in Clarksburg, Montgomery Co., two lots. Alfred FRAZIER.
Solomon DAVIS, adm'r. of John O'NEALE.

373. 19 Sep 1818
Sale of Surry Farm, late the property of Otho H. WILLIAMS, dec'd., near Woodsborough, 589 acres, with stone mill lately built. Wm. E. WILLIAMS.
Christian SCHOLL will sell his tract of land in Frederick Co., 3 miles from Emmitsburg, near the seminary, adjoining the lands of John STEWART, 50 acres.
Land, saw & grist mills for sale where he now lives near the turnpike from Westminster to Hagerstown, 250 acres in Harbaugh's Valley. William GREEN.
John CONNELL, anxious to retire from the management of the Brooke Furnace, offers sale with 570 acres for sale, on King's creek, Brooke Co., VA.
Fuller wanted. Apply to Isaac DERN at Joshua DELAPLAINE's Mills, Double Pipe Creek.

374. 26 Sep 1818
Hezekiah TRUNDLE, Montgomery Co., has taken up a stray mare.
Isaac DIEL offers reward for mare missing from Peter LIEKLIDER's pasture.
Francis S. KEY offers reward for horse which strayed from near Georgetown.
Joseph DELAPLANE, ex'r. of Joseph DELAPLANE, Frederick Co.

375. 3 Oct 1818
Sale of tract on Applepie Ridge, 6 miles from Winchester. Richard L. GALLOWAY.
Sale at the residence of Jacob LATE, dec'd. on Carrol's Manor, 4 horses, 5 cows, sheep and hogs, furniture. Michael LATE, John LATE, admr's.
Races to be held at Poolesville. Rodolph MAGINNIS.

376. 10 Oct 1818
Married Thursday evening, 1st inst., by Rev. P. DAVIDSON, Frederick KELLER to Miss Catharine HUGHES, dau. of Levi HUGHES, all of this co.
Candidates for sheriff: Daniel ARTHUR, Thomas W. MORGAN.

377. 17 Oct 1818. No new items.

378. 24 Oct 1818
Henry BECHLY cautions Henry MILLER or any of his family, from entering his premises, 4 miles above Middletown, for any purposes whatever.
Grist and saw mill for sale, 2 miles from Waterford, VA. Edward DORSEY, Waterford.
Sheriff's sale of tract of Patrick MAGRUDER called Dowell's Park, and large stone merchant mill, Montgomery Co., at the suits of George St. CLAIR use of Zachariah WALKER, Lewig G. DAVIDSON ex'r. of Samuel DAVIDSON.
Tobias BELT, near Berlin, Merryland Tract, offers reward for mare which strayed from Carroll's manor.

379. 31 Oct 1818
Died Saturday last, Mrs. Mary RITCHIE, in her 87th year.
Sale at the favor John HUGHES, 1 mile from Frederick-town, horses, cows and hogs. Thomas POWELL.
Ordered by the Court that the sale of the real estate of Israel PLUMMER, dec'd. at reported by Richard ROBERTS, the trustee, be ratified. Abm. SHRIVER.
Equity case: Devalt KESSELRING, John KESSELRING, Frederick KESSELRING, Louis KESSELRING, Wendal KESSELRING, George KESSELRING, Sophia KESSELRING, Ludwick RUMMAL and Magdalena his wife, Solomon BUSSART and Susanna his wife, John SLATES and Catherine his wife, John LITTLE and Mary his wife, Daniel YEISTER and Barbara his wife, George BAUGHER and Rebecca his wife vs. Michael KESSELRING, Elias CROSBY and Elizabeth his wife. Object of petition is to obtain a decree for sale of real estate of George Ludwick KESSELRING, late of Frederick Co., dec'd., who died intestate. Elias CROBY and Elizabeth his wife (dau. of dec'd.) moved to the western country many years ago, where it is supposed they both died, leaving an infant child.
Whereas John HOFFMAN of Henry, of Frederick Co, did report that a certain Frederick LUDWICK of the co. aforesaid, was guilty of the crime of meddling himself with a beast, said Ludwick hath brought suit against said John Hoffman of Henry for reporting the same. Both parties desire to discontinue the suit and John Hoffman of Hen. makes oath that he did not see Frederick Ludwick in the act above stated.

380. 7 Nov 1818
Sale of woodland called Polly's Habitation in Baltimore Co., joining tract called Buckhorn owned in part by James SMITH and joining tract called Bachelor's Refuge owned in part by Ely BENNETT. For William CAMPBELL, Wm. C. RUSSELL, at Bagdad, near Col. Beale OWING's, Baltimore Co.
Thomson M'CREA and Solomon RENNER, admr's. of Michael ECKHARD, Frederick Co.
Elizabeth HOOVER admr'x. of Jacob HOOVER, Frederick Co.

Sale in Cumberland Township, Adams Co., on Rock creek, near Black's mill, PA, 100 acres. Philip HEAGY.

381. 14 Nov 1818 ·
Miss Zulma MARCILLY has opened a millinery store in Patrick St., next door to John HOFFMAN.
John GLISAN adm'r. of Peter GOSSHOUR.

382. 21 Nov 1818
Died 12th inst. at his residence near Frederick, Joshua DORSEY, esq., long an inhabitant of this place.
Died on the 13th inst., Raymond REICH, in his 17th year, son of John REICH of this town.
Silvester COLBORN offers reward for red morocco pocket book.
Peter BRENGLE candidate for sheriff.
Farm for sale, 230 acres, 7 miles from Middle-town. George DELAUTER, living at Delauter's mill.
Sale at the dwelling of the subscriber, 3 miles from Taney-town, horses, cows, sheep and hogs, 170 acres. John RICHARDS.
Sale of 124 acres of Jacob DARNER, dec'd., 3 miles from Frederick-town. Frederick DARNER, ex'r.

383. 28 Nov 1818
Died 7th inst., aged 57, Mrs. Jane GUNTON, wife of Thomas GUNTON of the General Land Office.
Died Tuesday last in this town, Tobias HALLAR, mason.
George KLAY, adm'r. of Henry KLAY.
Chancery sale of farm of Frederick POOLE, dec'd., 199 acres, 4 miles east of Liberty, adjoining lands of Bruce POOL and John S. LAWRENCE. Frederick A. SCHLEY, Trustee.
Equity sale of 3 lots of John COPENHAVER, late of Frederick-town, dec'd., numbers 256, 257 and 258.
Sale pursuant to the last will of Thomas O. WILLIAMS, dec'd., at his residence in Prince George's Co., 50 Negroes, horses, cattle, hogs, sheep. Wm. B. WILLIAMS, ex'r.
Sale of 850 acres of woodland, 2 miles from Mechanicks-town and part of a saw-mill. J. GIST, Long Farm.
Charles HAMMOND cautions persons from trespassing on his property.
John SNOUFFER, adm'r. of Christena SNOUFFER.
William HAMILTON and James DOLAHITE, Adams Co., PA, jail, have applied for relief under the benefit of the Insolvency Act.

384. 5 Dec 1818
Chancery sale of 118 acres at the Poplar Spring; also mill seat on western branch of Patapsco Falls. Jacob SIDES, Trustee.

Sale by decree of the county court of Montgomery Co., at the residence of Mrs. Margaret WATERS, land devised to the late Dr. Richard WATERS by his father, dwelling plantation with 400 acres, subject to widow's dower. Zadok MAGRUDER, Trustee, Rockville.

Wm. GOLDSBOROUGH forewarns persons from dealing with his Negroes for any article without his permission.

To petition to open a road from M'FARLAND's Factory to the widow CRAFT's merchant mill, to Middletown between Adam ROUTZANG and Saml. BRANDENBURG, to run through the public alley, adjoining the property of Adam HERRING and Aaron SUMAN.

Jacob LEAB, near Frederick has taken up stray steers.

Friendship Factory (Woollen) for rent. Messrs. MARSH & O'NEILL have concluded to wind up their business. John S. LAWRENCE.

Sale by order of the Orphans' Court, at the late residence of James REID, dec'd., near Poolesville, personal property of the dec'd. Elizabeth REID and Henson REID, adm'rs.

Thomas G. MITCHELL, Frederick Co., applies for relief under Insolvency Act.

385. 12 Dec 1818

Married Tuesday evening last in this town, by Rev. Frederick W. HATCH, Alexander M'PHERSON, to Miss Matilda JOHNSON, dau. of the late Col. Baker JOHNSON.

Married by Rev. D. F. SCHAEFFER, Theophilus F. CONRAD, to Miss Eunice MORGAN.

Married same evening by Rev. Jon. HELFENSTEIN, John BALDERSTON, to Mrs. Mary EARLY.

Married Thursday evening by Rev. Jon. HELFENSTEIN, Doct. Henry STALEY of Woodsborough, to Miss Margaret KUHN, dau. of Henry KUHN, esq.

Died Saturday, 5th inst., Col. Daniel HUGHES, of Washington Co. in his 74th year.

Chancery case: Daniel COVER vs. Catherine GILDEA & others. Sale made by Richard BROOKE, Trustee, to sell the real estate of John GILDEA, dec'd., Frederick Co., ratified.

House and lot to rent at the low end of Church St. Joshua HALLER, on the premises.

Samuel DEVILBISS requests payment of accounts.

Philip HOPKINS has taken up a stray heifer which came to Maj. GRAHAM's farm, at Bush Creek Forge.

Rezin SIMPSON, near Liberty-town has taken up a stray heifer.

Samuel SLIFER, adm'r., gives notice to purchases at the sale of personal property of George BROWN, of Washington Co., that their notes are due.

Albert SUMAN, adm'r. of Eleanor SUMAN, Frederick Co.

James MORRISON, adm'r. of Samuel MORRIS.

Thomas W. JOHNSON, Elizabeth JOHNSON, ex'rs. of Joshua DORSEY.

386. 19 Dec 1818
Chancery case: Daniel HOOVER, John HOOVER, Christian HOOVER, Magdalena HOOVER, David HOOVER, Jacob CANDLE and Mary his wife, Martin HOOVER, Peter HOOVER, and Abraham MARTIN and Catherine his wife against David KAUFFMAN, Mary KAUFFMAN and Samuel KAUFFMAN. Object of the bill is to obtain a decree for sale of real estate of Christian HOOVER, dec'd. In the month of April 1809 Christian HOOVER died intestate, seized of a large real estate in Frederick Co. He left the following children and grandchildren his heirs at law, to wit, Daniel HOOVER, Christian HOOVER, John HOOVER, Magdalena HOOVER, David HOOVER, Mary who married Jacob Candle, Martin HOOVER, Peter HOOVER & Catharine who married Abraham Martin and all of whom are the complainants, also Nancy who married David KAUFFMAN; that Nancy died before the death of her father the said Christian HOOVER, leaving at the time of her death only two children, the one named Mary the other Samuel, both of whom are infants living in the state of Pennsylvania with their father the said David KAUFFMAN, and all of whom are the defendants in this case.

Committed to Frederick Co. jail, Negro man, who calls himself John William OYSTON, aged about 30 years.

Committed to the jail of Frederick Co., Negro man who calls himself Oz BUTLER, about 44 years old.

Christian BRENGLE, adjoining Frederick, has taken up a stray heifer.

Horse left at my house by a man named JONES, without paying his bill. Joseph TALBOTT.

Sale of plantation in Loudoun Co., adjoining the town of Waterford, estate of Joseph TALBOTT, dec'd., 136 acres. James MOORE, Asa MOORE, ex'rs.

387. 26 Dec 1818
Married Tuesday evening last, by Rev. ROSZELL, James RIED of Liberty-town, to Miss Susan SMITH of this place.

Two tracts of land for sale agreeable to last will of John M. DERR, on Fishing creek, adjoining Lewistown, 130 acres and 15 acres, respectively. John CRONISE, ex'r.

John WARNER, residing on Carroll's Manor, 1 1/2 miles below Buckey's town, has recommenced the pump and Pipe boring business.

Jacob LIGHDERT, 4 miles above Middletown, offers reward for stolen mare.

Tanyard for sale, now in possession of Robert M'CULLOCH, in town of Williams-port. M. Van LEAR, near Williams-port.

388. 2 Jan 1819
Married Thursday evening, 24th ult., by Rev. Curtis WILLIAMS, Jacob ANGEL, jr., merchant of Liberty-town, to Miss Julianna HAMMOND, dau. of Vachel HAMMOND, esq. of this co.

Married Tuesday evening, 22nd ult. by Rev. ARMSTRONG, David BRISH to Miss Ann LINTON, all of this place.

Store house for rent in town of Williams-Port, formerly owned and occupied by late John IRWIN. Samuel A. CHEW.

Escaped from jail of Frederick: (1) George C. CAMPBELL, about 5 feet, 7 inches high, 36 years of age, brown hair, a large nose and red face and some of his teeth out; his clothing consists of a short bottle green coat, striped vest, pea green overhalls, all much worn, an old low crowned fur hat, is very talkative and fond of drink, a mill-wright and miller by occupation and formerly resided in Philadelphia. (2) Samuel MACHER, about 5 feet, 6-7 inches high, 27 years of age, has large whiskers, dark brown hair, and is rather slow of speech; had on an old grey coat, light coloured pantaloons, striped vest, a red flannel doublet and an old fur hat with a scarf on it. (3) George AMEY, about 5 feet, 8-9 inches high, 30 years of age, fair complexion, light hair, long nose and has a family in Pennsylvania; had on an old bottle green coat, striped vest, corduroy overhalls and fur hat much worn.

Jacob WOLFE cautions persons from trespassing on his land.

Negro man for sale. John WHITE, 3 miles from Frederick.

389. 9 Jan 1819

William WORMAN has again got his mill in operation and gives the highest prices in cash for wheat, 4 miles below Liberty.

Chancery sale of lot of 7 1/2 acres, 5 miles from Liberty, adjoining lands of John KINZER. It will be shewn by Surratt D. WARFIELD who lives near it.

Mills, houses, lands, tavern stand and distillery for sale at the tavern now occupied by Adam BAUGHMAN, near Harper's Ferry: (1) 343 acres in Washington Co. (2) Merchant mill with three pair of stones with patent elevators. (3) Tavern stand and other - real estate of John ECARD. The property will be by Jonah BUFFINGTON.

390. 16 Jan 1819

Married Thursday evening, 7th inst., by Rev. John S. PITTS, Asa SWAMLY to Miss Mary WHITE, both of this co.

John C. GRAFF offers his services as an attorney.

Lewis CREAGER, Middletown, wishes to sell 100 cords of oak wood.

John SMITH, near Emmitsburg, has taken up 3 stray sheep.

Land for sale in Washington Co., 5 miles from Sharpsburg. Abraham SHOWER.

Sale pursuant to last will of John MATHIAS, Frederick Co., between Westminster and Petersburg, 3 miles from Westminster, 115 acres; also 100 acres in Baltimore co., 3 miles from Westminster. John MATHIAS, Jacob MATHIAS, ex'rs.

Chancery case: George HAIL vs. John COLLINS. Object of bill is to obtain decree for conveyance of the title to lot No. 81, in Creagers Town from COLLINS the defendant to George HAIL the complainant. The bill states that the defendant, being seized in fee of said lot on 17 Apr 1782 sold the same to Richard WOOD who sold same to John PRUTZMAN to sold same to John FRIEZE who sold same to Elizabeth STONER who sold same to David STONER who sold same to complainant.

Jacob STAUB, Middletown offers reward for apprentice to the wheel making named Anthony STORM.

391. 23 Jan 1819
Married Saturday evening last, by Rev. D. F. SCHAFFER, Isaac WYSONG, to Miss Elizabeth BAER, dau. of Henry BAER, all of this place.

Farm for sale, 340 acres, in Montgomery Co., 5 miles from Montgomery court House. Apply to Joseph CLAGETT, living near the property. Samuel CLAGETT, Pleasant Valley, Washington Co.

Sale by power of attorney from Miss Victoire VINCENDIERE, tract of 300-400 acres on west side of Monocacy River, 2 miles from Frederick; apply to major Peter MANTZ or subscriber, Leonard JAMISON.

392. 30 Jan 1819
Married Saturday evening last, by Rev. MAHVIE, Captain John R. CORBALEY, of the United States army to Miss Emerentienne VINCENDIERE, of this vicinity.

Chancery sale of woodland, 57 acres, for benefit of George SCHUERTZELL's heirs. George BALTZELL, Trustee.

Sale of mountain land, adjoining lands of Henry FRALEY, and 2-3 families of Negroes. James JOHNSON, Springfield.

Sale of tract of land, 207 1/2 acres, in Frederick Co., 2 miles from the turnpike, near Edward KENNEDY's tavern. Charles MULLINEAUX, ex'r. of Thomas MULLINEAUX.

James HARRITT, Emmittsburg, offers reward for apprentice to the hatting business, named James MARSHALL, aged about 19 years, stout made, dark hair, about 5 feet, 9-10 inches.

David DARKIS, near Woodsborough, has taken up a stray steer.

The following have applied to the court of common pleas of Adams Co, PA: Andrew GIFFEN, Conrad GEEZER, Samuel LEAMING, Adams Co. jail.

393. 6 Feb 1819
Lloyd SHIPLEY gives notice that his wife Sarah "had been running me so much in debt that I cannot put up with it... I am determined to pay no debts of her contracting."

Sheriff's sale at the house of Jonathan WOOD, 4 Negro men, 2 women and 2 children, late the property of Jonathan WOOD, taken at the suit of Peter BECRAFT, David WAGNER, William MUMFORD use of William LEEKINS and wife.

Farm for sale on which he now resides, 8 miles from Frederick-town, adjoining farms of Messrs. J. HOLTZ, COCKEY and POE, 318 acres; also Fleecy Dale Merchant and Saw-mills. Philemon CROMWELL.

John M'ANULTY has applied to judges of the Court of Common Pleas of Franklin Co., PA for benefit of Insolvency Act.

Chancery sale of tract, 1 1/2 miles from Frederick, 186 1/2 acres, occupied by John HELDERBRAND. Frederick A. SCHLEY, Richard POTTS, Trustees.

Sale of tract in upper part of the Middletown Valley, Frederick Co, adjoining lands of Levin HAYS and Jacob WOLF, 289 acres - land on which Hezekiah ROBINSON lately lived. Richard POTTS.

Chancery sale of farm, 127 acres, adjoining lands owned by Adam BURRIER, Major SOLLARS and Mr. POMPHREY. Land will be shewn by Adam BURRIER who lives adjoining or to John STEPHANUS who resides on it.

394. 13 Feb 1819

Married Thursday evening, 4th inst. by Rev. James L. HIGGINS, Basil DORSEY, to Miss Harriet, dau. of Rev. Joshua JONES, all of this co.

Died Sunday last, Mrs. Elizabeth SALMON, relict of the late Edward SALMON of this place.

Dorothea SHAFER has opened The Fountain Inn, Market St., Frederick-town, which she has repaired and fitted up.

F. & G. ENGELBRECHT inform the customers of their late father that the tailoring business is continued by them at his late shop in Market St.

Margaret ENGELBRECHT and George ENGELBRECHT, ex'rs. of Conrad ENGELBRECHT.

Town lots for sale in east Fourth St. Michael LATE and John LATE - for Catherine LATE.

Sale of tract, 310 acres on Evett's Run, 1 mile from Charlestown, VA; Anthony FULTON residing on the premises; apply to John R. COOKE, esq. in Martinsburg, or to the subscriber, John KENNEDY.

James WILSON (near the premises) is authorized to sell the farm late the property of Samuel CALDWELL, dec'd., 170 acres, part in Frederick Co, MD, and part in Liberty township, Adams Co., PA.

395. 20 Feb 1819

Married Tuesday evening last by Rev. WESTERMAN, Joseph JOHNSON, to Miss Eleanor HILLEARY, dau. of John HILLEARY, all of this co.

Married Thursday evening, by same, Fayette JOHNSON, of Baltimore Co., to Miss Catherine JOHNSON, dau. of late John JOHNSON, of this co.

Died Wednesday, 10th inst. at the advanced age of 80 years, Edward THOMAS, sen., long a citizen of this co.

Dry goods for sale at auction. STONEBRAKER & HOFFMAN who will continue to sell goods as usual. Middletown.

Wm. GOLDSBOROUGH will sell land about 3 miles from Frederick-town, 80 acres.

Stephen JOY, adm'r. of Henry GAVER.

Catherine SWOPE cautions persons from trespassing on her lands on which Mr. GILBERT now lives.

Trustee's sale of the real estate of Jacob DELAUTER, dec'd. in the neighbourhood of Godfrey LEATHERMAN and Mr. GROSNECKLE, in the northern part of Middletown Valley; grist and merchant mill, several tracts. The land will be shewn by George DELAUTER, on the premises.

Dennis POOLE, adm'r. d.b.n. of Luke POOLE, is available to make settlement on the estate.

Sheriff's sale of estate of James WAGERS, house and lot, now occupied by him as a tavern; Negro man, 2 women and 4 boys. Benjamin HAGAN, for the sheriff.

396. 27 Feb 1819

Died Saturday, 13th inst., at Liberty-town, Mrs. Margaret CRAPSTER, relict of Abraham CRAPSTER, aged 59 years and 7 months, from consumption.

Died Monday last, after a severe and lingering illness, in his 75th year, Joseph MILLER.

Sale of the estate of John KENEGE, dec'd., log house on upper end of Klinehart's Alley, 72 acres of woodland adjoining Hugh KNOB, another tract, 43 32/4 acres. Joseph KENEGE, Jacob SOUDER, ex'rs.

Sale of farm adjoining Emmitsburgh, 150 acres. Charles ROBERTSON, Emmittsburgh.

Samuel SLIFER, ex'r. of Elizabeth ARNOLD.

Seven horses for sale. J. FUNK, Patrick St.

Sale of lands of Thomas BEATTY, dec'd., adjoining Cregers-town, sundry houses and lots, tract of 215 acres. Samuel GRIMES will shew property. Also land in Allegany Co, 428 1/2 acres and other tracts. John RITCHIE, ex'r.

397. 6 March 1819

Married Sunday evening, 21st, by Rev. HELFENSTEIN, Ezra DILL, to Miss Margaret MORGAN, all of this city.

Died at his residence, about 2 miles from Frederick, Thursday, 25th ult, John BRUNNER, in his 75th year.

Dissolution of the partnership of M'QUAID & TOOL. The Union Factory, property of Mr. REMSBERG, 2 miles from Middletown, will be kept in operation by Patrick M'QUAID.

Sale of personal estate of Jonathan GARBER, dec'd., 1 mile from Herring's mill, horses, cows, hogs, sheep, furniture. John GARBER and Jacob SAYLER, adm'rs.

Land for sale, 180 acres, 2 miles from Emmitsburgh. Joseph OBOLD.

Sale of house and lot in Liberty-town. P. W. MARQUAM.

Henry STONER adm'r. of David STONER.

Elihu H. ROCKWELL, adm'r of William WINTER.

John M'HENRY, Allegany Co., MD, offers reward for mulatto boy named Patrick SMITH, about 18 years of age. His father is a free mulatto living in Frederick-town named SMITH, a carpenter, said to be a preacher.

Henry GEYER, Emmitsburgh, offers reward for Charles BOSS, apprentice to the Chair making business, about 18(?) years old.

398. 13 March 1819

Daniel YANTIS, Liberty-town to carry on plough making.

Mount Hampton Farm for sale, formerly the property of late Capt. Thomas SPRIGG, 800 acres. Otho SPRIGG.

Clement HILTON, living near B. JOHNSON'S glass manufactory, offers reward for an apprentice to the shoemaking trade, named John BAKER, about 20 years old.

144 *NEWSPAPER ABSTRACTS OF FREDERICK COUNTY*

399. 20 March 1819
Persons indebted to D. BENNETT are requested to make payment.
For rent - house occupied by J. LARKIN as an auction store. E. MURDOCH.
Jacob LITTLE continues plough and waggon making business at his shop at the south end of Market St., a few doors above John REICH's smith shop.
Dissolution of partnership of John THOMAS and William C. EMMIT, under the firm of THOMAS & EMMIT.
M. E. BARTGIS declining the tavern business, will sell furniture, milch cows, liquors and other.
George HAMMOND, 4 miles from Liberty Town, offers reward for Negro man named RAS, 25-30 year old; raised in Montgomery Co.; has a free brother in Baltimore.
Elijah BEALL, Libertytown, offers reward for Negro woman named AMELIA; may have gone off with her brother.
John J. M'CULLEY, adm'r. of Mathias KEYSER.
Farm for sale, 116 acres, 14 miles from Frederick, log house and kitchen, Samuel CLARY.
Chancery sale of house and lot of Edward SALMON, dec'd., in Frederick, in the rear of the Lutheran church; Raymer KOLB lives in said property.
Sale pursuant to order of Montgomery Co. court, all the real estate of Jesse HYATT, dec'd, tract of 156 1/4 acres; lots in the town; another tract of 290 acres - and other. Ephraim GAITHER, Bazil WATERS, Greenbury GRIFFITH, Howard GRIFFITH, Wm. WILSON of John, Commissioners. Call on Samuel SOAPER.
Sale of house and lot on south side of Main St., adjoining property and residence of Jesse WRIGHT, Esq. John DORSEY, New Market.

400. 27 March 1819
William MARKS has started a new line of stages to Frederick-town.
Lot for sale near the Court House Square. John BRIEN.
John BARRICK has rented Swan Tavern, Woodsborough, lately occupied by John B. STIMMELL.
Overseer wanted. T. W. JOHNSON, on Israel's creek, near Capt. WILLIAMS' mill.
Catherine KIMBOLL, wishes to sell 2 lots near Mr. THOMSON's brewery and to rent the store and cellar adjoining the dwelling of Michael HAUSER, formerly occupied by Henry THOMAS.
Mary Ann M'MILLEN and John W. MAIN, admr's. of Samuel M'MILLEN.
Christian SCHOLL, ex'r. of John BRUNNER.

401. 3 April 1819
Married Thursday evening last by Rev. Frederick W. HATCH, Joseph ADLUM, to Mrs. Mary CRUM, both of this co.
Controversy between Doct. Jacob BAER and Baltzer FOUT regarding the sale of a Negro woman called MATILDA. Resolved by arbitrators, Charles SCHELL, W. Bradley TYLER, Wm. ROSS. Witness: Hillary H. HALLEY.

Land for sale, real estate of Denton JACQUES, late of Washington Co., dec'd., 4000 acres. Lancelot JACQUES, jun., trustee.

Sale of the personal property of Daniel ETZLER, dec'd., 1 1/2 mile of Liberty, Negro woman, horses, cows, hogs and sheep. George FOX, Daniel ETZLER, exr's.

James DAUTY, Frederick Co., offers reward for indented apprentice to the blacksmith's trade named William HANNAH, about 17 years of age, about 5 feet, 8 inches, tolerable good weaver.

402. 10 Apr 1819

Married Tuesday last, by Rev. HAUSE, George SALMON of this city, to Miss Catherine SMITH, dau. of Capt. Daniel SMITH, of this co.

Married Thursday evening, 25th ult. by Rev. James L. HIGGINS, Henry WEBB, to Miss Eve FINE, dau. of Philip FINE, all of this co.

Died Monday morning last at his residence near Frederick, of a pulmonary disease, Charles HAMMOND, in his 38th year, leaving wife and 2 small children.

Sale of real estate of Edward SALMON, dec'd., postponed.

Rudolph MYERS near Frederick-town has lost a red morocco pocket book, containing two bonds, one on David GLENN, Alexander GLENN and Benjamin M'GATIAN, for 767 dollars, the other William MONROE, David GLENN and John SWALLER, for 433 dollars, residents of Cumberland Co., PA.

Dissolution of the partnership of Jacob CRONISE and Lewis REMSBERG, under the firm of CRONISE and REMSBERG.

SHERIFF'S sale of estate of John KURTZ, house and lot in Union Town, occupied by Charles HERSTONS - taken at the suits of David WARNER and George WINTER and Jacob LANDES, adm'rs. of John WINTER.

403. 17 Apr 1819

George Adam EBERTS, adm'r. of George EBERTS.

John L. POTTS offers reward of Joe THOMSON, slave of Mrs. E. POTTS, who absconded from Frederick-town.

Chancery sale of house and lot in New Market of Abraham B. WOODWARD in which he now resides.

Aaron OFFUTT, near Middle Brook Mills, Montgomery Co., offers reward for mulatto man named HENRY, about 24 years old; has a sister in Taney-town.

Sale pursuant to the will of Charles PERRY, Montgomery co., dec'd., farm, 1000-1100 acres, island in the Potomac, 50 acres, Negroes and stock. Thomas I. PERRY, ex'r.

The horse called Tom will stand this season for a few mares. George YANTES, manager at Surrey farm, 1 mile of Woodsborough.

Abellino, a maltese Jack-ass will cover mares at Ceresville farm. Daniel ELLIS, manager.

404. 24 Apr 1819
M'Kelvie HAMMETT has taken the Eagle & Review Tavern, formerly occupied by M. E. BARTGIS.
Bottled Porter for delivery. Andrew THOMSON.
R. G. M'PHERSON forewarns persons from trespassing.
3336 acres for sale on Cove Creek, Harrison Co., VA. Geo. BAER, Frederick.
700 acres of land in Frederick Co., VA. Fleet SMITH.
Sale of lot between Adam SCHISSLER and late Edward SALMON's property. Michael HAUSER.
Negroes for sale. Singleton WOOTTON, near New Market, or John WOOTTON at Montgomery Court House.
John WITHEROW, adm'r. of John STAMERS.

405. 1 May 1819
Died Thursday last in his 82nd year, Capt. John ADLUM, upwards of 50 years an inhabitant of this place; headed a company in Revolutionary War.
Walter POOLE forewarns persons from fishing on his premises.
SANBURN & DUSTIN are ready to commence carding at the mill near David KEMP's.
William DURBIN, jr., adm'r. of Frederick HOPPE.
Richard JOHNSON has taken up a stray gelding.
George SALMON, adm'r. of Elizabeth SALMON.

406. 8 May 1819
Married Thursday evening last, by Rev. Jonathan HELFENSTEIN, Jesse WRIGHT, jun. of New Market, to Miss Margaret MANTZ, dau. of Major Peter MANTZ of Frederick.
Died Monday, 3rd of May, Lewis HILL, in his 33rd year, resident of this co.
Doct. George HUGHES offers his services to the people of New Market and vicinity.
Dissolution of the partnership of David WEBSTER and Samuel WEBSTER (Shoes, boots, trunks, &c.).
Michael CROUSE, adm'r. of Paul RINECKER.
Sale at the store room (New-town, Trap), lately occupied by Prestley WARFIELD, dec'd., of dry goods, cutlery and groceries. John COST, Thomas JOHNSON, adm'rs.
Sale of 13 Negroes, horses, cows, hogs and other, part of the property of Charles HAMMOND. Thomas HAMMOND, adm'r.
Sale of personal estate of Joseph ETZLER, Frederick Co., dec'd., male slave, waggon makers tools, horse, milch cows, and other. John GLISAN, adm'r with will annexed.
Appointed commissioners by Judges of Frederick Co. court to open or straighten a road beginning at or near dwelling house of Christopher NEAT on Liberty road to run from thence by John BURGESS's mill, to intersect the Baltimore and Frederick town turnpike road at the 38th mile stone. Abraham STONER, Jesse WRIGHT, sen., John JIAMS, jun, New Market.

407. 8 May 1819
Chancery case: Albert SHUMAN, William SHUMAN, Garrot SHUMAN, Joseph ECARD and Gannett his wife against Jacob MACKLIN and Catolena his wife, Ely SHUMAN, Sarah SHUMAN, James SHUMAN and others. Object of the bill is to obtain a decree for sale of all the real estate of Peter SHUMAN, late of Frederick Co., dec'd., which was vested in his children by an act of the General Assembly of Maryland, passed at November session, in the year 1795, chap. 15, for their benefit. Vested in fee in the children of said Peter SHUMAN, subject to the dower of Eleanor SHUMAN, widow of dec'd. At the time of his death Peter SHUMAN left the following children: Aaron SHUMAN, Catolena SHUMAN, Albert SHUMAN, Jacob SHUMAN, Peter SHUMAN, John SHUMAN, Eleanor SHUMAN, William SHUMAN, Isaac SHUMAN, Gannett SHUMAN and Ann SHUMAN. Eleanor SHUMAN, dau. of said Peter has since married Samuel BUZZARD, one of the defendants. Catolena has married Jacob MACKLIN, another of the defendants. Gannett has married Joseph ECARD, one of the complainants. Samuel BUZZARD has purchased from Aaron, Jacob, John and Peter all their rights. Isaac SHUMAN long since removed to Ohio where he died leaving a widow named Sarah and three infant children named Eli, Sarah and James, all of whom are defendants. Jacob MACKLIN and wife have long since removed to Tennessee where they now reside. Eleanor SHUMAN, widow of said Peter SHUMAN has lately died.

408. 15 May 1819
Married in Emmitsburg, Tuesday last, by Rev. BRUTE, Joseph WHARFE to Miss Teresa C. NEVITT, of Frederick Co.

Died, 15th inst., Benjamin BIGGS, Esq., in his 59th year; twice represented Frederick Co. in the state legislature; for many years a magistrate, member of the levy court.

Died Tuesday last in her 47th year, Mrs. Sophia KOLB, wife of Mr. M. KOLB.

Died at his residence in Frederick, Saturday last, in his 44th year, Richard BROOKE, Esq., distinguished member of the bar of this state; received the holy sacraments of the Roman Catholic Church.

Died at Gisborough, Friday last, John T. SHAAFF, M.D., aged 56 years. After completing his professional education in Europe began the practice of Medicine in this city. *Md. Gaz.*

Sale of dry goods, a 2 story house, 4 lots and other. Peter STEVENSON, Liberty-town.

Land for sale, 175 acres in Botetourt Co., VA. D. SHANKS, Senr.

John C. DICKERSON, living near Goshen Mills, Montgomery Co., offers reward for Negro boy named PHIL, about 18 years of age.

409. 22 May 1819
James H. WILLIAMSON has rented Friendship Factory of Capt. John S. LAWRENCE, on Linganore, 5 miles from Liberty-town.

New Confectionery, next door to Henry KUHN, Esq., Market St. - G. F. TEUTO & Co.

Doct. G. WEISE, druggist, chemist and apothecary, late from Europe - at the above place.

Isaac CRUM, having last week has a number of sheep destroyed by dogs, cautions persons from trespassing on his premises.

John SMITH has purchased the Union Globe Tavern, Waynesburg, PA.

Sale made by Frederick A. SCHLEY, trustee for the sale of the real estate of Matilda SIMPSON, dec'd., ratified. John SCHLEY, clk.

Sale made by Frederick Augustus SCHLEY, trustee for sale of part of real estate of Edward SALMON, dec'd., ratified.

Joseph TANEY, adm'r. of John HUGHES.

410. 29 May 1819

Married 20th inst., by Rev. William CLINGAN, William DISON to Miss Ann DARNALD, both of Montgomery Co.

Married Thursday 20th inst., Peter HARDT, Editor of the *York Recorder*, to Miss Catharine SIDES, of Hanover PA.

Married Thursday evening last, by Rev. J. HELFENSTEIN, Christopher MYERS, to Miss Margaret BROWN, all of this place.

Died Wednesday night last, George William MURDOCH, Esq., only son of the late George Murdoch, dec'd., in his 32rd year, leaving wife and 2 infant children, mother and sisters.

Ice Creams. Mrs. WRIGHT near Mr. TALBOTT's tavern.

Cheap irish linens. A. THOMSON.

Chancery sale of real estate of Christian HOOVER, dec'd., 184 1/2 acres on Owen's creek, 1 1/2 miles from Graceham, Frederick Co.; also Graceham Mills; and other. Daniel HOOVER, Trustee.

Wanted at Tuscarora Paper Mill, 5 miles from Frederick, 2 journeymen paper makers. George BROADRUP.

Tract for sale in Washington Co., 300 acres. Thos. C. BRENT, Hancock.

Philip CULLER, 2 miles of New-town, Trap, offers reward for Negro woman named SALLY, upwards of 30 years of age.

Chancery case: Francis MANTZ against Matthias BARTGIS and John BEYER. Object of the bill is to obtain a decree for the sale of land conveyed to Francis MANTZ, the complaint, by John BEYER, one of the defendants, in order to satisfy a debt due to the complainant from the defendant.

Henry SPALDING, adm'r. of Robert JAMISON.

Lewis PRATZMAN, Graceham, offers reward for apprentice to the shoe-making business named John SHIFF, 19-20 years old, 5 feet, 7-8 inches, fair hair; had on blue cloth coat, brown vest and grey cassimere pantaloons.

411. 5 June 1819

Married Thursday, 27th ult., at Lancaster, PA, Walter KEMP, son of Christian KEMP, of this co., to Miss Catharine GLONINGER, dau. of Philip GLONINGER, Esq. of the former place.

Married Thursday last by Rev. David MARTIN, John LANE, of Baltimore Co., to Mrs. Barbara FOUT, of Frederick Co.

Daniel PRICE, carder, has formed a conveyance from CROMWELL's mill where he will take wool to HIBBERD's factory, New Market.

Appointed commissioners to open a public road from Taney Town to Middleburgh to store of George WEBB to Liberty Town, giving notice to Joseph TANEY, Edward J. WILSON, Leonard SIX, Christian SMITH, John DEAR, Henry MAYNARD that we will attend to the duties. Surratt D. WARFIELD, John DUDDERER, Wm. P. FARQUHAR.

Doctor L. J. SMITH, having taken an officer near Buckey's Town.

Samuel BAUGHER offers reward for steers which strayed from his plantation, Monocacy manor, near Nimrod OWINGS.

Jacob AMBROSE cautions persons that his wife Susannah has absented herself from his bed and board without just cause.

412. 12 June 1819

New Lumber Yard. A. THOMSON.

Andrew HOGMIRE, adm'r. of Jacob SPIELMAN. Persons with claims place them in the hands of Messrs. George and Jonathan HAGER.

Boarding house will be opened at Berkeley Springs. Ignatius O'FERRALL.

Edward MAGRUDER, 3 miles below Clarksburg, to sell screw, press plate, shears and kettle, belonging to a fulling establishment.

Sale of 2 story brick house now in the occupancy of Rev. HATCH. Apply to T. W. JOHNSON, living near Col. WILLIAMS' mill.

Basil D. STEVENSON, ex'r. of Beal SELMAN.

Jane HILL, ex'rx. of Lewis HILL.

John FLEMING, ex'r. of Lucy SOAPER.

413. 19 June 1819. No new items.

414. 26 June 1819

The Sunday School Society to meet. Rebeckah BYERLY, Sec'ry.

The German Reformed Congregation wishes to engage with a person as a teacher well versed in the German and English languages.

Dissolution of partnership of Lewis MOTTER and Isaac BAUGHER, under the firm of MOTTER & BAUGHER.

415. 3 July 1819

All Saints' Church, Frederick-town. The church being vacant by the resignation of Rev. HATCH, the vestry have appointed 1 Sep for the election of a Rector.

Gustavus H. SCOTT, Mulberry Mill, near Pleasant Valley Post Officer, Fairfax Co., VA, offers reward for mulatto man who calls himself Henry STUART, age 23.

Daniel RAGAN, to seek relief from debts under the Insolvency Act.

416. 10 July 1819

At a meeting of the executive the following appointments were made for this co.: Nicholas SNYDER, Philip W. MARQUHAM, Christian STEINER, justices of the peace for Frederick Co. Lewis MOTTER, justice of the levy court of Frederick Co. vice Benjamin BIGGS, dec'd. Jacob METZGAR, junr. armorer at Frederick-town, in the room of Jacob METZGAR, senr., resigned.

Died near the Navy Yard, Washington, 6th inst., after a painful and lingering illness, Mrs. Elizabeth HARRISON, wife of Dr. John HARRISON and dau. of John HOFFMAN, Esq., of this co., leaving husband and children.

Grist mill, saw mill & carding machine with 95 acres of land on Little Monocacy, belong to Ely DORSEY, Montgomery Co. Joshua PRESTON, living thereon. Christopher ZEIGLER, Hyatt's-town mill, Montgomery Co.

Dr. MACPHERSON, Bryan-town, Maryland, offers reward for Negro woman named ANN, about 25 years of age, in company with Negro man belonging to me, named NACE.

417. 17 July 1819

Died Friday evening last, after a lingering illness, Mrs. Lydia BROOKE, consort of Richard BROOKE, Esq., dec'd.; interred in the Roman Catholic burying ground.

Died yesterday morning, Leonard STORM, aged inhabitant of this town.

Sale at the residence of the widow Elizabeth SMITH, Carrol's Manor, all the stock and farming utensils. Leonard SMITH, Henry JENKINS.

Elizabeth THOMAS, near Carrol's Manor, offers reward for dark mulatto man named JACK, about 20 years old; taken up on 12th inst. by Samuel GAULT, near Taney-town, and brought to Frederick-town, where he made his escape again.

418. 24 July 1819

Equity sale of the real estate of Michael HAINES, dec'd., 3 tracts, one of 13 acres of woodland, the second of 47 1/2 acres near the head of Sams Creek; the other contains 1 3/8 acres. David HAINES, Trustee.

Dissolution of the partnership of H. H. WOOD and Wm. WINN, Baltimore.

John ARNOLD has taken up a stray gelding.

Edward LINTON has applied for benefit of the Insolvency Act.

Lewis CROSS, adm'r. of John BUCKIAS.

Joseph SMITH, Cumberland, offers reward for apprentice to the printing business named James BEACHEM, age 17, about 5 feet, 4 inches.

419. 31 July 1819

Died 4th inst., near Geneva, Ontario Co., N. York, Capt. George DERR, formerly a resident of Frederick Co., after a painful illness of two years, leaving a wife and family.

Died 7th inst., at the same place, Henry LAMBRECHT, late of this town, after an illness of 8 days with the quinsy.

Sale at the dwelling house of Leonard STORM, dec'd., in Bantz-town, personals estate of said dec'd., furniture, a few barrels of corn and other. Jacob GETZENDANNER, ex'r.

Trustees of the Lancaster and German School of Liberty-town give notice that they will have a large and commodious room ready for the reception of scholars about 1 Sep. Tho. SAPPINGTON, Sec'ry to the board.

Otho TRUNDLE, living near the mouth of the Monocacy, Montgomery Co., offers reward for Negro fellow named ARCH, about 28 years of age.

Sale at Woodbury, Frederick Co., VA, the temporary residence of the late John MOTTER, dec'd., all the personal estate of said dec'd., furniture, Negroes, stock, Woodbury estate, containing about 500 acres. John HOPKINS, Hill & Dale, Frederick Co.

Dissolution of the partnership of David HANE and John KINKERLEY, New Market, wagon-makers.

George HOFFMAN, ex'r. of Francis HOFFMAN.

420. 7 Aug 1819

John RIGNEY, saddler, has removed his shop from Market to Patrick St.

Sale of 18-20 Negroes at late residence of Thomas CRAMPTON, dec'd., near Dr. CLAGETT's, 1 mile from Rohrer's mill, Pleasant Valley, Washington Co. Elias CRAMPTON, ex'r.

Dwelling house for sale, late the residence of Joshua SIMPSON, dec'd., 3 miles from Liberty-town. Rezin SIMPSON.

George BAER forewarns persons from stealing his melons, cantaloupes, cucumbers and other vegetables.

Sheriff's sale at Captain Daniel SMITH'S saw mill, tract of Henry WELLER, called the Hammer, and part of a tract called Creager's Scheme, on Owing's creek, at the suit of Samuel OGLE.

Sheriff's sale of estate of John CREAGER of Lawrence, two lots in Graceham, numbers 11 and 12, taken at the suits of John EDMONDSON and Thomas EDMONDSON, John T. BARR, John F. KEYS and Thomas WELSH and George SEASE.

Sale of furniture, 2 carriages and horses. Mary SHAAFF, Wm. MARBURY, R. B. TANEY, ex'rs. of Jno. T. SHAAFF.

Solomon STICKEL has commenced the last-making business in Second St., Frederick-town, opposite Henry BANTZ's store.

421. 14 Aug 1819

The commissioners appointed for incorporating a water company in Emmitsburg, will attend at the hose of Henry WATERS. Daniel M. MOORE, Sec'ry.

Sale at residence of Christian BARRICK, dec'd., near Woodsborough, horses, cows, sheep, hogs, waggon and gears, ploughs, etc. Catherine BARRICK, Jacob BARRICK, Raphael JONES, ex'rs.

Wm. BIGGS of Benj. adm'r. of Benjamin BIGGS.

George FOX and Jacob BEARD, ex'rs. of Jacob BEACHT.

Joseph ADLUM, ex'r. of John ADLUM.

422. 21 Aug 1819
Watch making and silversmith business in Frederick-town, nearly opposite the Episcopal church. Joseph WHARFE.
Teacher wanted, lower end of Carroll's Manor. Thomas C. SCOTT, Clement T. HILLEARY, Joseph HERBERT, Ignatius JAMISON.
John HANE has for sale bacon, oats, bran, fish and leather shoes.
Wm. R. CHUNN, Lower Catoctin, about to remove from Frederick Co., wishes all persons having claims against him to call on him for settlement at Jacob MARTIN's tavern in New-town, Trap.
Solomon EADOR has taken up a stray mare.
Joseph MILLER, adm'r. of John TOMS.

423. 28 Aug 1819
Died Thursday morning, after a short but severe illness, William BAER, in his 60th year.
Sale of real property fronting the turnpike road in Middle-town of Philip CLONINGER, dec'd., 2 lots with 3 dwellings. Michael RUNER, residing on the premises. Jacob COBLENTZ, Middle-town.
George HARP, 7 miles from Middle-town, on the new cut road from Frederick-town to Greencastle, offers reward for stolen gelding.
William ALBAUGH, Liberty-town, offers reward for apprentice boy named William GAUSNELL, about 20 years old, 5 feet, 8-9 inches, bound to the blacksmith business.
Corn for sale at my farm on Monocacy near the mouth of Bennett's creek. Matthew BROWN.
Tract for sale in Washington Co., 300 acres. Thos. C. BRENT, Hancock, Maryland.
Peter ZIMMERMAN, 1 mile up the road from Emmitsburg, has taken up a stray mare.
Joseph NICKUM, Middle-town, offers reward for lost note of hand, signed by Samuel DUVALL and John CAMPBELL.
Joshua TODD, Baltimore Co., ex'r. of Zephaniah HARRISON of Frederick Co.

424. 4 Sep 1819
Married Thursday evening last, by Rev. P. DAVIDSON, Basil NORRIS, merchant of this town, to Miss Elizabeth CHARLTON, of this co.
Sale in pursuance of the order of the orphans' court of Montgomery Co., at late residence of Henry STRAUSE, dec'd., 2 miles from Montgomery Courthouse, 6 Negroes, horses, cattle and other. Christiana STRAUSE, Matthew MURRAY, ex'rs.
Sale of personal goods of Richard BROOKE, dec'd., in Frederick-town, furniture, law books, corn, wheat, oats in stacks, carriage, and other. John Thompson BROOKE, adm'r.
Henry HUMMER, living near Capt. Frederick EICHELBERGER's, has taken up a stray colt.

425. 11 Sep 1819
Sale of 3-acre lot in town of Frederick, and lot in City of Washington, furniture - John DOLL and Jacob BRUNNER, ex'rs. of Joseph DOLL.

James LEWIS, near Noland's Ferry, Loudoun Co., VA, offers reward for Negro man named NED, 24 years old, originally owned by Doctor GRAYSON, Winchester, VA, who sold him to Strother HELM of Loudoun Co. and HELM sold him to Doctor John H. LEWIS of Jefferson Co. "of whom I got him."

J. SCHREINER and HALLER have commenced the weaving business at the upper end of Patrick St.

Rudolph MYERS, 2 miles from Frederick-town, offers reward for light mulatto man, about 22 years of age, purchased about 12 months ago from Talbot SHIPLEY living near New Lisbon.

426. 18 Sep 1819
Walter SIMPSON, 1 mile from Frederick-town, offers reward for missing mare and a sorrel horse.

Abraham KEMP has taken up a stray calf which came to his farm (late John BRUNNER's).

R. POTTS will sell house in which he now lives in Market St.

B. S. PIGMAN, Atty. at Law, has opened his office in the house of Mr. DILL, Frederick-town.

Peter RHODES, near New-town, Trap, offers reward for missing mare.

Masonic meeting, Columbia Lodge, Frederick-town. Thos. W. MORGAN, Sec'ry.

Sale of farm adjoining Middle-town, late the property of Leonard STORM, dec'd., called Resurvey of Turkey Range, 180 acres; also tract of wood land, 86 acres. Philip WISE, the present tenants. John D. GROVE, John L. LEVY, Trustees.

Notice from Richard HOGGINS, defending his character from false story given by Robert DEAN.

John DEVILBISS of Casper has taken up a stray gelding.

Large brick dwelling house for rent at the Monocacy bridge, known as Gomber's Ferry. Benj. HERSH.

Chancery sale at William MYERS' tavern, Liberty-town, real estate of John Brice BURGESS, in upper part of Anne Arundel Co., 200 acres. West BURGESS, Trustee.

J. KEMP has commenced fulling, dying and dressing of cloth at his factory, 3 miles north of Frederick-town.

427. 25 Sep 1819
Died 11th inst., Mrs. Jane BEALL, consort of Elisha BEALL, in her 57th year.

Sale of personal goods of Abraham ROUZER, dec'd., in Mechanic's-town, furniture, saddlers' tools, mare, cows, hogs. Margaret ROUZER, adm'x.

Chancery sale of land, 155 acres, 1 mile from Middle-town, adjoining lands of John BOWLUS, Henry SCHLUSSER, Philip DERR and Nicholas HOUCK.

Samuel BUZZARD lives on the premises. Property will be shewn by him or Aaron SUMAN who lives near Middle-town.
William PERRY has fitted up 3-story brick house in Patrick St. occupied as a store by Mr. LEVY and opened a House of Accommodation.
Samuel PANCOAST, 1 mile from Buckey's-town, has taken up a stray steer.
Geo. BAER of Wm., adm'r. of William BAER.

428. 2 Oct 1819
Sale at the late residence of George COST, dec'd., near Burkett's store, 10 Negroes, cows, hogs and sheep, etc. Jacob BISE, George WHIP, ex'rs.
John HARRITT, Emmitsburg, offers reward for apprentice to the hatting business named James MARSHALL, about 20 years old, dark hair, stout, 5 feet, 9-10 inches.
Fulling, dying and dressing of blankets, cloths at Christian COST's new Fulling Mill, 1 mile of New-town, Trap.
Frederick HIGH, Liberty-town, offers reward for apprentice to the blacksmith business named Joseph MASON, about 18 years old, 5 feet, 6 inches, thick, well set fellow; on the same evening a horse was stolen a horse out of the stable of Thomas SAPPINGTON, nearly opposite to my house.
Jacob BISER and George WHIP, ex'rs. of George COST.

429. 9 Oct 1819
I do hereby certify, that at the time the British were besieging Baltimore, I heard William E. WILLIAMS, one of the present candidates for assembly, say at Major HALL's, in New Market, that Baltimore was in danger, and that the inhabitants of that place had better capitulate and make the best bargain they could with the British, and that he was on his way there, and would consent to an arrangement of that kind. Belt BRASHEAR. Samuel ENGLAND makes a related statement regarding Mr. WILLIAMS's comments.
Jacob ISH, Loudoun Co., VA, offers reward for Negro man named DAVID who calls himself David WILKINS or David BROWN, 30-35 years old.
Abraham PRESTON, manager for Major John GRAHAME, has taken up as stray mare.
Isaac PLUMMER has taken up a stray gelding.
Sale of personal property of Mary Magdalena SMITH, dec'd., mare, cow, heifer, 4 sheep. Henry BOSTIAN, adm'r.
David STOTTLEMEYER gives notice that his wife Catharine has left his bed and board; persons are cautioned against harboring her, or trusting her on his account.

430. 9 Oct 1819
Journeymen millwrights wanted. Peter BARKMAN, near the Three Springs, Carroll's Manor.
Sheriff's sale of estate of Barton HACKNEY, 150 acres called Merry Land on which he now resides, at the suits of Dennis O'BYRNE, Peter MARTIN use of Joseph M. CROMWELL, Philip BLESSING, Sarah LEARNED, extx. of Augustus LEARNED, Anna Maria COST, extx. of George COST, United

States, Alexander GRIM, Basil and Harper WILLIAMSON, use of Basil MULLIKEN, William DAUGHERTY use of George KOLB, Richard ENGLISH, Ann GARROT, Patrick O'BURNS use of John ECARD's adm'rs., Francis MANTZ and John C. FRAIM.

Sheriff's sale of Negro man named PLATO and Negro boy named HENLY, property John GARROTT, at the suits of Benjamin DEAVER, use of Joseph M. CROMWELL and George BUTT.

Dissolution of partnership of John THOMAS, William C. EMMIT, John N. PORTER and Valentine THOMAS, Murfreesborough, Tennessee, under the firm of THOMAS, EMMIT & Co.

Committed to Frederick Co. jail, Negro man who calls himself Joseph M'CORMICK, about 25 years old; says he was sold by John M'CUMBERLAND, Richmond Co., VA.

431. 16 Oct 1819

William MCFARLAND has commenced fulling and dying at his factory on the new road from Frederick-town to Greencastle, 4 miles north of Middle-town.

Committed to Frederick Co. jail, Negro man who calls himself Peter WINTER, about 35 years old; says he is a freeman from near Ironhill, New Castle Co., DE; manumitted by Joel HULET of New Castle CO.

Daniel ARTHUR will sell his tavern stand in Liberty-town, and other property including tract adjoining Winter's mill and William HAINES on Little Pipe Creek.

John MARTIN has commenced the tailoring business.

Sheriff's sale of estate of Greenbury KNOUFF, house and lot east side of Market St., Frederick-town, conveyed to his father Jacob KNOUFF by John PHILLIPS - at the suit of Frederick OTT, surviving partner of George SMITH.

Sheriff's sale of estate of James WOOD to lot with blacksmith's shop, devised to James WOOD by his father Joseph WOOD by will, dated 4 April 1817.

432. 23 Oct 1819

Died suddenly, Saturday, 2 Oct, at half past 7 o'clock p.m. at Taney-town, Miss Mary BROWN, aged 16 years, 6 months, 10 days. On the day of her death, she walked from home (6 miles), attended at the church as usual for instruction, at which last meeting she appeared to be much affected and sat weeping for a considerable time. As she wished to attend divine service next day, she accepted the invitation and accompanies Miss Elizabeth REIFSNIDER, to stay with her at her father's house. She supped with the family, enjoying perfect health. At an early hour the family and some of the neighbors assembled for family worship. Just as the mister was opening the bible she fell from her chair and expired!

Died 2nd inst., at his farm on Bush Creek, after a short illness, Robert ANDERSON, aged 56 years, husband and parent.

Married Thursday evening last by Rev. P. DAVIDSON, John DELAPLANE to Miss Sophia CHARLTON, both of this co.

Sale of the farm of the late Jacob BECHT, dec'd., adjoining Woodsborough, 186 acres. George FOX and Jacob BEARD, exrs.

Thomas BURROWS & Co., have commenced the book binding business over the post-office, Patrick St. Leave orders with James F. HOUSTON, postmaster.

Frederick FEAGA about to make arrangements to liquidate his debts.

Harriet BRISH has made considerable additions to her stabling at her old stand, sign of Thomas Jefferson, Market St.

Jacob WEIST has taken up stray steers, near Frederick-town.

Hugh MCMULLAN to open a school in Second St., opposite the Catholic Church.

Jacob OVELMAN, ex'r. of Henry OVELMAN.

433. 30 Oct 1819

Married Thursday evening last, by Rev. J. HELFENSTEIN, John OGLE to Miss Susan THOMAS, both of Frederick Co.

Died Tuesday morning, 26th inst. at Rose Hill, seat of John GRAHAME, near the close of his 87th year, revolutionary patriot, Thomas JOHNSON, Esq., native of Calvert Co., in this state, and for the last 40 years a resident of this co.; first governor of the state after the Declaration of Independence.

Committed to Frederick Co. jail, Negro man who calls himself Freeborn GARRETSON, 5 feet, 8 inches, 24 years old; says he was free born and bound to Rev. John ALLEN, Baltimore, Hanover and Market Sts.

Committed to Frederick Co. jail, Negro girl who calls herself Mary Ann COLE, 18-19 years old; says she was born free and bound to Alexander DEVALCOE of Charles St., Baltimore.

William CAMPBELL forewarns persons from purchasing anything from his Negroes, except old CHARLES his manager, commonly called Charles BOWEN.

Vachel of O., 5 miles from Frederick-town, offers reward for missing mares.

Sale of 11 slaves of Theodore MITCHELL, dec'd., Frederick Co., horses, cattle, sheep, furniture. Patrick MCGILL, adm'r.

Sale of 2 story brick house on Patrick St.; also fresh glade butter. Michael HAUSER.

Sale of personal estate of Levin HAYS, dec'd., 2 miles from DELAUTER's mill, and 4 from OATE's tavern - horses, milch cows, cattle, hogs, sheep. Wilson HAYS, adm'r.

Dissolution of partnership of Jno. STEWART and Jno. PITTENGER, under the firm of STEWART & PITTENGER. The business will be carried on (assortment of goods) by Jno. PITTENGER, Graceham.

434. 6 Nov 1819

Married Tuesday evening last, by Rev. SHAEFFER, Mr. G. M. CONRADT to Miss Margaret FESSLER, all of this place.

Married Tuesday, 26th ult., by Rev. BUCHANAN, Lewis A. BEATTY, of this co., to Miss Sarah B. MARSHALL, of Franklin Co., PA.

Died Tuesday morning last, Miss Rebecca KOLB, dau. of George KOLB, esq. of this place, in her 19th year, after a painful illness of 4 weeks.

Died Wednesday 17th ult, at Carlisle, Doct. John N. A. BOGEN, for many years a resident of this place.

Sale at the residence of Robert ANDERSON, dec'd. on Bush Creek, near Plummer IJAMS mill, personal property of dec'd., Negroes, horses, cattle, hogs and sheep, furniture. Mary ANDERSON, adm'rx.

Abrm. LICHTENWALTER, adm'r. of Charles HESS, Junr.

Sale on the farm where he resides, near Mr. LOWE'S mill, 4 Negroes, horses, cattle, sheep and hogs. Walter BEAVAN.

Thomas MOUNT, Hyatt's Town, Montgomery Co., offers reward for apprentice boy named Samuel W. READ, aged 14 years, 5 feet, 2-3 inches, bound to the waggon making business.

Dissolution of partnership of the firm of HUGHES & BIGHAM and SMITH & BIGHAM. Charles W. BIGHAM.

435. 13 Nov 1819

Died Tuesday morning, 9th inst., at Needwood, Frederick Co., Thomas Sim LEE, Esqr., in his 75th year, second gov. of Maryland.

Candidates for sheriff: George W. GIST, Peter MARTIN.

French tuition, having taught the French language during four years in Mount St. Mary's Seminary. F. MARCILLY, lawyer, late magistrate from St. Domingo.

J. A. RETZER, Professor of the French & German languages, lately from Europe, will commence lessons at The Frederick Academy.

Sale of 148 acres on main road from Frederick to MAYBURRY's Furnace, estate of late John M. DERR, adjoining Lewis Town, including blacksmith and waggon maker's shop. Call on John DERR, near the property, or John CRONISE, 3 1/2 miles north of Frederick-town, ex'r.

Chancery case, District of Columbia: Joseph NEVITT, complainant vs. Henry C. GAITHER, Beal GAITHER, Benjamin GAITHER, Frederick GAITHER and others, heirs and representatives of Henry GAITHER, dec/d. Complainant states he bought of Henry GAITHER on 22 Feb 1809, a lot in Beatty and Hawkins' addition to Georgetown, No. 266. Heirs of Henry GAITHER: Henry C. GAITHER, Beal GAITHER, Benjamin GAITHER, Frederick GAITHER and others.

436. 20 Nov 1819

Broke Frederick Co. jail, 3 Negro men: Freeborn GARRETSON [described earlier]; Joseph M'CORMICK, about 25 years old; ROBERT, mulatto about 25 years old, formerly property of William PERRY of this town and now the property of Justinian BARBERRY.

Henry BECKLEY, Senr., 4 miles above Middle-town, has taken up 2 stray heifers.

Sale of Negroes, property of Col. Thomas FLETCHALL, dec'd.; also horses, cattle, sheep, hogs, etc. Geo. W. FLETCHALL and William CHISWELL, ex'rs. of T. FLETCHALL.

Conrad MICHAEL, 4 miles above Middle-town, has taken up a stray heifer.

158   NEWSPAPER ABSTRACTS OF FREDERICK COUNTY

437. 27 Nov 1819
Married Thursday evening last by Rev. John KOLER, Doct. Jacob COBLENTZ, to Miss Melinda STALEY, both of this co.
Died Thursday last in his 70th year, Henry M'CLEERY, for many years a resident of this town.
George Wm. GRONLUND, will repair piano fortes during his stay in the city. (Mr. TALBOTT's, Washington Hotel)
Sheriff's sale of estate of Henry AMBROSE, 130 acres on which he now lives, belonging to two tracts called Hazle Bottom and Stephen's Hope, taken at the suits of Jacob HARP and George HOUPT use of Nicholas HOUPT.
Committed to Frederick co. jail, mulatto man who calls himself Joseph SMITH, about 30 years old.
Committed to Frederick Co. jail, black man who calls himself George BRAXTON, about 20 years old; says he was free born in Fincastle, VA.
Committed to Frederick Co. jail, mulatto man who calls himself Thomas THENS, about 25 years old; says he was born in Charleston SC.
Philip FLENARD and Michael BURNS, Adams Co. jail, have applied to the court of common pleas of Adams Co, PA, for benefit of Insolvency Act.
William W. PATTERSON has taken up a stray mare.
John HAMILTON, Frederick Co., VA, offers reward for Negro boy named COLEMAN, about 18 years of age.

438. 4 Dec 1819. [Pages 2 and 3 missing]

439. 11 Dec 1819
Land for sale in Berkeley Co., VA. Adam STEPHEN.
Eli TOWNE to sell his house in Woodsborough.
Sheriff's sale of Negro man, property of Abraham KARNES, at the suits of Eve M. REED and Joseph WALLING.
Abraham NUSBAUM, adm'r. of Jacob NUSBAUM.
Married Thursday last by Rev. HENRY, Henry LECKLITER to Miss Mary MEASLE, both of this co.
B. S. PIGMAN has removed his office to the room lately occupied by Joseph M. PALMER (Atty. at law) who has removed his office to room next door to John DILL's.
Susannah WHITMORE adm'rs. of John WHITMORE.
John CORBALEY to sell Negroes.
Dissolution of partnership of H. G. O'NEAL, F. RICHMOND, J. REMSBURGH, Middle-town; settle accounts with Levi CAIN.
Sale of real estate of George Ludwick KESSELRING, dec'd., lying on Silver Run, 4 miles from Taney-town, 300 acres, and other property. George OTT, Trustee.
Purchasers at the sale of Hugh GRIFFIN are informed that the notes are due.

440. 18 Dec 1819
Dissolution of partnership of Jacob ANGLE, John ANGLE and Isaac ANGLE,

Liberty. Business to be carried by Jacob ANGLE at the stand occupied by Messrs. HAMMOND, known as the Red House.
36 town lots to be sold, laid off adjoining Middle-town as Grove's Addition to Middle-town. Jacob GROVE, senr. Apply to David BOWLUS, Middle-town.
Persons are cautioned against taking assignment on note given by late Joshua DORSEY, dec'd., given to her. Catharine KIMBOLL.
Benjamin MACKALL, adm'r. of William JONES.
Pocket book lost near Camp Meeting, near John DEVILBISS, with notes given by John MEAZEL. Peter WILE, 3 miles from Middle-town.
Otho TRUNDLE, near the mouth of the Monocacy, Montgomery co., offers reward for Negro fellow named ARCH, about 28 years old.
Michael NULL, ex'r. of Michael NULL.

441. 25 Dec 1819
Married Tuesday evening, 14th inst. by Rev. PHINNEY, David SCHLEY, of Frederick-town to Miss Anna Mary, dau. of Peter HOKE, of Harford Co.
Lumber for sale. Andrew THOMSON, Frederick.
Chancery case: John COOK vs. Thomas N. BINNS, Benedict DARNALL, Charles F. MERCER and Meschach RICHARDS. Object of bill is to charge the land conveyed by Benedict DARNALL to Thomas N. BINNS, and by him since sold to Charles F. MERCER, being part of the tract of land called The Hope, in Frederick Co., MD. Thomas N. BINNS, Benedict DARNALL and Charles F. MERCER, do not reside in this state.
Chancery case: David HILL and George H. STEWART, adm'r. of Barnard FAGAN vs. Richard FALLS & Washington VANBIBBER. Bill states that certain mills in Frederick Co., now in the occupation of Washington VANBIBBER, were leased by Isaac VANBIBBER to above named Richard FALLS for 10 years, commencing on 6 Apr 1818 and which said lease was afterwards assigned by said FALLS to Washington VANBIBBER.

INDEX to Paragraph Number 161

-A-
A PART OF ADDISON'S CHOICE, 345
A. & H. BURNSIDE & CO., 358
ABRAHAM, 56
ADAMS, Benedict L., 125
 James, 27
ADDISON, Rev., 278
ADLUM, John, 23, 302, 405, 421
 Joseph, 13, 401, 421
AGER, Samuel, 65
AGNEW, Andrew, 55, 67
 John, 18, 254, 269
 Samuel, 288
AILSEY, 67
AISQUITH, S., 256
ALBAUGH, Abraham, 14, 230, 299
 Christian, 363
 David, 75
 Margaret, 163
 Philip, 257
 William, 289, 367, 423
ALEXANDER, Ashton, 123
 Gerard, 26
 Jacob, 23
ALEXANDER & PHILLIPS, 298
ALFRED, 355
ALLEN, 283
 Isaac, 59
 James, 290
 John, 433
 Mathew R., 246
ALTOGETHER, 232
AMBROSE, Henry, 437
 Jacob, 411

 Susannah, 411
AMELIA, 399
AMEY, George, 180, 388
ANCHLING, Henry, 232
ANDERSON, 125
 Edward, 245, 277
 F., 18
 Joshua, 238
 Lucy, 277
 Mary, 434
 Mr., 228
 Richard, 319
 Robert, 432, 434
ANDREW, Richard, 257
ANDREWS, John, 228
ANGEL, Jacob, 59
ANGLE, Isaac, 440
 Jacob, 440
 John, 440
ANN, 416
ANNAN, Doctor, 44
 R. I., 274
 Robert I., 276
 Robert L., 64, 301, 327, 355
APPLER, Elizabeth, 62
 Jacob, 58, 59, 62
APPOLOW, Lewis B., 158
 Lewis G., 149
ARCH, 419
 Otho, 440
ARCHER, John, 299
ARMISTEAD, George, 159
ARMOUR, David, 212
ARMSTRONG, Isaac, 282, 304
 James, 282, 304
 John, 304

 Mr., 97
 Quinton, 304
 Rev., 38, 86, 91, 356, 388
ARNEST, J., 302
ARNOLD, David, 243, 257
 Elizabeth, 396
 John, 418
ARTHUR, Daniel, 1, 68, 234, 245, 276, 321, 349, 376, 431
ARTNER, Peter, 132
ARTUR, Charles, 123
ASH, George, 62
ASKIN, George, 238
ASKINS, George, 237
ATKINS, John, 125
ATLEE, Isaac, 67, 108, 234
AUSTIN, William W., 232
AYLE, Valentine, 144

-B-
BACHELOR'S REFUGE, 380
BADEN, Acquilla, 368
BAER, Adam, 255
 Elizabeth, 97, 391
 Ezra, 355
 George, 22, 37, 120, 146, 154, 164, 223, 236, 240, 243, 255, 404, 420
 George of William, 164, 243, 427
 Henry, 103, 164, 243, 250, 391
 Jacob, 1, 14, 73, 230, 243, 258, 276, 401
 John, 55, 120, 141, 159, 278, 342, 355
 Michael, 355
 Michael of John, 286

William, 2, 41, 120, 243, 423, 427
BAILY, Abraham, 56
John, 1
Samuel, 55
BAITHER, Benjamin, 247
BAKER, Abednego, 52, 82
  Brooke, 26
  Frederick, 48, 53, 120, 234, 304, 370
  Henry, 26, 254, 299
  Jacob, 332
  John, 122, 264, 275, 398
  Nathan, 254
BALDERSTON, John, 385
BALDERSTONE, John, 91
BALDWIN, Elijah, 68, 124, 167
BALL, Daniel, 78, 287
  Dr. H., 177
  John, 14, 230
BALLARD, James, 37
BALLINGER, William, 40
BALTZEL, J., 192
BALTZELL, Barbara, 144
  Catharine, 252
  Charles, 48
  David, 145
  George, 9, 243, 252, 320, 392
  John, 231, 243, 249
  Michael, 144
BANKS, Allen, 247
  Samuel, 247
  William, 243
BANTZ, Gideon, 1, 21, 22, 240
  Henry, 36, 140, 420

John, 134, 318
BARBERRY, Justinian, 436
BARKMAN, Peter, 430
BARNDOLLAR, Michael, 183
BARNES, Catharine, 334
  Jacob, 136
  John, 290
  S., 28
  Samuel, 3, 22, 38, 44, 45, 140, 146, 164, 344
  Thomas, 334
BARNETT, Mr., 2
BARNHARD, Philip, 107
BARNHART, Jacob, 236
  Philip, 236, 257
BARR, 199
  John T., 420
  William, 126
BARRICK, Catherine, 421
  Christian, 421
  Elizabeth, 269
  Frederick, 253
  Jacob, 421
  John, 400
BARRICKMAN, Christopher, 276
BARTELSON, John, 358
BARTGIS, M. E., 16, 63, 64, 120, 264, 399, 404
  Mathias E., 146
  Matthias, 123, 125, 132, 410
BARTHOLOW, Michael, 234
BARTON, Absolom, 124

Charlotte, 124
Joshua, 55
BASH, Catherine, 355
  John, 158, 355
  Michael, 355
BASIL, 72
BASIL NORRIS & CO., 120, 271
BAST, John, 129, 161
BAUCHMAN, Frederick, 9
BAUER, 2
BAUGHER, George, 379
  Isaac, 414
  Rebecca, 379
  Samuel, 27, 411
BAUGHMAN, ADam, 7
  Adam, 15, 84, 195, 308, 389
BAXTER, Eliza, 240
BAYER, Catherine, 35
  Jacob, 40, 328
  Michael, 328
BAYLES, John B., 130
BAYLY, John, 9, 231, 243, 324
BAYLY & JOHNSON, 120, 253, 324
BEACHEM, James, 115, 418
BEACHT, Jacob, 421
BEALL, Asa, 265
  Eden, 308
  Edward, 308
  Eli, 308
  Elijah, 308, 399
  Elisha, 356, 427
  Enoch, 308, 353
  Esther, 277
  Gustavus, 265
  Isaac, 265

James A., 250
Jane, 427
John, 164, 299, 338
Josias T., 250
Levin C., 277
Margaret, 299, 338
Mary, 265
Perry W., 283
Peter, 132, 169, 313
Rebecca, 356
Richard of Samuel, 265
Robert A., 250
Robert B., 265
Samuel, 248
Samuel B., 265
Theodore, 242
Thomas, 265
Thomas B., 265
Walter B., 265
William M., 5, 9, 16, 47, 49, 68, 204, 243, 298, 321, 331
BEALMEAR, Lewis, 319
BEAM, John, 77
BEAR, George, 2, 146
John of Henry, 192
BEARD, Jacob, 219, 421, 432
BEATTY, Elie, 276
Elijah, 143
John M., 261, 276, 277
L. A., 7
Lewis A., 52, 244, 434
Sarah, 143, 244
Thomas, 103, 154, 228, 235, 250, 278, 396
BEAVAN, Walter, 434
BEAVINS, Walter, 9
BECHLY, Henry, 378
BECHT, Jacob, 219, 432

BECKENBAUGH, George, 247
BECKLEY, Henry, 436
BECRAFT, Aquila, 370
  Peter, 99, 218, 393
BEDFORD, 181
BEDFORDSHIRE CORNER, 77
BEEKENBAUGH, Jacob, 349
BEESON, Edward, 326
  Jesse, 326
  Micajah, 326
BELL, John B., 100
  William D., 90
BELT, Delia, 232
  Evan, 245, 251, 257
  Jeremiah, 9, 17, 152
  Sarah, 152
  Tobias, 3, 9, 17, 378
BEN, 60, 129
BENNET, David, 123
BENNETT, Benjamin, 90
  D., 399
  David, 146
  Elisha, 90
  Ely, 299, 380
  Robert, 90
  Sarah B., 265
BENSON, John, 297
  Robert, 75
BENTLEY, Eli P., 1, 5, 31, 68, 146
  Israel, 88
BENTZ, Elizabeth, 291
  George, 146, 243, 247, 265, 283, 291
  Jacob, 247, 265
  Mr., 86
  William, 288

BERGER, Frederick, 13, 259
  Henry, 66
  Jacob, 164
BERKLEY, Robert, 163
BERRY, James, 123
BETTS, Solomon, 279
BETWEEN TWO BARRENS, 82
BEVANS, Walter, 349
BEYER, John, 410
BIAYS, Ned, 21
BIERLY, Frederick, 268
  George, 82
  Lewis, 23
  Mrs., 297
BIGGS, Benjamin, 14, 26, 123, 230, 287, 357, 408, 416, 421
  Joseph of John, 243
  William of Benjamin, 421
BIGHAM, Charles W., 49, 434
BILL, 233, 243
BINNS, Thomas N., 61, 143, 233, 277, 312, 313, 441
BINS, Elvira, 138
  Ninian, 138
  Thomas N., 138
BIRELEY, Lewis, 52
BIRELY, Elizabeth, 208, 242
  Frederick, 208, 243
  Lewis, 14, 51, 146, 257
BIRNIE, C., 341
BIRNSIDE, Ann, 244
  Aquilla, 244
  Henry, 244
  Joseph, 244
BISE, Jacob, 428

BISER, Daniel, 328
  Jacob, 328, 428
  John, 262, 319, 328
BIVEN, John, 254
BIXLER, Emanuel, 283
BLACK, Adam, 15, 16
  Henry, 15, 16, 56, 326
  John, 16, 56, 326
  Michael, 16
  Samuel, 204
BLACKFORD, Benjamin, 146
BLAIR, Hugh, 2
  William, 327
BLAKE, James H., 37
  Rev., 107
BLESSING, Michael, 18, 278
  Philip, 12, 223, 252, 430
BLESSINGER, Michael, 28
BOB, 168, 274, 302
BOERSTLER, G. W., 230, 245
  Mr., 66
BOGEN, John N. A., 243, 355, 434
  John N. Andrew, 221
  Thomas, 294
BOGLY, Henry, 293
BOHN, Jacob, 40
  Mr., 23
BOMGARDNER, Jacob, 117
BONAFFON, A., 20
BOND, Thomas, 98
BONER, John, 115, 170
BOONE, Robert, 76
BOOSER, Catherine, 85
BOSS, Charles, 397

BOSTIAN, Andrew, 349
  Anthony, 349
  Henry, 429
BOSWELL, William, 58
BOTELAR, Henry, 242
BOTELER, Edward, 4
  Edward L., 200
  Henry, 39, 181
  Thomas, 236, 334
BOWEN, Charles, 51, 433
BOWER, John, 93
BOWIC, Peter, 258
BOWIE, Thomas H., 126, 128
  Washington, 297
BOWLUS, David, 14, 56, 230, 278, 350, 440
  Jacob, 234, 330
  John, 46, 427
  Nicholas, 23
  Valentine, 6, 338, 362
BOWMAN, Captain, 283
BOWNEY, Edmund, 1
BOYCE, Daniel, 126
BOYD, David, 31, 243, 277
  Frederocl 124
  Marmaduke W., 139
  Mr., 365
  Reuben T., 312
  William, 239
BOYER, Daniel, 300
  John, 132
  Thomas, 21, 86, 108, 139
BOYLE, Daniel, 341, 351
  Peter, 10

BOYLE & DARBY, 341
BRADFORD, William, 25, 196
BRADFORD'S REST, 308
BRANDENBURG, Samuel, 5, 43, 384
BRANDENBURGH, Matthias, 320
BRANDY HALL, 58
BRANGLE, Nicholas, 345
BRASHAER, Ann, 55
  Belt, 2, 47
BRASHEAR, Belt, 7, 14, 230, 331, 429
  Dr., 259
  Elizabeth, 331
  William, 259
BRAXTON, George, 437
BRENGLE, Amelia, 142, 331
  Christian
  Daniel, 331
  Jacob, 110, 142, 199, 331
  John, 124, 247, 347
  Lawrence, 151, 164, 247, 298, 321, 356, 359
  Nicholas, 288, 326
  Peter, 5, 52, 382
BRENT, Thomas C., 410, 423
BRIEN, John, 38, 103, 175, 236, 400
BRISCOE, Hanson, 138
BRISH, David, 388
  Harriet, 432
  Harriot, 67
  Henry, 67, 149, 156, 243, 254, 348

BROADRUP,
George, 288, 369, 410
BROADRUP &
MORGAN, 168, 361
BRODERICK, John
M., 166
BROOK PARK, 59
BROOK PINEY
GROVE, 59
BROOKE, John
Thompson, 41, 424
Lydia, 34, 417
Richard, 7, 15, 25, 34, 41, 259, 322, 370, 385, 408, 417, 424
Roger, 230
Samuel B., 346
BROOKES, Walter, 170, 371
BROOKGROVE, 59
BROOKS, E., 302
Henry, 38
James Hall, 257
BROTHERLY
LOVE, 16
BROWER, David, 78
John, 82
BROWN, David, 429
Elias, 368
Frederick, 241
George, 385
Ignatius, 23
Jane, 165
Jean, 297
John, 82, 255, 297
Joseph, 258
Juliana, 297
M., 122
Margaret, 28, 410
Mary, 297, 432
Mathew, 252
Matthew, 121, 123, 242, 262, 268, 423
Robert, 297

Thomas, 297
William, 4, 48, 73, 261, 297, 368
BROWNE, Henry, 84
BROWNING, James, 238
Jesse, 238
Nathan, 259
BRUCE, Harry, 276
Rachel, 276
BRUNER, Elias, 30
Jacob, 40, 243, 299
John, 14, 102
Peter, 30
Valantine, 86
Valentine, 146
BRUNNER, Elias, 354
Jacob, 238, 425
John, 186, 256, 304, 397, 400, 426
Margaret, 186
Mary Magdalena, 238
Mr., 350
Peter, 186
Valentine, 164, 243
BRUTE, Rev., 408
BUCHANAN, Rev., 52, 434
BUCK LODGE, 122
BUCKEY, Daniel, 275, 300
David, 14, 230
George, 300, 356
Jacob, 124, 291, 296
John, 164, 250
Michael, 14, 124, 125, 238, 296
Peter, 314
Rebecca C., 356
Valentine, 284
BUCKHORN, 380
BUCKIAS, John, 418
BUCKIUS, John, 229, 327

BUCKY, John, 251
BUFFINGTON,
Jonah, 5, 7, 12, 15, 42, 117, 389
Josiah, 65
Magdalena, 117
BUNKERS HILL
FORTIFIED, 247
BURCHINAL, William, 121
BURGEE, Thomas, 107
BURGESS, Caleb, 333
Edward, 124, 232
Ephraim, 124
John, 23, 72, 406
John Brice, 426
John H., 121, 132
Samuel, 333
Thomas, 2, 278
West, 141, 426
William P., 69, 135
BURGISS, Shadrach, 162
BURKE, William B., 146
BURKETT, 243
BURKHART, Margaret, 288
BURKITT, Henry, 271
BURKITT AND
MORGAN, 271
BURNIE, C., 6
BURNS, Michael, 437
BURRIER, Adam, 10, 263, 393
Jacob, 64
John, 64
BURROWS, Frances
Harriet, 278
Thomas, 47
BUSSARD, Daniel, 12, 63, 283
Henry, 47, 63, 283

BUSSART, Solomon, 379
Susanna, 379
BUTLER, Henry, 157
  Ormand, 251, 302
  Oz, 386
  Tobias, 66, 132
BUTT, George, 223, 430
  John, 321
  Mr., 351
BUXTON, John, 16
BUZZARD, Samuel, 46, 407, 427
BYERLY, Rebeckah, 32, 414
BYERS, Benjamin, 154, 312

-C-
CAIN, Levi, 55, 439
CALAME, Oliver, 48
CALDWELL, Samuel, 394
  Samuel B. T., 130
CALHOUN, James, 42
CAMP, William, 1
CAMPBELL, Adam W., 178
  Captain, 154
  George C., 7, 388
  John, 132, 254, 313, 352, 423
  Rebecca, 304
  Richard, 352
  Richard C., 355
  William, 6, 51, 345, 380, 433
CANDLE, Jacob, 386
  Mary, 386
CANNON, Catharine, 210
  Grace, 210
  Mary, 210

  Moses, 210
  Nace, 210
  William, 210
CARBERRY, 16
CAREY, Mr., 212
CARLTON, Thomas, 2, 6, 65, 78, 84, 124, 146
CARMACK, Mary, 179
  Samuel, 162
  William, 289
CARNAGY, William, 283
CARNES, Henry, 284
CARR, Catherine, 363
  John, 103
  Joseph, 125
CARRICO, Alexander, 232
  Elexander, 232
CARRINGTON, John, 73
CARROLL, Charles, 353
  Daniel, 353
  H., 353
CARTER, Bernard M., 272
  Charles, 243
  Charles L., 260
  George, 265
  James P., 21
CARY, Cyrus, 164
CASSADAY, J. H., 44
CASTLE, Thomas, 293, 358
CASTLEMAN, David, 13
  John, 339
  William, 354
CATLETT, Gradison, 252
CATO, 283
CATON, Richard, 238

CAYLAR, Abraham, 89
CAZIER, Thomas, 259
CEILY, 67
CHAMERHORN, John N., 302
CHAMPER, Basil, 154, 344
  Christian, 154, 344
CHANEY, Charles, 137
  Robert, 101
CHARLES, 51, 126, 312, 314, 319
CHARLTON, Elizabeth, 42, 424
  Sophia, 432
CHARN, Jacob, 23
CHASE, Samuel, 259
CHEW, Samuel A., 388
CHISWELL, William, 436
CHOLLET, Cecelia, 192
CHRIST, Jacob, 62, 71
CHUNN, William R., 39, 251
CHYNOWATH, William, 180
CLABAUGH, Elizabeth, 82
  Jacob, 14, 64, 107, 192, 230, 274, 327
  John, 251
CLAGETT, Dr., 420
  Joseph, 391
  Samuel, 391
CLAGGETT, Joseph, 58
  Ninion, 124
  S., 228
CLAGHORN, John, 152

INDEX to Paragraph Number 167

CLAPSADDLE,
Michael, 77
Paul, 254
CLARK, Daniel, 107
John, 354
Richard, 23, 31, 47
Samuel, 85
Seth, 234
William, 337
CLARY, Samuel, 399
CLEAN SHAVING, 286
CLEMMENS, Abraham, 59, 60
CLEMSON, 108
John, 65, 102, 181
Mordecai, 65
Mr., 251
Sarah, 102
CLIFTON, 371
CLINGAN, James, 251, 257, 356
Rev., 77, 260
William, 28, 356, 410
CLONINGER, Mary Magdalena, 350
Philip, 55, 302, 423
CLOPPER, Abraham D., 9
F. C., 311
Nicholas, 5, 233, 247
CLOUD, Jesse, 41
CLOUDE, Jesse, 311
CLUDE, Mr., 311
COAL, William, 84
COBELER, Rev., 248
COBLENTZ, Catharine, 117
Elizabeth, 117
Jacob, 117, 234, 423, 437
John, 117
John Philip, 23
Peter, 111, 165

Philip, 234
COCKEY, John C., 21
Mr., 10, 393
COE, Thomas, 63
COFFMAN, James, 173
COGHLIN, William, 14
COKERY, Bernard, 272
COLBORN, Silvester, 382
COLE, John, 279
Mary Ann, 433
COLEGATE, George, 21, 299
COLEMAN, 52, 437
Charles, 353
Jacob, 23, 48
James, 353
William, 353
COLL, Joseph, 425
COLLINS, Abraham H., 308
Frederick, 250
Henry, 320
John, 390
COLSTON, Edward, 236, 249
COMBS, Henry, 251
Joseph, 89
CONCLUSION, 232
CONDON, David, 234
John, 345
Zachariah, 345
CONGO, 333
CONNELL, John, 373
CONNER, Thomas, 146, 243
CONNOLLY, Michael, 204
CONNOR, Thomas, 106

CONRAD,
Theophilus, 385
CONRADT, G. J., 261, 304
G. M., 50, 249, 434
George J., 82
Jacob G., 139
Mr., 66
T., 50
Theoliphus R., 91
CONTEE, Thomas, 124
CONWAY, W. T., 4
COOK, John, 6, 55, 61, 82, 121, 258, 272, 351, 441
John K., 2
Thomas, 5, 55
COOKE, John R., 368, 394
Stephen, 368
COOKERLY, 3
Jacob, 235, 247
John, 146
Margaret, 235, 247
William, 10, 71, 72, 167, 247
COPELAND, Charles, 299
COPENHAVER, John, 383
CORBALEY, John, 439
John R., 98, 392
COSKERY, John, 14, 110, 119
COST, Anna Maria, 223, 430
Christian, 46, 247, 428
George, 223, 296, 428, 430
John, 24, 406
COTTERELL, John, 27
William, 27

COUGHLIN, William, 230
COVENTRY, Mely, 48
COVER, Daniel, 40, 53, 79, 95, 385
 John, 270
COX, George, 283
COX & WRIGHT, 283
CRABB, Charles H., 242
 General, 242
CRABEL, Ann, 270
CRABS, Peter, 238
CRAFT, Widow, 5, 43, 384
CRAGHILL, Nathaniel, 176
CRAIG, John, 315
CRAIGE, Seth, 212
CRAMER, Cornelius, 198
 David, 269
 Jacob, 23, 238
CRAMPTON, B. A., 290
 Elias, 420
 Thomas, 420
CRAPSTER, Abraham, 57, 396
 John, 57, 67, 68, 115, 157, 196, 312
 Margaret, 396
CRAVER, George, 369
 John, 285
CRAWFORD, F. L., 344
CREAGER, Daniel, 43, 254
 George, 14, 68, 230, 345
 Henry, 132
 John, 82
 John of L., 139
 John of Lawrence, 420

Lewis, 8, 23, 390
CREAGER'S SCHEME, 420
CREEGER, Henry of John, 23
 J. of L., 23
 John L., 23
 John of Lawrence, 199
 Joseph, 23
 L., 23
 Lawrence, 23
CREEGERS SCHEME, 208
CRIGLER, Lucy, 248
 Major, 248
CRISE, Jacob, 23
CRIST, Jacob, 23
CRITZER, Jacob, 6, 338, 362
CROBY, Elias, 379
 Elizabeth, 379
CROCKETT, Robert, 296
CROMWEL, John, 217
CROMWELL, 411
 J. M., 235, 278
 John, 89, 143, 145, 153
 John C., 271
 Joseph, 79
 Joseph M., 5, 99, 143, 181, 223, 229, 243, 270, 349, 430
 Philemon, 10, 393
 Richard, 323
CRONIS, John, 435
CRONISE, 24
 J., 351, 356
 Jacob, 260, 273, 291, 351, 402
 John, 387
 Simon, 286
CRONISE AND REMSBERG, 402

CROSBY, Elias, 379
 Elizabeth, 379
CROSS, Bill, 323
 Catharine, 307
 John V., 35, 318
 Lewis, 243, 251, 302, 418
CROUSE, Elizabeth, 122
 John, 308
 Joseph, 122
 Mary, 307
 Michael, 406
 Mrs., 170
 Paul, 308
CRUM, Isaac, 26, 302, 409
 John, 279, 310, 312
 Mary, 401
CRUMBACKER, Abraham, 62, 64
 Jonas, 64, 95
CRUMBAKER, Abraham, 110
 Elizabeth, 110
 Ephraim, 110
 Jacob, 110
 John, 110
 Jonas, 110
 Lydia, 110
 Mary, 110
 Peter, 110
CRUMMELL, John, 182
CRUMPACKER, Jonas, 230
CRUSHAN, John, 122
CRUTCHLEY, Elias, 296
 Mr., 371
CUBLER, Henry, 253
CULLER, Henry, 123, 349
 Jacob, 349

Michael, 349
Philip, 27, 410
CULP, Philip, 72
CUMMING, General, 297
John, 277, 337
CUN, John, 129
CUNNINGHAM, Charles, 231, 341
CUPPET, Isaac, 257
CURFMAN, Henry, 86
William, 249
CURL, James, 354
CUSHMAN, John H., 274, 277
CUTTS, Richard, 309

-D-

D. & F. HINES, 307
D. & G. MANTZ, 314
D. & S. WEBSTER, 284
DADISMAN, Jacob, 186
Sarah, 186
DAGEN, John, 229
DAILEY, James, 249
DALAPLAINE, Joshua, 299
DALAUTER, George, 100
DALL, James, 297
DANIEL, Jonathan M., 14
Stephen, 300
DANNER, Jacob, 254
Zachariah, 234, 268
DARBY, Adan, 232
John, 169, 232, 263, 341, 363
Samuel, 232
DARCUS, Henry, 286
DARKIS, David, 392

DARNAL, Benedict, 138
Robert, 143
DARNALD, Ann, 28, 410
DARNALL, Benedict, 61, 143, 313, 441
Charles, 143
John, 143
Major, 247
Raphael, 143, 262
Robert, 60, 118, 143, 233, 320, 369
Thomas, 143, 233, 312
William, 143
DARNELL, Raphael, 229
DARNER, Frederick, 176, 357, 382
Jacob, 176, 357, 382
DARNES, William, 290
DARNEY, 320
DAUGHERTY, William, 430
DAUTY, James, 401
DAVAU, William, 125
DAVENPORT, John, 354
DAVID, 429
DAVIDSON, Lewis, 378
Mr., 249
P., 42, 52, 77, 119, 123, 169, 198, 243, 278, 363, 376, 424, 432
Samuel, 378
DAVIS, Catharine, 210
Denton, 210
Eliza, 210
Elizabeth, 210
George, 210
Gilbert, 210, 237
Henry L., 251, 269

Ig., 232
Ignatius, 14, 230, 255, 274
Isaac, 234
John, 5, 277
Joseph, 210
Luke, 23
Maria, 237
Robert, 149
Samuel, 267
Sarah, 300
Solomon, 233, 310, 372
Susanna, 210
Thomas, 309
Walter, 210
DAVISON, P., 292
DAWDEN, Martia B., 58
Zachariah, 58
DAWSON, Nicholas, 312
DAY, James, 47
Rev., 165
DE LA VINCENDIERE, Madame, 31
DEAL, John, 16, 103
DEAN, Barney, 210, 274
Catharine, 210, 274
James, 210
Joahua, 210
John A., 271
Robert, 43, 426
Sarah, 210
Thomas, 91, 210
William, 249, 339, 341
DEAR, John, 199, 411
DEAR STONES, 77
DEAVER, Benjamin, 223, 430
DEB, 248
DEBIS, Jacob, 196

DEGRANGE, Peter, 14
DELAPLAINE, Joshua, 373
DELAPLANE, Daniel, 306
　John, 432
　Joseph, 374
　Joshua, 9, 139, 248, 306
DELASHMUT, Basil, 283
DELAUTER, 433
　George, 12, 382, 395
　Jacob, 12, 31, 100, 395
DEMBO, 42
DENNY, Edmond, 315
DERN, Isaac, 373
　William, 123
DERR, George, 37, 419
　Jacob, 296
　John, 23, 435
　John M., 387, 435
　Philip, 46, 427
DERTZBACH, John, 120, 249
DERTZBAUGH, George, 125
DEVALCOE, Alexander, 433
DEVELSBERGER, Jacob, 76
DEVER, Levi, 285
DEVILBISS, Alexander, 324
　George, 324
　John, 331, 440
　John of Casper, 426
　Michael, 35
　Samuel, 385
DEVITT, David B., 13
DEWESE, Lewis, 169, 362
DICK, 350

DICKERSON, John C., 408
DIDENHOVER, William, 275
DIEHL, Frederick, 264
　Samuel, 275
DIEL, Isaac, 374
DIETRICK, Philip, 2
DIFFENDALL, Samuel, 255
DIGGES, Edward, 76, 302, 304
DIGGES LOT, 218
DIGGS, Esther, 152, 352
　James, 5
　Jane, 21
DILL, Andrew, 261
　E., 47
　Ezra, 397
　Ezrea, 14
　John, 11, 47, 243, 273, 278, 439
　Mr., 11, 41, 426
　Sarah Ann, 261
DINSMORE, Patrick, 29
DISON, William, 28, 410
DIXON, Haines, 122, 235
DOFFLER, George, 302
DOLAHITE, James, 383
DOLL, Jacob, 297
　John, 425
DONSON, 76
　Henry, 291
DONSTON, Henry, 120
DORSEY, Allen, 287, 312, 344
　Basil, 12, 238, 314, 393
　Bazil, 368

　Benjamin, 6
　Caleb, 99
　Caroline, 91
　Col., 237
　Edward, 378
　Elizabeth, 245
　Ely, 233, 297, 416
　Ely C., 245
　Ely of Ely, 65, 268, 306
　Evan, 119, 298, 301, 304
　Evelina, 77
　Harry W., 360
　Hill, 243
　John, 276, 323, 399
　John of John, 238
　John W., 53, 65, 254
　Joshua, 2, 6, 382, 385, 440
　Mary, 245
　Nicholas W., 275
　Otho, 245
　Samuel, 276
　Tabitha, 248, 259
　Vachel W., 302, 303
DOUD, John, 232
DOUGHERTY, William, 58, 276, 283
　Willliam, 223
DOUGLASS, Samuel, 48
DOUP, John, 9
DOWDEN, Maria Beall, 283
　Martia Beall, 283
　Zachariah, 283
DOWELL'S PARK, 378
DOWNEY, Michael, 237
　William, 23
　William A., 210
DOYLE, Henry, 243, 288

John, 146
Lawrence, 146
DRAPER, Thomas, 1, 9, 48, 153, 355
DRUMMOND, James, 274
DRUNENBERGER, John, 223
DRURY, William, 327
DUANE, Mr., 212
DUBOIS, Rev. J., 378
DUDDERAR, John, 199
DUDDERER, John, 411
DUDDERIR, George, 42
  Mary, 42
DUFFIN, James, 305
DUGAS, Lewis J., 120, 240
DUHAMEL, Charles, 345
DUNAVIN, William, 243
DUNHAM, Isaac, 85, 110
DUNLAP, James, 2, 10
DURANG, F., 121
DURBIN, William, 14, 21, 230, 234, 299, 405
DURST, Elizabeth, 153, 344
DUSTIN, Jonathan W., 356
  Jonathan W., 273, 317
DUSTIN & SANBURN, 28
DUTRO, Peter, 291
DUTROW, Peter, 120
DUVAL, Singleton, 11, 99
DUVALL, Daniel, 108
  Grafton, 236
  Marsh Mareen, 132

Samuel, 23, 153, 423
Thomas, 23
William, 153
DUVELL, Grafton, 334

-E-

EADOR, Solomon, 422
EARLY, John, 228, 237
  Mary, 91, 237, 385
  William, 233
EASTBURN, Robert, 121
  Robinson, 23
  Robison, 9, 23, 43
EASTERDAY, Christian, 48, 53
  Jacob, 308
EATON, Elisha, 246
  Job, 91
EATOR, David, 124
EBBERT, George Adam, 153
  John, 164
  Joseph, 124
  Margaret, 153
EBERT, George A., 14
  George Adam, 153
  John, 6, 328
  Margaret, 153
  Valentine, 343
EBERTS, George, 403
  George Adam, 403
ECARD, Gannett, 407
  John, 5, 12, 42, 389, 430
  Joseph, 407
ECARDS, John, 223
ECKARD, Henry, 117
  John, 236
  Michael, 117

ECKER, Christopher, 78, 251
  Elizabeth, 192
  George, 192
ECKERSON, Frederick, 367
ECKHARD, John, 334
  Michael, 380
ECKLER, John, 258
  Ulrich, 258
ECKMAN, Jacob, 233, 237
ECKMOND, George, 358
EDMONDSON, John, 199, 420
  Thomas, 199, 420
EDWARD, 296
  Ninian, 138
EDWARDS, Elvira, 138
EICHELBERGER, Frederick, 9, 238, 297, 302, 424
  G. M., 6
  George M., 9, 23, 56, 64, 327
EICHOLTZ, I., 67
EILER, Conrad, 281
  John, 281
EILIE, John, 242
ELDER, Aloysius, 351
  Joachim, 14, 251
  Mr., 157
ELGIN, Major, 370
ELIAS, 360
ELLEN, 250
ELLICOTT, Andrew, 236
ELLIOT, Joel, 141, 251
ELLIOTT, Eli, 245, 250, 257
  John, 293

Robert, 35, 55
Sarah, 254
Thomas, 3, 254
ELLIS, Daniel, 21, 403
  Joseph, 345
  Mr., 245
ELLMAKER, Jacob C., 254
ELSRODDS, Frederick, 337
  John T., 337
ELVINS, William T., 1
ELY, 313, 336
EMMIT, William, 230, 243
  William C., 17, 47, 399, 430
EMMIT & PORTER, 47
EMMITT, William, 347, 355
ENGA.., Richard, 146
ENGELBRECHT, Conrad, 12, 99, 243, 394
  F., 12
  G., 12
  George, 12, 394
  John, 271
  Margaret, 12, 394
ENGLAND, Amos, 251
  Nathan, 234, 251, 254, 353
  Samuel, 429
ENGLAR, Daniel, 333
  Philip, 165
ENGLE, David, 110
ENGLEBRECHT, John, 121
ENGLEMAN, John, 321
ENGLISH, Richard, 140, 223, 243, 320, 430

ENOUGH AND TO SPARE, 242
ENSEY, William, 229
ENT, George W., 22, 146, 164, 361
ERB, Peter, 42, 347
  Peter of Christopher, 14, 230
ERNSBERGER, Christopher, 18
ERNST, Matthias F., 58
ESTHER, 56, 126
ETZLER, 327
  Andrew, 123, 124, 234, 289
  Daniel, 401
  John, 108
  Joseph, 406
  Magdalena, 108
EVAN, Samuel, 180
EVANS, 126
EVELAND, David, 229
EVERHARD, Lawrence, 331
EVERHART, Jacob, 111
  John, 165
  Lawrence, 126
EVERSOLE, Catharine Magdalena, 297
  George, 297
  Jacob, 297
  Solomon, 297
EVERT, George A., 153
EVITT, Woodward, 128
EWELL, Thomas, 282
EYLER, John, 23
EYRE, Franklin, 212

-F-
F. & G. ENGELBRECHT, 393
F. & T. SAP, 349
FAGAN, Barnard, 441
FAHNESTOCK, Benjamin, 199
  Henry, 28
FAIRHILL, 59
FALLS, Richard, 441
FANNY, 314
FARE, Jacob, 126
FAREWELL, 313
FARQUHAR, James, 315
  Moses B., 62
  William, 10
  William P., 14, 67, 86, 199, 230, 358, 411
FARQUHAR AND GRIFFITH, 62
FARRE, Jannaro S., 245, 320
FARROE, Jannaros S., 239
FAUBLE, Jacob, 208
FAY, Billy Gardner, 176
FEAGA, Frederick, 123, 206, 253, 432
FEAGLER, Henry, 132, 234
FEASTER, Jacob, 253
FEBY, 77
FEEZER, Conrad, 392
FENWICK, Helena, 87, 309
FERGESON, Amos, 333
FESSLER, John, 122, 123, 274
  Margaret, 50, 434
  Michael, 272
FICK, Daniel, 300
  John, 300

FIELDEREA, 242
FIEROR, Jacob, 23
FILLER, Lucy, 221
FINE, Eve, 20, 402
  Philip, 20, 402
FINK, Daniel, 149
  John, 42
  John W., 338
FIRER, Jacob, 23
FIREY, John, 56
FISCHER, John, 239
FISHER, David, 212
  Eleanor, 212
  George, 183
  Jacob, 228
  James, 148
  John, 21, 212, 218, 299, 345
  Philip, 218
  Samuel, 274
FISTER, Jacob, 236
FITTERLING, John, 132
FITZHUGH, Giles, 259
FLANIGAN, Malachi, 305
  Thomas, 305
FLANNER, Abraham, 122
  Hannah, 122
FLAUTT, Christian, 274
  Hannah, 274
FLECK, George, 28
FLEEK, A., 9
FLEMING, Caleb, 251, 362
  John, 412
FLENARD, Philip, 437
FLENNER, Abraham, 97, 353
FLETCHALL, George W., 436

Thomas, 436
FLETCHER, Thomas, 212
FLICKINGER, John, 347
  Peter, 299
FLOOK, Conrad, 7, 303
FLUCK, Adam, 125
FLUHART, John, 338
FOGLE, Baltzer, 120
FOGLER, Henry, 132, 146
  Jacob, 177
FOOT, Anna, 367
  Peter, 367
FORMWALT, Solomon, 192
FORNEY, Samuel S., 157
FORREST, Jonathan, 212
FORWOOD, John, 299
FOSS & BAILEY, 164
FOUT, Ann, 153
  Baltzer, 11, 266, 401
  Balzer, 153
  Barbara, 29, 328, 411
  Elizabeth, 153
  John Henry, 153
  Margaret, 292, 371
  William, 153, 331
FOUTZ, David, 108
  Solomon, 271
FOX, George, 180, 219, 300, 401, 421, 432
  John, 160
FRACIN, John C., 223
FRAIM, John C., 430
  Richard, 286
FRALEY, Henry, 151, 392
FRANCIS, Joseph, 52

FRANKLIN, Charles, 90
FRAZIER, A., 255
  Alfred, 338, 372
  John S., 10, 14, 48, 230, 255
  Luke, 267
  Maryland, 251, 273
FREEMAN, John, 55
FREESE, Sarah, 276
FRIEND IN NEED, 313
FRIEZE, John, 390
FRITCHIE, John C., 243
FRIZEL, Ann, 212
  Nimrod, 212
FRRAZIER, James, 48
FRY, William, 212
FULLER, Caleb, 186
  Margaret, 186
FULTON, Amelia, 198
  Anthony, 394
  Robert, 26
FUNDENBURG, Daniel, 28
  Henry, 146, 303
  L., 245
FUNK, J., 396
  Joel, 231, 240, 254, 351
  Joseph, 16, 239
  Solomon, 273
FUNSTUN, John, 353
-G-
G. F. TEUTO & CO., 26
  Henry, 409
GAITHER, 1
  Beal, 435
  Benjamin, 435
  Col., 247
  Ephraim, 254, 399
  Frederick, 435

George, 60
Henry, 247, 435
Henry C., 435
S., 50
Stuart, 46, 271
William, 267
GALEZIO, Charles, 64, 122
GALLOWAY, Richard L., 375
GALT, John, 242
  Moses, 251
  Samuel, 114, 157
  William, 235
GANTE, Daniel, 331
GANTT, Daniel, 228
  Thomas T., 248
GARBER, John, 397
  Jonathan, 397
GARDINER, James, 15
GARDNER, Mr., 64
GARNHART, Henry, 149, 367
GARRET, Erasmus, 285
  John P., 285
GARRETSON, Freeborn, 52, 433, 436
  Jaser, 267
GARRETT, Ann, 270
  Elizabeth, 238
  Erasmus, 238, 338
  John P., 238
  John Philpott, 338
  Joseph, 261, 270, 300
GARROT, Ann, 430
GARROTT, Ann, 9, 223
  Edward, 9, 354
  Elizabeth, 67, 84
  Erasmus, 354
  John, 223, 430
  John P., 67, 84

Joseph, 9, 354
GASSAWAY, Charles, 85, 290
  Thomas, 252
GATES, Maria, 35
GATTON, Benjamin, 345
GAULT, Samuel, 417
GAUSNELL, William, 289, 367
  Willliam, 423
GAVER, Henry, 6, 338, 362, 395
  Mary, 42
  Peter, 152
  Samuel, 39, 152
GEBHART, Catharine, 210
  Elizabeth, 350
  George, 28, 210
  John, 226, 350
GEISINGER, David, 252
GELWICKS, George C., 254
GEORGE, 300, 327, 354
GEORGE BUCKEY & SON, 300
GEPHART, F. A., 225
  John, 243
GESEY, Jaocb, 17
  John, 150
GETTINGS, John F., 314
  Mary, 314
GETZENDANNER, Catharine, 278
  Henry, 146
  Jacob, 36, 40, 152, 249, 419
  Jacob of Gabriel, 291
  John, 47, 231, 278
  Mrs., 152

GETZENDENNER, Jacob, 22
  John, 4
GEYER, Henry, 397
  Samuel, 15
GHISELIN, Miss, 255
GIBBENS, M., 9
GIBBONEY, John, 66
GIBBONS, Jacob, 19, 106
GIBBONY, John, 63
GIBSON, John, 10
  Solomon D., 186
  Stephen Decatur, 186
  William, 10, 29, 188, 347
GIFFEN, Andrew, 392
GIFT, 359
GILBERT, Mr., 395
GILBREATH, Thomas, 66
GILBRETH AND RUSSELL, 347
GILDEA, Catherine, 385
  John, 322, 385
GILL, Mr., 173
  Walter F., 369
GILLMEYER, Catharine, 257
  Francis, 257
GIST, David R., 368
  George W., 52, 103, 435
  Independent, 359
  J., 176, 383
  Job, 338
  Joshua, 230, 244
  Joshua C., 14, 103
  Thomas, 14, 69, 230, 259, 303, 358
GITTING, Thomas, 286
GITTINGER, John, 22

GITTINGS, Benjamin, 265
James, 265
Jane, 320
Jeremiah, 320, 366
John F., 80
Richard, 265
GLEIM, Jacob, 59
GLENN, Alexander, 402
David, 402
GLETCHALL, T., 436
GLISAN, John, 14, 230, 239, 277, 337, 363, 381, 406
GLISSON, Sarah, 347
GLONINGER, Catharine, 29, 411
Philip, 29, 312, 411
GOLDSBOROUGH, Mr., 319
William, 12, 243, 329, 384, 395
GOMBER, Josiah, 243
GOOD, John, 315
GOODMAN, Philip, 124
GOSHOUR, Barbara, 363
Henry, 363
Mary, 363
Peter, 363
Susanna, 363
GOSSHOUR, Peter, 381
GOSSOM, Oliver C., 319, 329
GOTT, Eleanor, 305
GOULDING, James, 6
GOWENS, George, 69
GRABILL, John, 64, 162
GRAFF, Andrew, 60
John C., 97, 390

Marcus Y., 302
Sebastian, 262
GRAHAM, Augustus, 268
Larry, 267
Major, 385
Martha, 268
GRAHAME, Ann Rebecca, 235
J., 228, 245, 249
John, 154, 230, 235, 429, 433
GRANDADAM, Regena, 139, 327
GRAVES, John, 287
GRAYBILL, John, 9, 327, 358
GRAYSON, Doctor, 425
John W. B., 247
R. O., 121
GREAGH, Thomas B., 363
GREASON, William, 307
GREEB, John, 26
GREEN, Francis, 82, 85, 278
John, 64
Lewis, 140, 253, 288
Maria, 48
Sophia Susannah, 378
William, 373
GREENSHAW, Nathaniel, 73
GREENWELL, Enoch, 126
GREENWOOD, John, 321
GREFFIN, Hugh, 38
GREGG, William, 336
GRIFFIN, Hugh, 439
Jacob S., 167
Mr., 66

GRIFFITH, Abraham, 6
Greenbury, 399
Howard, 331, 399
Ignatius, 336
Isaac
Mary, 259
Philemon, 230, 325
Philip, 62, 64, 65
Samuel, 7
Thomas, 327
GRIM, Alexander, 223, 236, 430
GRIMES, Elizabeth, 331
S., 235
Samuel, 15, 48, 103, 154, 396
William, 14, 40, 53, 230, 286, 306, 321
William H., 65, 251, 329, 331
GRIMMITT'S PROSPECT, 55
GRONLUND, George Willliam, 437
GROSNECKLE, Mr., 12, 100, 395
GROSS, Jacob, 115, 172
GROVE, Godfrey, 171
Jacob, 56, 269, 440
John D., 43, 426
GROVER, George, 218, 297
Jacob, 247
GROVES, Joshua, 344
GRUBBY THICKET, 77
GRUMBINE, George, 73
GRUSHON, Abraham, 23
John, 23
GUEST, Job, 299

GUEST & BAKER, 299
GUILLARD, Henrietta, 162
GULICK, George, 21
GUMP, GEorge, 9
GUNDERMAR, C. L. D., 33
GUNN, Christopher, 186
  John, 186
  John Curry Cunningham, 186
GUNNEL, W. H., 44
GUNTON, Jane, 383
  Thomas, 383
  William, 2, 89, 140, 146, 243

-H-
HAAS, Frederick C., 320
  Jacob, 188
  Mr., 15
HAASE, Frederick C., 232
  Rev., 297
HABLING, Abraham, 82
HACEY, 126
HACKE, Nicholas, 4
HACKNEY, Barton, 65, 84, 223, 308, 430
  Mary B., 65
HAFF, Abraham, 287
  Priscilla, 52, 119
HAGAN, Benjamin, 16, 47, 84, 200, 395
  Dennis, 120, 234, 253
HAGER, George, 412
  Jonathan, 412
HAIL, George, 390
  Henry, 272
  William, 272

HAINES, Daniel, 80
  David, 6, 98, 418
  Elizabeth, 97
  Henry, 126
  Job, 97
  Michael, 98, 418
  William, 72, 431
HALE, H., 71
HALL, Baruch, 2
  Benjamin, 229
  John S., 24
  Major, 429
  Nehemiah, 229
  Nicholas, 248, 252, 292, 301
  Warfield, 229
HALL AND REABUS, 164
HALLAR, Joseph, 302
  Philip, 243
  Tobias, 383
HALLER, 425
  Christopher, 123, 333
  George, 290
  Henry, 12
  Joseph, 139
  Joshua, 91, 326, 385
  Mary, 351
  Tobias, 12, 164, 290
HALLER & LEATHERWOOD, 125
HALLEY, Hillary H., 401
HALLINBERGER, Elizabeth, 333
  William, 333
HALLOWAY, Ephraim, 255, 285
HALTLERMAN, Jacob, 180
HAMAN, Jacob, 347
HAMBLETON, Francis, 14

HAMILTON, G., 76
  John, 52, 437
  William, 383
HAMILTON'S RECOVER, 218
HAMMER, 420
HAMMET, M. K., 2, 84
HAMMETT, M'-Kelvie, 404
  M., 276
HAMMOND, Ann, 304
  Charles, 20, 23, 106, 192, 251, 383, 402, 406
  Eden, 304
  George, 11, 399
  John, 226, 331
  Johnsey, 89, 314
  Julianna
  Mary, 110, 297
  Mordecai L., 59, 281
  Mr., 440
  Nathan, 3, 86, 368
  Ormond, 302
  Polly, 11
  Rezin, 102, 305
  Thomas, 14, 23, 226, 297, 406
  Thomas I., 110
  Upton, 254, 290, 360
  Vacel, 51
  Vacel of O., 51
  Vachel, 52, 119, 331, 388
  Vachel of O., 433
  Walter C., 287
HAMMONS, Mordecia L., 226
HAMPSTON, William H., 74
HAMTON, John, 314
HANDSOME WIFE, 55

INDEX to Paragraph Number 177

HANDY, Sam, 319
HANE, D., 192
Daniel, 146
David, 419
Jacob, 243
John, 126, 299, 422
William, 3, 86, 146
HANKY, Isaac, 317
HANNAH, William, 401
HANSON, Alexander C., 22, 243
HAPE, George, 139, 322
HARBAUGH, Christian, 107
Henry, 166
Jacob, 82, 107, 166
Mary, 88, 107
HARDESTY, Joseph, 354
HARDIN, Charles F., 267
E. H., 251
HARDING, E. H., 347
Eleanor, 244
Elias H., 14
John L., 154, 164, 228, 243, 244, 302
Lewis, 242
Mr., 26
HARDMAN, George, 57
HARDT, Peter, 28, 410
HARDY, Isidore, 368
HARGESHEIMER, John, 182
HARGROVE, Rev., 37, 116
HARLEY, Mr., 47
HARMAN, Christian, 82
HARP, George, 423
Jacob, 437

HARR, Isaiah, 6
HARRIS, 357
Elizabeth, 146, 206
James, 146, 206
John, 63, 146
Thomas, 40, 74
William C., 178
HARRIS & LIVERS, 59
HARRISON,
Elizabeth, 34, 416
John, 34, 212, 416
Kensey, 182
Mary, 320
Sarah, 48
Thomas, 48
Zephaniah, 313, 314, 320, 351, 423
HARRITT, James, 392
John, 308, 428
HARRY, 3, 57, 58, 86, 126, 231, 299
Silas, 256
Susanna, 90
HARSNIPT, Matthew, 308
HART, Ellis, 254
Patrick, 290
William, 14, 230
HARTMAN, Jacob, 126
HARTSOCK, Daniel, 60
David, 234
John, 247
Mary, 247
HARVEY, David, 48
Mary, 48
HATCH, F. W., 91, 262, 269
Frederick W., 331, 385, 401
R. W., 152, 243, 302
Rev., 33, 36, 412, 415

HATLEY, Hilleary, 164
HAUER, Adam, 121
Daniel, 123, 243, 263, 275
George, 164, 243
HAUER & MANTZ, 50, 146, 275
HAUPTMAN, Philip, 11, 146, 296
HAUSE, Michael, 400
Rev., 20, 402
HAUSER, Frederick, 339
Michael, 14, 22, 49, 106, 153, 230, 243, 361, 404, 433
Mr., 3, 86
William, 205, 243
HAUSER & LEVY, 15
HAVNER, John, 308
HAWKINGS,
Thomas, 175
HAWKINS, Francis W., 350
James L., 236
Thomas, 28
HAWMAN, Peter, 23
HAYDEN, Basil, 251
HAYS, Levin, 14, 188, 230, 393, 433
Wilson, 300, 433
HAZLE BOTTOM, 437
HEABY, Philip, 380
HEAD, John, 348, 378
William B., 14, 16, 230
HEAD & SPALDING, 348
HEAGY, Henry, 148
HEARN, Lewis, 4
HEARTHERLEY, Benjamin
HEBB, Richard T., 14

HEBBERD, Allen, 108
HEDGES, Isaac, 132
　Joseph, 13, 26, 120, 235, 284
HEFFNER, Jacob, 22
　Michael, 48
HEIM, Andrew, 31
HEISELY, Catharine, 244
　Frederick, 243, 244
HEISLER, Joseph, 35
HELDERBRAND, John, 11, 393
HELFENSTEIN, J., 28, 243, 252, 269, 276, 283, 284, 286, 302, 410, 433
　John, 347, 385
　Jonathan, 25, 30, 91, 339, 356, 406
　Rev., 14, 84, 179, 250, 275, 397
HELFFENSTEIN, Jonathan, 162
　Rev., 163
HELM, Strother, 425
HELMUTH, Rev. Dr., 257
HEMP, Christian, 246
　Henry, 158, 301
　Philip, 158, 301
HEMPSTEAD, William, 297
HEMPSTON, Christian T., 283
HEMPSTONE, William, 353
　William E., 108
HEMPTON, Christian T., 58
HENCK AND ELIOTT, 353
HENDERSON, James, 72, 311, 337
　R. H., 311

Richard H., 259
　Robert, 254
　Sarah, 337
HENLY, 223, 430
HENNING, Catharine, 28
　Catherine, 35
HENNY, 53, 67, 367
HENRY, 21, 84, 86, 403
　Hugh, 212
　Rev., 439
HENSHAW, Rev., 25, 196
HENSON, 5
HERBERT, Joseph, 40, 422
HERD, Aaron, 132
　William, 132
HERMAN, George, 23
HERR, John P., 33
HERRING, Adam, 5, 43, 384
　Ludwick, 242
　Mr., 157
HERRY, Alexander, 210
　Sarah, 210
HERSH, Benjamin, 43, 214, 426
HERSHMAN, Christian, 300
　Jonathan, 300
HERSTONS, Charles, 29, 402
HESS, Charles, 434
HETIZ, Jacob, 200
HEUISLER, Joseph, 319, 337
HIBBERD, 411
　Benjamin, 327
　Silas, 58, 59, 63, 80
HIBBIRD, Joseph, 98
HICHU, William, 256

HIDGKISS, William, 64
HIGGINS, George W., 238
　James L., 12, 20, 265, 393, 402
　Rev., 89
HIGH, Frederick, 428
HILDEBRACK, Jacob, 274
HILL, David, 441
　George, 347
　James, 351
　Jane, 412
　Lewis, 25, 406, 412
HILL IN THE MIDDLE, 286
HILLEARY, Clement T., 40, 255, 371, 422
　Eleanor, 395
　Henry, 352
　John, 395
　Mrs., 255
　Perry, 9
　William, 236, 252
HILLEN, Thomas, 345
HILLERAY, Eleanor, 100
HILLERY, Clement T., 91
　Thomas, 252
HILRY, Jack, 258
HILTEBRAND, Joseph, 307
HILTIBRAKE, Jacob, 9
HILTON, Clement, 398
HIME, 181
HINCKLE, John, 242
HINCKS, Joseph, 247
HINDS, John, 296
　Martin, 296
HINES, David, 9, 52, 307, 353

INDEX to Paragraph Number   179

Philip, 218
HINKS, William, 208
HINTEN, William, 109
HISS, George, 308
HITCHCOCK, Charles B., 341
HITCHEN, Hannah, 110
  Isaac, 110
HITCHEW, Barbara, 122
  Christopher, 122
  Conrad, 77
  Hannah, 110
  Henry, 122
  Isaac, 110
  Jacob, 122
  John, 122
  Philip, 122
  William, 122
HITECHEW, Bernard, 122
  David, 122
  Eliza, 122
  Elizabeth, 122
  Gideon, 122
  Henry, 122
  Israel, 122
  Susanna, 122
  William, 122
HITESHEW, Isaac, 64
HITON, Nancy, 136
HOBBS, Dr., 64
  Horatio, 28, 63, 305
  William, 126, 314
HOCKENSMITH, Jacob, 9
  John, 9
  William, 9
HODGKISS, William, 14, 59, 63, 103, 305
HOFF, B., 77
  Benjamin, 161, 326, 355

HOFFMAN, Adam, 126
  David, 44
  Francis, 419
  Frederick W., 243
  George, 230, 236, 252, 279, 333, 419
  George William, 29, 30, 200
  Henry, 159, 243
  Jacob, 5, 252
  John, 1, 4, 5, 9, 22, 29, 30, 34, 146, 199, 236, 296, 324, 334, 381
HOFFMAN, John, 416
  John of Henry, 379
  Mrs., 320
  Nelson, 371
  Peter, 254
HOGEN, John N. A., 350
HOGGINS, John, 304
  Richard, 43, 106, 426
HOGMIRE, Andrew, 412
HOKE, Anna Mary, 57, 441
  Peter, 57, 358, 441
HOLDRY, George, 298
HOLLAND, Nathan, 262
  William, 262
HOLLOWAY, Ephraim, 246
HOLTER, John, 291
HOLTS, Nicholas, 48
HOLTZ, J., 10, 393
  Jacob, 29
  Nicholas, 22, 132, 149, 317
HOLTZES, Nicholas, 132
HOLTZMAN, 15
HOOD, James, 6

Rachael Howard, 196
Robert, 55
Thomas, 196
W., 91
HOOK, James, 231, 243
  James S., 290
  Polly, 243
HOOPER, John, 226
HOOVER, Christian, 28, 386, 410
  Daniel, 28, 386, 410
  David, 386
  Elizabeth, 380
  Jacob, 380
  John, 386
  Magdalena, 386
  Martin, 386
  Peter, 386
HOPE, 229, 441
HOPE HILL, 268
HOPKINS, Evan, 89, 100, 367
  John, 419
  Philip, 385
HOPPE, Frederick, 405
HORATIO HOBBS & CO., 258, 305
HORN, Henry, 212
HORRELL, Henry B., 257
HOSE, Peter, 126
HOUC, John, 55
HOUCH, John, 227
HOUCK, George, 146, 243
  Jacob, 23, 123, 308
  John, 4, 139, 146, 243, 252
  Nicholas, 46
HOUCK, Nicholas, 427
HOUK, Peter, 9

HOUPT, George, 437
Nicholas, 55, 437
HOUSE, Anna, 48
Caleb, 48
Daniel, 48
Edward, 59
George, 48
John, 59, 368
Marandah, 48
Nelson, 48
Rebeckah, 48
Sarah, 48
William, 48
HOUSTON, F., 164
J. F., 66
James F., 47, 432
HOUSTON & RUSSELL, 18, 105
HOUX, George Jacob, 164
HOW, Joseph, 3, 86
HOWARD, Cornelius, 82
Elisha, 62
Elizabeth, 61
George, 341
John E., 236
Joseph, 222
Joshua, 61, 300
Luke, 129
Martha, 251
Richard, 251
Samuel, 346
Thomas W., 320
Widow, 222
HOWSER, William P., 283
HOY, Nicholas, 326
HUBBS, Charles, 63
Clement, 63, 95
HUBLEY, Samuel, 228
HUFF, Priscilla, 119
HUGHES, 43

Catharine, 376
Daniel, 361, 385
Edward, 271, 286, 328
Elizabeth, 51, 286, 316
George, 25, 406
Hugh, 51
James, 49
John, 19, 192, 228, 243, 249, 276, 316, 327, 366, 379, 409
Joseph, 28, 278
Joseph A., 245, 306
Levi, 355, 376
Mr., 180
Richard, 361
Thomas, 297
HUGHES & BIGHAM 49, 434
HUGHES & POGUE, 67
HULET, Joel, 431
HULL, Andrew, 59
Peter, 59
HUMMER, Henry, 424
HUMPHREYS, George, 86
HUMSTOTT, Abraham, 159
HUNSBERRY, Frederick, 200
HUNTER, Edward, 315
James, 148
Moses T., 243
William, 315
HURD, John, 318
HUSTON, J. F., 232
James F., 4, 132, 140, 243
John, 120, 152, 228, 243
HUTTON, Enos, 113
HYATT, Elisah R., 257

Ezra, 252
Jesse, 399
Joseph, 6
William, 66, 101, 251
HYDER, John, 59
HYE, Frederick, 353
HYLAND, Nathaniel, 47
HYMES, John, 84

-I-

IAMS, Plummer, 23
ICKES, Samuel, 75
IGLEHART, Edward T., 248
IIAMS, John, 200
Plummer, 28, 200
IJAMS, Plummer, 434
ING, Frances, 308
Thomas, 308
INGELS, John, 97
INGLE, John P., 5
INGLIS, James, 39
INGMAN, Mr., 23
IRVINE & BARNES, 45
IRWIN, John, 388
ISAAC, 1, 55
ISH, Jacob, 429

-J-

J. S. EICKELBERGER & CO., 89
J. SCHREINER & HALLER, 38
JACK, 114, 248, 314, 341, 417
JACKSON, Jacob, 331, 358
JACOB, 125, 248, 258, 347
JACOB BAER & CO., 240
JACOBS, A., 47

Joel, 14
William, 48
JACQUES, Denton, 401
  Lancelot, 401
JAMES, 304
  Daniel, 119, 166
JAMISON, Benjamin, 253
  Ignatius, 40, 233, 422
  John, 40, 67
  Leonard, 9, 86, 341, 391
  Robert, 410
JANNEY, George, 315
  Jacob, 59
JARBOE, Alexander, 289
  Catharine, 289
  Henry, 86, 273
  Raphael, 286, 289
JASON, 65
JEFFERSON, Thomas, 360
JEMISON, John, 308
JENKINS, Elizabeth, 35
  Henry, 35, 87, 309, 417
  William, 195, 229, 231, 243
JENNINGS, Dr., 271
JESSOP, William, 236, 315
JIAMS, John, 230, 406
JIM, 67, 302
JOHN, 58, 62, 66, 254, 296, 319
JOHN BAER & CO., 146
JOHN FESSLER & SON, 122
JOHN ROSS & CO., 329
JOHN TOM'S LUCK, 188, 334

JOHN'S FANCY, 278
JOHNSON, Andrew, 275
  B., 398
  Baker, 231, 349, 385
  Benjamin, 226, 319
  Catharine, 100
  Catherine, 395
  Elizabeth, 385
  Fayette, 100, 395
  George, 58
  J., 153
  James, 1, 349, 392
  John, 12, 100, 246, 254, 255, 395
  Joseph, 55, 100, 233, 251, 277, 299, 395
  Joshua, 226, 250, 319
  Lydia, 29
  Major, 320
  Matilda, 385
  Matilda C., 91
  Molly, 123
  Mrs., 262
  Olive, 91
  Richard, 246, 255, 290, 405
  Roger, 268
  Samuel, 28, 48
  T. W., 400, 412
  Thomas, 24, 49, 406, 433
  Thomas W., 243, 385
  William, 243, 279, 324
  William of Jeremiah, 251
JOHNSTON, Joseph, 74
JONATHAN, 231
JONES, Abraham, 68, 248, 254, 342, 349
  Benjamin, 157, 304
  Harriet, 12, 393
  Hezekiah, 296, 302

J., 252
James E., 50
Jeremiah, 200
John, 9, 57
John P., 243
Joseph J. W., 257
Joshua, 12, 14, 230, 299, 393
Lat, 22
Levi, 294
Morris, 238, 273, 285
Raphael, 421
Sarah, 257
Thomas, 164
Thomas Ap. C., 177
Thomas B., 230, 243
William, 440
JOSEPH, 269
JOSIAH, James, 212
JOY, Stephen, 395
JUDE, 121, 258
JULIET, 263
JUST AS YOU LIKE, 233

-K-

KALB, Absalom, 249, 295, 297
KARNES, Abraham, 439
KARNEY, James, 31
KARNS, Abraham, 225
KAUFFMAN,
  Andrew, 229, 284
  David, 386
  John, 229, 255
  Mary, 386
  Nancy, 386
  Samuel, 386
KAUFMAN, Conrad, 320
  Henry, 371

KEAFAUVER, John, 247
KEARNEY, James, 111, 307, 358
  Patrick, 307
KEEDY, George, 360
KEEFER, Frederick, 274
  Samuel, 171
KEEPERS, james, 293
  Michael, 251
KEILER, George, 14, 230
KEISER, Deterick, 235
KELIN, Lewis, 334
KELLENBERG, George, 290
KELLENBERGER, George, 319
KELLER, Absalom, 363
  Conrad, 22, 123
  Daniel, 363
  Eleanor, 363
  Frederick, 376
  Jacob, 9, 244, 297
  John, 363
  Peter, 363
  Susan, 371
KELLY, Allen, 64
KEMP, Abraham, 426
  Bishop, 170
  Christian, 15, 29, 275, 285, 411
  David, 28, 405
  Dorothy, 153
  Evelina, 275
  Frederick, 122, 153, 311
  Gilbert, 9, 122, 132, 311
  Henry, 8, 13, 14, 38, 159, 352, 367, 369
  J., 43, 426

Jonathan, 301, 351, 356
  Lewis, 356
  Margaret, 122, 159, 311
  Walter, 29, 411
KENAGE, John, 238
KENDALL, Jacob, 327
KENEGE, D., 351
  John, 229, 396
  Joseph, 396
KENNADY, Edward, 236
KENNEDY, Dennis, 289
  Edward, 7, 233, 392
  John, 394
  Rev., 76
KEPHART, 77
  Charlotte, 286
  David, 108
  George, 277
  John, 286
KEPPART, Solomon, 10
KERR, Thomas, 159
KESSELRING, Devalt, 379
  Frederick, 379
  George, 379
  George Ludwick, 379, 439
  John, 379
  Louis, 379
  Michael, 379
  Sophia, 379
  Wendal, 379
KESSLER, Andrew, 13
  Jacob, 301
  Rachel, 301
KEY, Anne, 308
  Anne Arnold, 308
  Edmund, 326
  Elizabeth R., 308

Emily, 308
  Francis S., 374
  Louisa, 308
  Mary L., 308
  Philip B., 308
  Rebeca Ann, 308
KEYS, John F., 420
KEYS & WELSH, 199
KEYSER, Mathias, 399
KIEFER, C., 286
  Charlotte, 286
KILB, Ann Catherine, 153
  George, 274
  William, 153
KILGOUR, Charles J., 165
  John A. T., 58, 59, 68, 252
KIMBOLL, C., 353
  Catharine, 97, 440
  Catherine, 243, 400
  Mrs., 2, 18, 25, 283
KING, William B., 288
  William R., 14
KINKERLEY, John, 419
KINKERLY, J., 192
KINZER, John, 8, 16, 26, 103, 389
KINZEY, Henry, 311
KIPHART & PETERS, 261
KISER, Philip, 318
KITTY, 311
KLAY, George, 383
  Henry, 383
KLINE, Casper, 192
  John, 101
  Stephen, 19, 106
KLINEHART, Francis, 164
KLISE, John, 160

Mr. 182
KLUNK, Andrew, 9
Henry, 9
KNIFE, Elizabeth, 334
Michael, 334
KNIGHT, Eleanor, 169, 362
KNOB, Hugh, 396
KNODE, John, 263, 317
KNOTT, Caleb, 238
Edward, 314
KNOUFF, Greenbury, 47, 431
Jacob, 47, 431
John, 354
KNOX, John, 179, 308
Robert, 308
William, 157, 308
KOCH, John, 119
KOHLENBERG, Adam, 261
Justus, 261
KOHLENBURG, Justus, 23
KOLB, Elizabeth, 283
George, 2, 14, 50, 123, 221, 223, 230, 243, 259, 283, 296, 302, 430, 434
M., 408
Michael, 26, 53, 217
Michel, 48
Peter, 83
Raymer, 16
Rebecca, 50, 221, 434
Reomer, 83
Sophia, 26, 408
William, 14, 132, 182
KOLER, John, 437
KOONS, George, 303
Peter, 303
KOONTZ, Catharine, 283

Henry, 14, 164, 230, 243, 283
Jacob, 251
KRAUTH, J., 371
KREBS, John, 153
KREPS, Catharine, 257
KUHN, Eliza, 348
Elizabeth, 156
Henry, 21, 22, 26, 91, 106, 153, 156, 283, 348, 356, 385, 409
Jacob, 226
Lieutenant, 283
Margaret, 91, 385
Zebulon, 23
KUHNS, Jacob, 157
KUNKLE, 113
John, 22
KURTZ, John, 29, 59, 402

-L-

LABES, James, 236
LACKLAND, George Z., 281
J. C., 281
James, 281
Samuel W., 65, 80
LAMBERT, George, 108
Mary, 155, 176
LAMBRECHT, Henry, 37, 419
LAMBRIGHT, Michael, 308
LANDES, Abraham, 328
Jacob, 29, 59, 402
LANDIS, Isaac, 105
LANE, James B., 138
John, 29, 411
LANE & RUTHERFORD, 21, 25
LANG, Hannah, 334

Robert, 334
LANGSTROTH, J. D., 212
LANSTON, Joseph, 63, 77, 88
LARKIN, J., 19, 146, 399
John, 274
Joseph, 37
LARNED, Augustus, 1, 77
Sarah, 1, 77
LARRY, 267
LATE, Catherine, 394
Jacob, 168, 230, 254, 305, 322, 341, 375
John, 322, 341, 375, 394
Michael, 315, 322, 341, 375, 394
Mr., 46
LAURENCE, 154
LAWE, William, 47
LAWRENCE, 299
John S., 26, 276, 383, 384
Joseph W., 132
S., 409
U., 271
LEAB, Jacob, 66, 90, 384
LEAMING, Samuel, 182, 392
LEAPLEY, George, 62
Mary, 38
LEARNED, Augustus, 223, 430
Sarah, 223, 430
LEASE, Catherine, 158
George, 273, 293
Jacob, 153, 296, 302
Nicholas, 179
LEATHERMAN, Godfrey, 12, 23, 395

Godfried, 180
Godrey, 100
Jacob, 41
John, 230
LEATHERWOOD,
Jesse, 36, 250, 251
S. B., 66, 139
Samuel B., 326
LEBY, Mr., 43
LECHLIDER,
George, 139
LECKLITER,
George, 309
Peter, 279
LECKLLITER,
Henry, 439
LEE, Daniel, 265, 286
Richard Bland, 309
Richard H., 251
T. L, 311
Thomas S., 293
Thomas Sim, 52, 435
William, 44
LEEKINS, William, 99, 393
LEIPER, George R., 368
Thomas, 176
LEISTER, David, 60
John, 63, 108
LEMMON, Hugh, 276
LEMOINE, Hyacinth, 286
LEMON, Nicholas, 60
LEMONNIER, A. L., 247
LEN, 309
LESHORN, Widow, 323
LEVERING, Nathan, 64
LEVY, David, 369
John L., 1, 19, 43, 63, 426

Mary Ann, 1, 19
Mr., 427
Mrs., 75, 369
LEWIS, James, 425
John H., 425
Joseph, 371
Philip, 177
William, 263
LEWIS BIRELY & CO., 242
LICHTENWALTER, Abraham, 434
LIEKLIDER, Peter, 374
LIGHDERT, Jacob, 387
LIGHTER, Henry, 307
LILLY, Samuel, 352
LIND, Rev., 90
LINEBAUGH, Mary, 146
Mary Ann, 206
Samuel, 146, 206
LINK, John, 221
LINN, Henry, 105
Isaac, 105
LINSTEAD, Ann Maria, 58
Thomas, 58
LINSTID, Thomas, 242
LINTHICUM, Frederick, 121
LINTON, Ann, 388
Edward, 418
John, 168, 361
LITTLE, Jacob, 304, 346, 399
John, 379
Mary, 379
LITTLEJOHN, George, 6
Leonard J. M., 243
LITTLER, Charles W., 322

Elijah, 322
LIVERS, Catharine, 206
Catherine, 146
Ignatius, 146, 206
Thomas, 40, 74
LIZAR, George, 175
William, 175
LLOYD, William A., 258
LODGE, Johannah, 77
John, 283
LOEHR, Frederick, 243
LOGSDEN, John, 304
LOGSDON, John, 101
LOGSDON'S AMENDMENT, 181
LONDON, 238
LONG, William, 44, 230
LONG MOUNTAIN, 371
LONG POINT, 232
LORENTZ, Adam, 123, 302, 312
Elizabeth, 369
LOUX, George J., 4
LOVE, Charles K., 67
Philip, 64
LOWE, John, 353
John M., 146
John W., 283
Mr., 434
Patrick, 64, 327
Philip, 25
Robert, 248
William, 237, 262, 353
LUCAS, Aquilla, 67, 298
LUCKETT, Lloyd, 296
William, 42
LUDWICK, Frederick, 379

INDEX to Paragraph Number

LUGENBEEL, John, 345
LUKENBEEL, Samuel, 313
LUKENS, Jonathan, 212
LUPTON, William B., 6, 289
LUSCALLEED, John, 98
LUTEN, Henry, 296
LYND, Joseph, 298
LYON, Isaac, 55, 121, 151, 271

-M-

M. BROWN & BROTHER, 252
MCANULTY, Cornelius, 48
M'ANULTY, Cornelius, 255
John, 393
M'ATEE, Archibald, 254
James, 14, 263
John R., 242
M'BELL, Ninian, 311
M'CANNON, Ann, 300
James, 300
M'CARTY, John, 11
M'CHIRGAN, William, 157
M'CLAIN, Eliza, 297
William, 297
M'CLANE, Joshua, 244
M'CLARY, Benjamin, 254
Zachariah, 254
MCCLEERY, Henry, 164
M'CLEERY, Henry, 225, 243, 437
Robert, 254, 356
William, 169, 362
M'CONKEY, James, 139
M'CORMICK, Charles, 13
Joseph, 52, 430, 436
MCCREA, Mary, 117
Thompson, 117
M'CREA, Thomson, 380
William, 157
M'CREADY, F., 160
MACCUBBIN, Zachariah, 335
MCCULLEY, John J., 164
M'CULLEY, John J., 17, 31, 302, 399
M'CULLOCH, Robert, 387
M'CUMBERLAND, John, 430
MCDANIEL, James, 115
M'DANIEL, James, 234, 243
John, 245
Jonathan, 230
William, 303
M'DEVITT, Philip, 182
M'DONALD, John, 141
M'ELFRESH, Henry, 230
P., 336
Ruth, 336
M'ELROY, James, 182
M'FARLAND, 5, 384
William, 4, 43, 247, 269
MCFARLAND, William, 47, 431
M'GATIAN, Benjamin, 402
MCGILL, Mr., 46
Patrick, 49, 433
M'GILL, Miss 231
Patrick, 231, 236, 243, 251, 334
M'GREED, Joseph, 3
M'GRUDER, Rezin, 188
M'GUIRE, Col., 18
M'HAFFIE, James, 139, 148, 288, 299, 327, 345
MCHENRY, Henry, 40
M'HENRY, Henry, 218
John, 397
MACHER, James, 300
Samuel, 7, 388
M'ILHANEY, Louisa, 165
MCILHENNY/M'ILHENNY, A., 93
Alexander, 14
M'KALEB/MCKALEB John, 44, 64, 253, 260, 274, 304, 356
Mary, 260
Mary Ann, 356
M'KALEN, John, 327
MACKALL, Benjamin, 440
M'KELFRESH, John H., 313
Philip, 157
M'KELL, Patrick, 212
M'KENNEY, Samuel, 274
M'KENNIE, John Harris, 145
M'KERNEY, Francis, 361

M'KESSON, James, 314
MACKLIN, Catolena, 407
　Jacob, 407
M'LAUGHLIN, Ervine, 256
M'MILLEN, Mary Ann, 400
　Samuel, 400
MCMULLAN, Hugh, 48, 432
M'NULTY, Cornelius, 278
MCPHERSON/M'PHERSON, Alexander, 91, 385
　Col., 11, 276
　Dr., 416
　John, 14, 38, 67, 122, 146, 153, 175, 230, 236, 311, 334, 351
　R. G., 107, 404
　Robert G., 27, 237
　William S., 67, 351
M'QUAID, Patrick, 1, 15, 66, 346, 397
M'QUAID & TOOL, 397
M'SHERRY, William, 319
MAGERS, Greenbury, 230
　Lawrence, 78
MAGILL, John, 32
　Patrick, 195
　S., 126
　Samuel, 156
MAGINNIS, Rodolph, 375
MAGRUDER, Edward, 412
　John M., 114
　John R., 23
　John Rezin, 263

Lloyd, 77
Martha, 337
Patrick, 378
Robert P., 242
Samuel C., 263
Zadock, 337
Zadok, 359, 384
MAGRUDER AND BEALLS HONESTY, 77
MAHONEY, James, 247
MAHORNEY, Lewis, 295, 296
MAHVIE, Rev., 392
MAIN, John W., 400
MAJORS, Greenbury, 14
MALAMBRE, Jacob, 4, 214
MALOVA, Rev., 98
MANCHA, Solomon, 64
MANN, Charles, 121, 230, 242, 243
　William, 13
MANNACAY, Catharine, 210
MANRO, Major, 365
MANSION PLACE, THE, 56
MANTZ, 2
　Amie C., 302
　Casper, 38, 175
　Cyrus, 123, 156, 275, 348
　E., 38
　Emanuel, 269
　Ezra, 123, 140, 230, 234, 252, 296, 310, 312
　Francis, 55, 73, 123, 132, 153, 161, 223, 275, 283, 410, 430
　Gideon, 165
　Isaac, 21, 29, 243, 273

John, 15, 208, 283
Margaret, 25, 406
Mary, 77, 161
Peter, 9, 14, 24, 236, 269, 283, 391, 406
MARBURY, William, 38, 420
MARCHALL, James, 308
MARCILLY, E., 350
　F., 435
　Zulma, 5, 381
MARCKEY, David, 345
MARGERY, 309
MARIAH, 122
MARITN, Peter, 52
MARK, James, 117
MARKELL, Charlotte, 302
　Jacob, 249
　John, 35, 146, 244, 252, 271
　Mr., 249
　Sophia, 249
　William, 249, 271
MARKER, George, 23, 247
MARKEY, 2
　David, 120
MARKS, William, 17, 400
MARLOW, Thomas, 48
MARLOWE, Thomas, 332
MARQUAM, P. W., 397
MARQUHAM, Philip W., 416
MARRIOTT, William H., 368
MARSH, Henry H., 304
　J., 351, 356

Joel, 121, 254, 321
MARSH & O'NEILL, 384
MARSH, SANBURN & O'NEILL, 304
MARSHALL, James, 392, 428
  Sarah B., 52, 434
MARTIN, Abraham, 386
  Catherine, 386
  David, 14, 29, 77, 136, 146, 161, 243, 271, 298, 411
  George, 281
  Jacob, 39, 422
  John, 41, 243, 281, 431
  Luther, 58
  Peter, 5, 51, 65, 223, 229, 430, 435
  Rev., 82
  Robert N., 29
  Thomas J., 296
MARTINS, John, 130
MARTZ, Daniel, 2
MARY, 122
MARYLAND, 255, 285
MASON, A. T., 130
  Armistead T., 11
  Joseph, 428
  W., 304
  William T. T., 237
MATHEWS, Benjamin, 206
  Elizabeth, 206
  Henry, 206
  James, 9
  Peter, 206
MATHIAS, Francis, 92
  Jacob, 390
  John, 390
  Joseph, 9
  Rev., 67

MATILDA, 401
MATTERN, Philip, 9
MATTHEWS, James, 255, 302
  Jane Maria, 125
  Jesse, 230, 236, 285, 334
  Jonas, 297, 300
MATTHIAS, Jacob, 14, 230, 357
MAULSBY, Benjamin, 302
MAUZY, Thomas, 358
MAY, Michael, 358
  Thomas P., 192
MAYBERRY, 150
  J., 355
  Jesse, 363
  Justinian, 52, 233, 243, 252
  Mr., 153
  Willoughby, 48
MAYBURRY, 435
  Will'y, 349
MAYBURY, Thomas, 250
MAYNADIER, Henry, 231
MAYNARD, E. H., 64, 305
  Henry, 199, 411
  Nathan, 132, 360
MAYNARD & CO., 84
MEASEL, Rosanna, 182
MEASLE, Mary, 439
MEAZEL, John, 440
MEDTART, Jacob, 243
  Mr., 121, 253
MEIXSEL, Jacob, 270, 297
MEIXSELL, Frances, 346

  Jacob, 277, 302, 341, 346
MELSHEIMER, C. T., 259
MENSER, Michael, 128, 293
MERCER, Charles F., 369, 441
  Charles Fenton, 143, 312
  W. F., 143
MERITT, Samuel, 197
MERKELL, John, 243
MERRYLAND, 17, 299
MERRYMAN, John, 162
MESNER, Christian, 206
  John, 206
MESNOR, Christian, 206
  George, 206
MESSONIER, Christian, 146
  George, 146
  John, 146
METCALF, Enos, 345
  Joshua, 59
  Rachel, 349
METCALFE, Joshua, 63
METZGAR, Jacob, 416
METZGER, Elizabeth, 288
  Margaret, 250
MEYERHEFFER, M., 248
MICHAEL, Catherine, 84
  Conrad, 436
  George, 139, 314
  Henry, 314
  Lewis, 258

William, 123, 146, 243, 252, 275
MICHAEL HAUSER & SONS, 65, 329
MICHAEL LEE & CO., 256
MILBURN, James, 33
  Stephen, 33
  William, 33
MILHOFF, Philip Jacob, 126
MILLER, Abraham, 293
  Adeline Frances, 342
  Christiana, 186
  Elizabeth, 60
  George, 342
  George W., 283, 305
  Henry, 30, 378
  John, 60, 132, 144, 186, 263, 317, 347
  John S., 243
  John W., 153, 171
  Jonathan, 181
  Joseph, 120, 178, 236, 267, 269, 396, 422
  Leonard, 122
  Martin, 153
  Michael, 194
  Peter, 124
  Sarah, 264
  Susanna, 153
  William, 256
MILLIGAN, John, 55
MILLS, Joseph, 60
MITCHEL, John, 341
MITCHELL, James A., 49
  Theodore, 49, 433
  Thomas G., 384
MITTEN, John, 78, 109
MITTER, Samuel, 146

MITZGER, Maria Catharine, 120
MIXELL, Jacob, 152
MOCKBEE, Ninian, 232
MOGAHAN, Elizabeth, 324
MONECAY, Catharine, 274
MONROE, William, 402
MONTGOMERY, Elizabeth, 179
MOONEY, William, 324
MOORE, Andrew, 13
  Asa, 386
  Daniel M., 421
  Daniel W., 38
  F. B., 168
  James, 315
  Jehu, 80
  Maria, 212
MORE, 16
MORGAN, 265
  David, 271
  Euenice, 91
  Eunice, 385
  Margaret, 14, 397
  Thomas W., 1, 6, 14, 334, 376, 426
MORRIS, Samuel, 385
MORRISON, James, 14, 230, 366, 385
MORSE, C., 4, 73
MORSELL, William, 124
MORT, Matthias, 302
MOSES, 228
MOTTER, Catharine, 296
  Christianna, 153
  Elizabeth, 30
  Henry, 30, 297

  John, 153, 296, 419
  Lewis, 14, 336, 414, 416
  Michael, 123
  Mr., 263
  Valentine, 296
MOTTER & BAUGHER, 414
MOUGHT, John, 299
MOUNT, Thomas, 434
MOURER, Paul, 24
MOYER, Abraham, 345
  John, 23
MULLEN, William, 48
MULLICAN, Mrs., 359
  William of John, 359
MULLIKEN, Basil, 223, 430
MULLIKIN, Edward, 45
  Henrietta B., 91
MULLINEAUX, Charles, 392
  Thomas, 392
MULLINUX, Charles, 236
  Thomas, 236
MULLOY, Elizabeth, 283
  John, 283
MUMFORD, William, 99, 393
MUNDEEL, Thomas, 368
MURDOCH, E., 399
  Eleanor, 293
  G. W., 31
  George, 28, 278, 287, 410
  George W., 198, 243
  George William, 28, 287, 410
  William, 300, 324

MURDOCH'S INHERITANCE, 300
MURET, James, 139
MURPHY, Eleanor, 294
  James, 14, 230, 294
  Mary Ann, 294
  Mr., 232
  Orell, 305
  Thomas, 45
  William, 14
MURRAY, Daniel, 245
  Matthew, 24, 41, 267, 424
  Thomas Gist, 324, 328
MUSGROVE, Jacob, 279
  Zachariah, 60
MYER, Caspar, 8
MYERHEIFER, Peter, 164
MYERS, Adam, 317
  Andrew, 273
  Christopher, 28, 164, 410
  Israel, 208
  Jacob, 240, 333
  Joseph, 240
  Mary, 333
  Michael, 238
  Rudolph, 402, 425
  William, 3, 197, 426

-N-

NACE, 126, 232, 416
NANCY, 314
NAPEY, Mr., 16
NATHAN, 86
NEAT, Christian, 251
  Christopher, 72, 406
NED, 425
NEIDIG, John, 231

NEILL, John, 240
  Lewis, 326
NELSON, Burges, 86, 165
  Eliza, 240
  General, 240
  Henry, 102, 333
  John, 28, 37-39, 146, 242, 243, 278
  Joseph S., 55
  Robert, 258, 122
NEVITT, Joseph, 435
  Teresa C., 408
NEW BREMEN, 341
NEWCOMER, Christopher, 139
  Henry, 239, 300
NEWENS, Thomas, 37, 250
NEWPORT, John, 4
NICEWANGER, Christian, 251
NICHOLAS, 248
  John, 356
  Peter, 83
NICHOLLS, Thomas C., 311
NICHOLS, Jacob, 253
  Mr. 46
  Mrs., 235
  Peter, 2, 25, 67, 132, 243, 306
NICK, 248
NICKUM, Jacob, 336
  Joseph, 331, 423
NICODEMUS, John, 234
NIMROD, 231
NIXDORFF, Samuel, 229
  Tobias, 238, 252
NOKES, Richard, 199, 250

NOLAND, Dade P., 242, 278
  Elizabeth, 366
  William, 333
NORRIS, 1
NORRIS, Basil, 42, 46, 243, 271, 424
  John, 260
  Jonathan, 14, 230
  Puton, 58
  William, 271
NORRIS & GAITHER, 31, 50, 271
NORRIS & MARTIN, 271
NOTTINGHAM, 242
NULL, Abraham, 305, 328,
  346
  John, 359
  Mary, 359
  Michael, 55, 440
NUNNEMAKER, John, 346
NUSBAUM, William, 297
NUSEWANGER, Christian, 48
  Ruth, 48
NUSZ, Frederick, 2, 89, 146, 180, 243, 249
  Jacob, 120
NUXBAUM, Abraham, 439
  Jacob, 439

-O-

O BURN, Patrick, 223
OARE, Thomas, 288
OATE, 300, 433
OATS, George, 23
OBOLD, Joseph, 397
O'BURNS, Patrick, 430

O'BYRNE, Dennis, 223, 430
ODEN, Charles, 123, 296
O'FERRALL, Ignatius, 362, 412
O'FERRELL, Mary, 252
OFFUTT, Aaron, 251, 257, 403
  Andrew, 309
  Basil, 265
  Charles, 64
  Mordica B., 68
OGLE, Eli, 164, 298
  John, 433
  Samuel, 14, 44, 139, 230, 359, 420
OILER, Conrad, 120
O'NEAL, H. G., 439
O'NEAL & CO., 46, 66
O'NEALE, Ferdinand, 7, 328
  John, 310, 372
O'NEALL, H. G., 55
O'NEILL, Bernard, 76, 272
  Mary, 76, 272
  Patrick, 304
OPELO, Louis B., 32
  Mary, 32
OPPELLO, Louis B., 175
OPPOLOW, Mary Ann, 67
ORNDORFF, Christian, 242
  Eve, 242
OTT, Elizabeth, 208
  Frederick, 47, 122, 319, 336, 431
  George, 439
  John, 23
  Michael, 208

O'TUEL, Erasmus, 117
OVELMAN, Henry, 432
  Jacob, 432
OWING, Beale, 380
OWINGS, Christopher, 67, 336, 367
  Edward, 6, 230, 231, 236, 305, 331
  Joseph W., 58
  Joshua W., 103
  Mary Govane, 331
  Minerva, 305
  Nimrod, 6, 27, 236, 411
  Patrick, 14
  Thomas, 125
OYSTER, George, 346
  Jacob, 254
OYSTER & CO., 346
OYSTON, John William, 386

-P-

PAGE, Alexander, 159
PALMER, Joseph, 211
  Joseph M., 58, 439
PANCOAST, J., 98, 302
  John, 98
  Samuel, 274, 427
PARKER, 358
PARRISH, Barbara, 347
  Joshua, 347
PARSONS, John, 265
PART OF DUNGHILL, 283
PART OF RESURVEY ON BRANDY MAL, 283
PART OF THE PINES, 283
PART OF THREE MILL SEATS, 278
PASCAULT, Lewis, 315
PATTAN, Thomas, 155
PATTERSON, Thomas, 20
  William, 64, 327
  William W., 437
PAYNE, George, 229, 243, 277
PAYSON, Henry, 236
PEARCE, Josiah, 108
  Russell, 252
PEARRE, Charles W., 63
  James, 231, 300, 327
  Lemuel, 63
  William, 243, 276
PEARRE & ROHR, 68, 120
PEARRE AND ROHR, 146
PECK, Hiel, 245, 256
  Mr., 275
PEIRCE, Rachel, 338
PENDLETON, William, 316
PENN, Joseph, 14, 230
  Mary, 299
  Samuel, 299
  William G., 247
PENNEBAKER, 302
PEPPLE, Elizabeth, 288
  Joseph, 288
PERKINS, Daniel M., 86
PERREL, Thomas, 13
PERRELL, Samuel, 275
PERRY, 82, 129
  Charles, 403
  Roger, 336

Thomas I., 403
William, 23, 43, 52, 78, 427, 436
PETER, 140, 162, 248, 358
George, 93
Thomas, 50, 251, 257, 262
PETERS, Michael, 270
PETRE, Mr., 58
PFUND, Godfried, 130
PHIL, 309, 408
PHILIP, 6
PHILIPS, Eli, 259
Levy, 61
PHILL, 298
PHILLIPS, Charlotte, 256
Eli, 274
George, 298
James, 48, 256
Jason, 14, 230
John, 47, 283, 431
Leah, 48
Levi, 138
Levy, 313
Maria, 48
Mely, 48
Rachael, 48
PHILPOT, Barton, 223
PHILPOTT, Barton, 44, 86, 285
PHINNEY, Rev., 57, 441
PICKENS, George, 181
Margaret, 181
Mary, 181
Robert, 181
PICKETT, George B., 22
PICKING, John, 56
PIGMAN, B. S., 29, 31, 41, 58, 68, 120, 124, 150, 200, 234, 276, 426, 439
PINKNEY, Jonathan, 120
PITTENGER, Benjamin, 240
Daniel, 240
James, 240
Jeremiah, 240
John, 240, 305, 433
PITTINGER, John, 28
PITTS, John, 82, 265
John S., 390
Susannah, 234
PLAINE, Jacob, 48, 324
PLATER, George, 308
Thomas, 308
PLATO, 223, 430
PLEASANT HILL, 16
PLEASANT VALLEY, 345
PLUMMER, Evan, 55, 316, 319
Isaac, 429
Israel, 379
Ruth, 331
POE, Jacob, 257
Mr., 10, 393
POFFENBARGER, John, 132
POFFINBARGER, Henry, 12
POLE, William, 230
POLLY'S HABITATION, 380
POLLY'S INHERITANCE, 226
POMFREY, Mr., 10
POMPHREY, Mr., 393
POOL, Bruce, 383
Henry, 262
Phileman, 207
POOLE, Dannie, 230
Dennis, 14, 185, 233, 254, 344, 395
Frederick, 234, 383
George, 328
John, 237
Joseph, 371
Luke, 344, 395
Samuel, 314
Walter, 317, 405
POPE, William, 146
PORTER, James, 250, 365
John Alfred, 125
John N., 47, 430
Peter, 162
PORTERFIELD, John, 316
POSEY, John, 314
POTTS, Doctor, 24
E., 20, 403
E. C., 14, 354, 358
Eleanor, 124, 232
Elizabeth C., 358
John L., 20, 403
John T., 341
Joseph, 55
Philip, 149
Philip T., 120, 246, 338, 341
R., 14, 24, 124, 354, 358, 426
Richard, 11, 28, 38, 52, 124, 175, 188, 243, 296, 300, 329, 338, 354, 358, 371, 393
William, 14, 243, 286, 305, 351, 354, 358
POWEL, Thomas, 14, 15
POWELL, John, 327
Samuel, 164
Thomas, 23, 120, 228, 379

POWER, Francis, 286
POWLES, Henry, 176
PRATZMAN, Lewis, 410
PRESTON, Abraham, 429
  Joshua, 416
PRETZMAN, Jacob, 101
PRICE, Daniel, 327, 411
  George, 14, 117, 185, 230, 259, 322
  William, 279
PRIESTLEY, Edward, 45
PRINCE, William, 77
PRINTZ, Michael, 185
PROTZMAN, Jacob, 299
  Mary, 299
PROUTZ, Jacob, 86
PRUTZMAN, John, 390
PUMPHREY, Vachel, 235
PUMPKIN HILL, 300
PURDY, Joseph, 157
PUSEY, Ann, 181
  Joel, 123, 181
PYFER, John, 336
  Philip, 37, 217, 243

-Q-
QUEEN, John, 182
  Mary Ann, 67
QUYNN, A., 9
  Catharine, 302

-R-
RADCLIFFE, Elizabeth, 210
  James, 210
  Joseph, 210
  Joshua, 210
  Mary, 210
  Sarah, 210
  Thomas, 210
  Upton, 210
  Willliam, 210
RADFORD, Thomas, 218
  William B., 87
RAGAN, Daniel, 415
  John, 249
RAHAUSER, Jonathan, 322
RAITT, Elizabeth, 181
  Hammond, 16, 103
  Margaret, 181
  Nathan, 181, 233, 289
RAMSAY'S REST, 278
RAMSBURG, Casper, 308
  Sebastian, 42
RAMSBURGH, George, 9
RANDALL, Beal, 54
  Elizabeth, 124
  Nicholas, 54
  Vachel W., 14, 230
RANDELL, James, 297
  William, 297
RAS, 399
RATCLIFF, Joseph, 237
RATRIE, William, 62
RAYNALS, Caleb, 331
RAYS ADVENTURE, 59
READ, Jacob, 132
  Samuel W., 434
REED, Eve M., 225, 439
  Jacob, 186
  Mr., 13
  Patrick, 79

REEDER, Alexander Washington, 94
REEDY, John, 256
REEP, John, 181
REESE, Adam, 19, 209
  Jacob, 19, 209
  John, 19, 209
REICH, John, 164, 302, 382, 399
  Philip, 164
  Raymond, 382
REID, Elizabeth, 384
  Henson, 384
  James, 384
  John, 84
  Patrick, 230
  Patrick of Alexander, 235
  Rev., 77
  Upton, 258
REIFSCHNEIDER, John, 92
REIFSNEIDER, David, 93
REIFSNIDER, Elizabeth, 432
REIGH, John, 222
REISNER, Susannah, 244
REITCH, John, 164
REITZEL, John, 243
REITZELL, John, 14
REMICK, John O. M., 350
REMSBERG, Charlotte, 238
  Christian, 245, 247
  George, 233
  John, 22
  Lewis, 351, 402
  Mr., 397
  Sebastian, 233
  Stephen, 238

REMSBURG, Christian, 39
John, 149
Mr., 15, 66
Sebastian, 242
Stephen, 247
REMSBURGH, J., 55, 439
RENN, Barnard, 367
Barnet, 8
Catherine, 352
George, 13
Isaac, 13
RENNEF, Barbara, 117
Solomon, 117
RENNER, Abraham, 352
John, 5
Solomon, 380
RENNGER, Daniel, 328
RENS, Barnard, 367
RES, Catherine, 156
RESURVEY OF TURKEY RANGE, 43, 426
RESURVEY ON BROTHERS' AGREEMENT, 181
RESURVEY ON PART OF BEDFORD, 308
RESURVEY ON PART OF MT. PLEASANT, 367
RESURVEY ON STONY LEVEL, 299
RESURVEY ON VALUE IN TIME, 300
RETIREMENT CORRECTED, 181
RETZER, J. A., 51, 435

REYNALDS, John, 341
Samuel, 278
REYNOLDS, David, 284
Samuel, 229
RHODES, Jacob, 31
John, 244
Peter, 44, 426
RICE, Benjamin, 260, 319
George, 181, 243
James, 26, 124
Perry, 26
RICH LAND, 257
RICHARDS, Elizabeth, 254
George, 122, 274
Jane, 300
John, 382
Mark, 212
Meschach, 441
RICHARDSON, Davis, 2, 14, 77, 85, 230, 369
Meridith, 77
Samuel P., 14, 230, 239
RICHIE, Robert, 323
RICHMOND, F., 55, 439
RIDDLE, William, 326
RIDENOUR, Martin, 82, 85, 278
RIDGE, Cornelius, 251
RIDGELY, David, 238
Jacob, 242
James, 133
Joshua, 133, 286
Noah, 256
Phebe, 260
Samuel, 133, 286
Thomas, 253, 260, 320

RIDGWAY, David, 326
RIDINGER, Andrew, 334
RIDOUT, Joseph, 257
Polly, 257
RIECH, Christian, 273
RIED, Catharine, 363
Catherine, 169
Francis, 257
James, 387
Patrick, 14
Patrick of Alexander, 278
RIFE, Jacob, 255
Sophia, 255
RIGGS, Amon, 232
George, 35
John, 35
John H., 257, 309
Susanna, 35
William, 35
RIGHT AND GOOD REASON, 262
RIGHTMYER, Conrad, 243
RIGHTS OF MAN, 210
RIGNEY, John, 39, 52, 146, 164, 243, 420
RIGNY, John, 49
RILEY, Anna, 232
Frederick, 232
Mary, 77
Rebecca, 232
William, 232
RINE, John, 141
RINECKER, Paul, 406
RINEHART, Israel, 80
RINES, 58
RINGGOLD, Jane, 25, 196
Tench, 121

RITCHIE, Frances, 211
  John, 15, 103, 123, 154, 250, 254, 278, 287, 396
  Mary, 2, 251, 254, 379
  Mrs., 254
  R., 38
  Robert, 164
  William, 38, 100, 211, 251, 254, 309
ROBERT, 52, 274, 436
ROBERTS, Isaac, 125
  John, 309
  Richard, 29, 55, 98, 188, 293, 316, 345, 379
  William, 234
ROBERTSON, Alexander, 77
  Charles, 396
  James, 2, 14, 85, 86, 124, 137, 146, 243, 288, 319, 336, 346, 348
  Samuel, 309
  William, 309
ROBINSON, Charles, 235
  Hannah, 334
  Hezekiah, 188, 334, 393
  John, 126
  M., 354
ROCHE, Mr., 68
ROCKWELL, Elihel, 14
  Elihu H., 257, 397
ROCKY FOUNTAIN, 341
RODGERS, Henry, 8
  Rev. Dr., 237
RODKEY, George, 108
RODRICK, Benjamin, 313
ROGERS, Thomas, 45

ROHR, David, 67
  George, 14, 243
  Jacob, 30, 243
  Philip, 230
ROHRER, John, 9
ROHT, George, 283
ROLLINGS, Elias, 360
RONALDSON, James, 212
RONEY, Bartley, 241
ROOP, Christian, 181
  David, 16, 103, 181
  Elizabeth, 181
  John, 86
  John of Joseph, 86
  Sally, 181
ROOT, Daniel, 123, 254, 300
ROSENMILLER, Lewis, 36, 207
ROSS, C. B., 2
  James, 264
  William, 38, 57, 106, 175, 243, 299, 401
ROSSEL, Stephen C., 370
ROSZEL, Stephen C., 350
ROSZELL, Rev., 387
ROUSH, John, 277
ROUTZANG, Adam, 5, 43, 384
ROUZER, Abraham, 427
  Margaret, 427
ROW, Frederick, 8
  George, 307
ROWE, Elizabeth, 285
  Michael, 285
ROWLINGTON, John, 62
ROZELL, Widow, 300
RUDISELL, Ludwick, 278

RUDISIL, John, 299
RUMMAL, Ludwick, 379
  Magdalena, 379
RUNER, Michael, 423
RUNKEL, Catharine, 276
  W., 276
RUNKELS, Joseph, 276
RUSSEL, John, 286
RUSSELL, 12
  Abel, 326
  P., 220
  William C., 6, 331, 380, 302
RUSSELL & GRAFF, 121, 253, 302, 308, 331
RUST, George, 304
RUTHERFORD, Benjamin, 21, 146, 229, 243
RYAN, William, 234

-S-

SAFER, John, 246
SAILOR, Christian, 181
ST. CLAIR, George, 378
SALKELD, John, 283
  Lucy, 283
SALLY, 27, 77, 410
SALMON, Edward, 22, 345, 402, 404, 409
  Elizabeth, 345, 405
  George, 20, 402, 405
  Sarah, 240
  William, 240
SAM, 73, 247, 262
SANBURN, Daniel, 304

SANBURN & DUSTIN, 405
SANDERSON, William R., 146, 243
SANDS, Samuel, 45
  Thomas, 371
SANDY, 364
SAPPINGTON, F. B., 14
  Francis B., 230
  Thomas, 37, 419, 428
SARAH, 6, 258
SAWYER, Ruth, 91
SAYLER, Jacob, 397
SCHAAFF, Arthur, 306
SCHAEFER, John A., 278
SCHAEFFER, D. F., 179, 270, 288, 351, 385
  David F., 68, 153, 155, 156, 158, 159, 244, 348, 371
  Rev., 36, 50, 91, 97, 207, 221
SCHAFFER, D. F., 391
  David F., 243
SCHAUB, Jacob, 100
SCHELL, Charles, 204, 243, 401
  Ezra, 164
  Joseph, 5, 164
SCHILLER, John, 226
SCHISSLER, Adam, 22, 404
SCHLEY, Captain, 126, 303
  David, 57, 441
  Eliza, 278
  F. A., 154, 278
  Frederick A., 11, 24, 128, 238, 243, 249, 259, 293, 355, 383, 393, 409

Frederick Augustus, 409
  John, 126, 251, 409
  William, 164
SCHLEY AND SEWELL, 199
SCHLOSSER, Henry, 48
  Peter, 43, 48
SCHLUSSER, Henry, 46, 427
SCHNEBLY, Henry, 15
  John, 15
  Mr., 50
SCHNERTZELL, 16
  George, 9, 259
  Margaret, 269
SCHOFIELD, A. J., 259
SCHOLL, Christian, 48, 53, 78, 231, 373, 400
  Henry, 68, 164
SCHREINER, J., 425
SCHRINER, Peter, 276
SCHRIVER, Jacob, 229
  John, 58
SCHROEDER, Henry, 279
  John, 152, 279
SCHUERTZELL, George, 392
SCHULTZ, Conrad, 353
  George, 146, 164
  Henry, 146
  Martin, 164
SCHUMACHER, Maurice, 298
SCHVEIGART, Elizabeth, 307
  Peter, 307
SCISS, Godfrey, 79

SCOTT, Gustavus H., 415
  John, 59, 295, 306, 337
  Rolly, 126
  Sarah, 123, 292
  Thomas C., 14, 40, 230, 422
  Thomas W., 249, 261
SEAMERS, Betsey, 266
  Joseph, 266
SEASE, George, 199, 420
SEATON, James, 272
SEDGEWICK, Captain, 324
SEDWICK, Thomas, 232
  William, 232
SEEVERS, Henry, 185
SELMAN, Beal, 412
SELMON, Edward, 16
SENLEY, George, 164
SENSENEY, Mary, 59
SENSENY, Peter, 71
SERGEANT, Jacob, 239
  Polly, 239
SEUCABACH, Mottelena, 82
SEVER, Elizabeth, 153
  Frederick, 153
SHAAF, Arthur, 303, 304, 316, 325
  John T., 38
SHAAFF, Arthur, 38, 255, 261
  Dr., 11
  J. T., 306, 355, 366
  John T., 25, 408, 420
  Mary, 38, 420
SHAEFFER, Rev., 124, 434

SHAFER, Conrad, 60, 65, 129, 232, 260, 273, 278, 285, 299, 320
  Dorothea, 11, 393
  John, 48
  John A., 273
  Leonard, 287
  Mrs., 20, 220
  Nicholas, 212
  Philip, 293
SHAFFER, Conrad, 229, 315
  John, 319
SHAFFNER, Jacob, 284
SHANKS, D., 408
SHARER, John, 55
SHARRER, John, 92
SHAW, George, 296, 311
  Hugh, 253
  Moses, 86
  Thomas, 38, 97, 119, 120, 233, 236
SHAWEN, Cornelius, 306, 338
  Daniel, 23
  David, 86
  James, 47
  Moses, 63
SHAYNBOLTER, Frederick, 243
SHECKLES, Richard F., 36
SHEETZ, John, 302
SHELDMERDINE, John A., 27
SHELLMAN, Jacob, 13, 243
  John, 244, 256, 304
SHELMERDINE, Edward, 212
  John A., 198
  Mr., 248
SHEPHERD, David, 354
  James, 339
  Joseph, 339
SHEPPARD, Solomon, 80
SHEREDINE, Upton, 259
SHERMAN, 86
  Conrad, 45
SHIELDS, John, 14
  William, 3, 14
SHIFF, John, 410
SHINDLE, Lawrence, 124
SHIPLEY, Lloyd, 393
  Sarah, 393
  Talbot, 425
  Thomas C., 301
SHOEMAKER, Henry, 123
  John, 305, 328, 346
  William, 286, 346
SHOOK, Peter, 199
SHOPE, George, 180
SHORB, Frances, 196
  Jacob, 218
  John, 64, 274, 327
SHOUP, Christian, 180
  Jacob, 122
SHOWER, Abraham, 390
SHOWERS, Abraham, 9
SHRINER, Michael, 334
  Peter, 26, 108
SHRIVER, Abraham, 154, 379
  David, 26
  Isaac, 235
  Jacob, 22, 43, 146, 226, 234
  John, 60
  Judge, 68
SHROEDER, Elizabeth, 89
SHRUNK, Joseph, 157
SHRUP, Matthias, 238
SHRUPP, Henry, 132
SHUEE, Daniel, 321, 359
SHUFF, Rachel, 206
  Thomas, 206
SHULTZ, George, 243
  Henry, 243
SHUMAN, Aaron, 407
  Albert, 407
  Ann, 407
  Catolena, 407
  Eleanor, 407
  Eli, 407
  Ely, 407
  Gannett, 407
  Garrot, 407
  Isaac, 407
  Jacob, 407
  James, 407
  John, 407
  Peter, 407
  Sarah, 407
  William, 407
SHUTE, Lee, 355
  Michael, 91
  Philip, 355
SHUTS, Peter, 42
SIDES, Catharine, 28, 410
  Eliza, 165
  Jacob, 308, 384
SIMMONS, Abraham, 107
  Elizabeth, 107
  James, 230, 236, 274, 369
  John H., 230
  William, 71

SIMMONS & BE-
CKENBAUGH, 111
SIMON, Adam, 160
SIMPSON, Basil, 327
  Harrison, 333
  James, 312, 365
  Joshua, 420
  Matilda, 275, 409
  Rezin, 275, 306, 385, 420
  Walter, 261, 426
SINGER, Eve, 16
  Jacob, 16, 370
  Samuel, 370
SINN, Mrs., 298
SIX, Leonard, 199, 411
SLAGEL, 267
SLAMON, Edward, 393, 399
  Elizabeth, 393
SLATES, Catherine, 379
  John, 379
SLAYMAKER, Alexander, 276
  Daniel, 123
SLEMMONS, Margaret, 330
  Robert, 330
  Thomas, 330
SLICER, Walter, 262
SLIFER, John, 80, 236, 255, 285, 360
  Samuel, 274, 385, 396
SLINGLUFF, Jesse, 15, 21, 95, 299
SLOTHOUR, Francis, 307
SLOTHOW, Francis, 254
SMALL GAINS, 341
SMALLEY, W., 342
SMALLWOOD, John, 257

SMELSER, John, 107
  Michael, 58, 63, 108
SMELTZER, Jacob, 82
SMELZER, George
  Jacob, 14
  John, 14
SMITH, 397
  Adam, 9, 97
  Andrew, 14, 230, 278
  Bob, 302
  Caroline, 162
  Catherine, 20, 402
  Christian, 37, 199, 411
  Daniel, 20, 208, 402, 420
  Doctor, 124
  Elizabeth, 35, 417
  Fleet, 404
  George, 23, 31, 47, 156, 255, 336, 431
  Harriett, 284
  Henry, 98, 243, 247, 284, 301
  Jacob, 156
  James, 53, 154, 345, 380
  John, 23, 175, 259, 296, 365, 390, 409
  John D., 243, 308
  John H. M., 23
  John of Daniel, 230
  Joseph, 38, 115, 125, 223, 418, 437
  Joseph S., 117, 230
  Joseph Sim, 14, 157
  L. J., 29, 109, 411
  Leonard, 35, 63, 318, 347, 417
  Lewis, 314
  Mary, 156, 163
  Mary Magdalena, 429
  Obadiah, 124
  Patrick, 397

  Philip, 231
  Samuel, 80
  Samuel R., 331
  Seth, 300
  Susan, 387
  Widow, 47
  William, 225, 240
SMITH AND BIGHAM, 49
SMITHERS, William, 63
SNECK, Adam, 23
SNEEDER, Jacob, 98
SNETHEN, N., 331
  Nicholas, 283
SNIDER, Christian, 264
  Nicholas, 86, 237, 274, 304, 351
SNODER, Jacob, 24
SNOHLE, Joseph, 85
SNOOK, Adam, 125
  Simon, 120, 124, 242
  Solomon, 124, 242
SNOUFFER, Christena, 383
  John, 383
SNOWDEN, Gerrard H., 60
  Henry, 368
SNURR, Charles, 320
SNYDER, Jacob, 179, 299
  John N., 256
  Nicholas, 416
  Simon, 53
SOAPER, Lucy, 412
  Samuel, 399
SOERS, Peter, 1
SOLLARS, Dennis, 85
  Major, 393
SOLLERS, Dennis, 245, 365
  Major, 10

SOLOMON, 231
SOUDER, Benjamin, 370
  Jacob, 396
SOWER, Charles, 59, 63, 229
  David, 192
SOWERS, Peter, 1, 164, 229
SPALDING, Francis, 6, 274
  George, 334
  Henry, 64, 327, 348, 410
SPANGLER, Zachariah, 126
SPIELMAN, Jacob, 412
SPONSELLER, Jacob, 124
SPOTSWOOD, Lindsay, 159
SPRENGLE, 2
  David, 164
  Michael 9
SPRIG, Otho, 2
SPRIGG, Joseph, 271
  Otho, 2, 16, 58, 85, 230, 250, 398
  Ozburn, 302
  Samuel, 302
  Thomas, 2, 16, 85, 398
SPRINGER, Catharine, 276
  William, 144, 214
SPURRIER, Eliza Sophia, 170
  John T., 163
STALEY, 229
  Frederick, 232
  H., 71, 91, 365
  Henry, 26, 385
  Jacob, 23, 122, 153, 311
  John, 30, 154
  Joseph, 153
  Maria Julian, 153
  Melchior, 232
  Melinda, 437
  Peter, 126, 202, 232
STALLINGS, Benjamin, 243
STALY, Peter, 163
STAMERS, John, 404
STANLEY, John, 82
STANSBURG, William, 120
STANTON, John, 182
STAPLETON, Joseph K., 298
STATTLEMEYER, John, 336
STAUB, Jacob, 390
STAUFFER, Joseph, 234
STAUNTON, John, 182
STECKEL, Solomon, 242
STEINER, 12
  Capt., 336
  Christian, 3, 416
  David, 77, 366
  George, 326
  H., 152
  Hannah, 3, 4
  Henry, 48, 153, 165, 243, 328, 333
  Henry of John, 302
  Jacob, 12, 14, 146, 243, 331
  Richard M., 165
  Stephen, 14, 19, 89, 106, 230, 239, 245, 298, 326
  William, 164, 243, 331
STEINER & GRAHAME, 250, 331
STEM, Jacob, 86
  John, 59, 86, 333
  Lydia, 333
  Margaret, 333
  Nathan, 59
  Salome, 333
  Samuel, 333
STEMBEL, Frederick, 23, 121
  Henry, 1
  John, 1
STEMBELL, Frederick, 285
STEMBLE, John, 5, 86, 155, 320
  Josephus, 155
STEMMEL, John B., 329
STEPHANUS, John, 10, 393
STEPHEN, Adam, 439
STEPHENS, John, 251
  Thomas H., 302
STEPHEN'S HOPE, 437
STEVENS, Horatio, 80
  James, 304, 306
  John, 306
  Susannah, 306
STEVENSON, Basil D., 412
  James, 322
  Peter, 353, 408
  Samuel, 294, 299, 344
  William, 322
STEVESON, Benjamin, 136
STEWARD, John, 28
  Robert, 240
STEWART, Adam, 21
  Ann, 7
  George H., 441
  John, 305, 311, 373, 433
STEWART & PITTENGER, John, 433

STICHER, Peter, 251
STICKEL, Solomon, 420
STICKER, Jacob, 71
STICKLE, Solomon, 36
STIEMMEL, Jacob, 181
STIER, Frederick, 301
  Henry, 301
  John, 18, 247, 301
STIERS, John, 55
STIFER, Eve, 30
  John, 30
STILES, George, 31
STIMBELL, John, 199
STIMMEL, John B., 65
STIMMELL, John B., 400
STINCHCOMB, 4
  Beal C., 154, 256
  Elizabeth, 154
STITEBY, Jacob, 289
STOCKMAN, Betsy, 176
  George, 283
  Jacob, 176
  William, 179, 283
STODDERT, Benjamin, 248
STOLTER, Henry, 61
STONE, Nehemiah, 256
STONEBRAKER, 63, 318
  Christian, 65, 273, 285
  Sebastian, 229
STONEBRAKER & HOFFMAN, 395
STONER, Abraham, 243, 311, 406
  Christina, 339
  Daniel, 248
  David, 99, 390, 397
  Elizabeth, 390
  Frederick, 14, 243
  Henry, 243, 397
  John, 72, 352
  Mary, 86
  Polly, 179
  Rachel, 251
  Samuel, 86, 251
  Sarah, 65
  Stephen, 319
  Upton, 251
STORM, Anthony, 390
  James, 346
  Leonard, 34, 36, 40, 43, 417, 419, 426
  Mr., 304
  Peter, 30
STOTTLEMEYER, Catharine, 429
  David, 429
  John, 23
STOUFER, Henry, 139
STOUFFER, Henry, 67, 358
STOVER, John, 181, 337
  Michael, 107
  Philip, 181
STRAUSBERGER, John, 365
STRAUSE, Christiana, 41, 424
  Henry, 24, 41, 424
STRAVER, Michael, 4, 132
STRIBLING, Francis, 322
STRIDER, Philip, 9, 65, 67, 80, 246, 255, 260, 273, 285
STRODE, Thomas, 13
STRONG, Col., 324
STROTHER, George F., 13
  George S., 13
STUART, Henry, 415
STUMP, John, 299
  John W., 299
STURM, Mr., 346
SUGAR LOAF PLAINS, 268
SULL, Catharine, 208
  Peter, 208
SUMAN, Aaron, 5, 43, 46, 384, 427
  Adam, 229
  Albert, 385
  Arthur, 128
  Eleanor, 385
  William, 128
SWAIDNER, Andrew, 181
SWALLER, John, 402
SWAMLEY, Mariam, 357
SWAMLY, Asa, 390
SWANN, Thomas, 44
SWARTZWALDER, Philip, 121
SWEADNER, Jonathan, 363
SWEARINGEN, Joseph, 21, 23, 43, 243
SWIFT, George Washington, 38
  Jonathan, 38
SWIGARD, Adam, 108
SWIGART, Daniel, 41
SWIGER, Daniel, 120
SWINEHART, Peter, 73
SWITZER, Ulrick, 80
SWOPE, Catharine, 128
  Catherine, 395
  Christopher, 128

SWOTSCOAP, Joseph, 353
SYCAMORE ISLAND, 16

-T-

TABLER, Jacob, 369
TAILS, Margaret, 179
TALBOT, Joseph, 208
TALBOTT, Charles, 230
  John, 55, 316
  Joseph, 9, 15, 53, 62, 92, 146, 251, 277
  Mr., 27, 100, 103, 410, 437
TANEHILL, Lindley, 347
TANEY, Augustus, 75, 262, 277, 283, 286, 317, 334
  Dorothy, 61
  Elizabeth, 272
  Joseph, 14, 61, 64, 117, 199, 230, 272, 274, 303, 315, 327, 409, 411
  Mary, 317
  Michael, 114
  R. B., 38, 58, 420
  Roger B., 75, 122, 249, 283
TANNEHILL, Verlender, 348
TANZEY, Arthur, 23
TASKER'S CHANCE, 273
TAYLOR, Enoch, 123, 161
  Hezekiah, 58
  R. I., 259
TEENER, George, 98
TEMLIN, Samuel, 120
TEMPLIN, Richard, 86, 123
TEMPLING, Elizabeth, 371
TEUSY, Thomas, 55
THENS, Thomas, 437
THOMAS, Archibald, 272
  Benjamin, 272, 276
  Catharine, 245
  Catherine, 269
  Dr., 236, 249
  Ed, 100
  Edward, 14, 395
  Elias, 276
  Eliza, 276
  Elizabeth, 114, 417
  Henry, 13, 15, 58, 65, 120, 121, 203, 231, 243, 252, 312, 329, 334, 353, 400
  J. H., 59
  Jacob R., 63
  Joe, 20
  John, 17, 19, 47, 170, 399, 430
  John H., 249, 252
  Joseph, 313
  Levin, 364
  Mary, 78, 276
  Mary Ann, 76
  Mary I., 236, 249
  Mary J., 353
  Notley, 272
  Otho, 272
  Philip, 236, 266
  Richard, 276
  Richard of Samuel, 230
  Richard W., 276
  Samuel, 76, 278
  Samuel H., 276
  Samuel S., 290
  Susan, 312, 433
  Valentine, 47, 430
  William, 120, 243, 245, 269, 276
THOMAS & EMMIT, 63, 308, 399
THOMAS BURROWS & CO., 443
THOMAS, EMMIT & CO., 47, 430
THOMPSON, George, 29
  Hugh, 297, 353
  James, 336
  John P., 164
  John W., 121
THOMSON, A., 410, 412
  Andrew, 1, 24, 127, 284, 332, 346, 404, 441
  Joe, 403
  John P., 3, 140, 146, 227, 243, 344
  Mr., 400
  Samuel, 274
THRELKELD, John, 353
TICE, Barbara, 341
TIERNAN, Luke, 236
TILLARD, William, 274
TIMBER PLEMTY, 290
TIMBLE, Mary, 347
TITLOW, George, 23
TODD, Joshua, 423
  Lucinda, 347
  Warfield, 347
TOKINS, Guy, 269
TOM, 62, 196, 360
TOMS, Abraham, 334
  Catharine, 334
  Daniel, 251
  David, 334
  Elias, 334
  George, 334

John, 28, 334, 422
Jonathan, 334
Margaret, 334
Polly, 153, 334
Samuel, 334
Solomon, 334
William, 153, 334
TOM'S SAFE GUARD, 28, 188, 334
TOOL, Mr., 15
TOOLE, Peter, 1, 66
Peters, 346
TORRANCE, James, 15, 162
TOWNE, Eli, 37, 268, 305, 439
Elie, 14
TOWNSEND, William, 232
TRAIL, Frances, 271
James of William, 271
TRAIL'S JAUNT, 293
TRAVERS, John, 328
TRENT, 170
TRESLER, Sebastian, 283
TRISLER, George, 1, 2, 71, 121, 146, 233, 243, 296
TRISSLER, Catherine, 67
TROAZEL, Michael, 274
TROGLER, Frederick, 45
TROXALL, Jacob, 152
TROXEL, George, 23
Jacob, 255, 278
Mary, 278
Peter, 255
TROXELL, George, 41
Jacob of John, 281
Peter, 281

TRUNDLE, David, 277
Hezekiah, 289, 374
Otho, 419, 440
TRUSTY, Benjamin, 64
TUCK, Samuel J., 26
TUCKER, Rachael, 48
TURBETT, Nicholas, 146
TURBUTT, 302
Nicholas, 5, 17, 67, 126, 303
TURER, London, 238
TURNER, Delilah, 48
Elenor, 2, 85
James, 125
John, 2
Rev., 240
Thomas, 2, 85
TWO BROTHERS, 319
TYLER, John, 38, 175, 243, 328
W. Bradley, 278, 401
William, 17, 299
William B., 243
TYSON, Isaac, 236
Jesse, 331

-U-
UMBAUGH, George, 9, 42
UMSTEAD, Nicholas, 157
UNION FACTORY, 15
UNKEFER, Abdiel, 53, 218, 276
Frederick, 230, 276
UPTON, 278
URNER, Hannah, 98
Jonas, 24
Samuel, 24

-V-
VALENTINE'S GARDEN ENLARGED, 319
VAN LEAR, M., 387
VANBIBBER, Isaac, 441
Washington, 14, 230, 441
VANCE, John, 45
Thomas, 45
VANFOSSEN, Mary, 89
VEATCH, John T., 256
VEITCH, Richard, 13
VENCIENDIER, Emerentienne, 98
VINCENDIERE, Emerentienne, 392
V., 231
Victoire, 9, 391

-W-
W. R. ELVINS & CO., 87
WADSWORTH, Samuel, 194
William, 251
WAGERS, James, 16, 185, 234, 395
Upton, 68
WAGGONER, John, 108
WAGNER, David, 99, 393
John, 11, 234, 254, 312, 353
Mary, 254
Mr., 311
WAKEFIELD, 371
WALKER, Andrew, 157

John, 231, 309
William, 157
Zachariah, 378
WALLACE, Charles, 77
WALLICK, Christian, 318
WALLING, James, 227
  Joseph, 77, 225, 227, 243, 439
WALNUT RIDGE, 303
WALSH, John, 1, 290, 299
WALTERROTH, James, 121
WAMPLER, Ludwick, 21, 299
WARD, Ignatius P., 86
  Joel, 65, 67
WARENFELS, Jacob, 236
  Peter, 236
WARFIELD,
  Alexander, 58, 283, 294, 300, 344
  Alexander of Charles, 14, 230
  Bela, 298
  Charles, 259, 300, 312
  Charles A., 315
  Charles D., 266
  Henry H., 175
  Henry R., 77, 99, 255
  Mr., 46
  Peregrine, 257
  Prestley, 24, 406
  Surat D., 14
  Surratt D., 8, 103, 199, 230, 389, 411
WARING, Henry, 255, 341
WARNER, Amaria, 296
  David, 402
  George, 296, 300
  Henry, 228
  John, 387
  William, 366
WARREN, Harry, 6
WARRING, Henry, 126, 302, 311
  Mr., 126
WARTHEN, Francis, 288, 336
WARTZWALDER, Philip, 270
WASHEY, Jacob, 285
WASHINGTON,
  George, 354
  John, 228
WAT, 66, 350
WATERS, Baker, 319
  Bazil, 399
  Benjamin, 304
  Charles, 248
  Henry, 38, 421
  Henry G., 125
  Horace, 59, 72, 124
  Joab, 125
  Margaret, 384
  Nathaniel, 59
  Nathaniel M., 124
  Richard, 384
  William, 59, 124
  Zachariah, 238
WATSON, Edward M G., 64
  Sandy, 364
WATT, John, 287
  William, 287
WAY, William S., 64
WAYMAN, Henry, 82, 233
WEAKLEY, Thomas, 306
WEAKLY, Benjamin, 285
  Otho, 253
WEAVER, Adam, 255
  Catharine, 91
  David, 340
  George, 278
  Lewis, 82, 85, 235, 276
WEBB, Even, 335
  George, 199, 308, 411
  Henry, 20, 402
WEBER, John B., 3, 75, 206, 225, 258
WEBSTER, Cassandra, 272
  David, 25, 243, 406
  George, 146
  Hezekiah, 186
  Liddy, 186
  Samuel, 25, 123, 243, 272, 292, 406
  William, 325, 366
WEEDON, 256
WEISE, G., 26, 409
  Godfrey, 37, 116
  Susanna Louis, 116
  Susanna Louisa, 37
WEISER, Charles, 126
WEIST, Jacob, 48, 432
WELCH, Henry, 336
WELKER, John, 349
WELLER, Henry, 208, 420
  Jacob, 23, 153
WELSH, Thomas, 420
WELTY, Bernard, 283
  Casper, 56
  John, 139, 283
WENRICK, John, 35
WERSTHERN, Philip, 164
WERTENBAKER,
  George, 208
  Jacob, 208
  John, 208
  Michael, 208

INDEX to Paragraph Number 203

William, 1, 4, 208
WERTMAN, Henry, 137
WEST, Benjamin, 236, 334
  Horrace, 9
  Joseph, 349
  Levin, 63
  Norman, 58
WESTERMAN, Rev., 100, 395
  William, 47
WEVER, Adam, 246
WEYLIE, John V., 231, 288, 296, 311, 354
  Martha, 296
  Martha M. J., 311, 354
  Mr., 249
WHARF, Joseph, 119
WHARFE, Joseph, 408, 422
WHEELER, Clement, 87
  Lucretia, 86
  Odel, 91
WHIFFING, James, 316
WHIP, Barney, 293
  George, 428
WHITE, Addison, 240
  Burgess B., 240
  Captain, 311
  James, 58, 240, 262
  John, 292, 388
  Mary, 390
  Rev., 302
WHITEFOOT, Thomas, 312
WHITEHALL, John, 181
WHITENECK, John, 246, 255
WHITMORE, Ann, 16
  Anne, 16
  Catharine, 16
  Elizabeth, 16
  Jacob, 16
  John, 439
  Mary, 16
  Susannah, 439
WICKHAM, Jacob, 23
WIKE, Jacob, 308
WILE, Peter, 440
WILES, Elizabeth, 48
  Thomas, 48, 126
WILHELM, Elizabeth, 358
  Peter, 358
WILHIDE, John, 124
WILKINS, David, 429
WILLARD, Daniel, 29
  Elias, 29
  George, 29
WILLIAM, 58, 64, 122
  Captain, 400
  Col., 412
WILLIAM BAER & CO., 252
WILLIAMS, 4
  Absalom
  Basil, 223
  C., 65
  Charles P., 129
  Curtis, 62, 85, 89, 97, 327, 388
  Edward O., 320
  G. M., 290
  George, 231, 232, 243
  Harper, 223
  Henry, 14, 230
  Henry L., 352
  James, 18
  Mr., 64
  Otho H., 1, 274, 297, 352
  Thomas O., 50, 383
  William B., 50, 383
  William E., 1, 28, 38, 48, 175, 250, 256, 352, 429
WILLIAMS & STINCHCOMB, 17, 146
WILLIAMSON, Basil, 430
  Harper, 430
  James H., 26, 409
WILLIARD, Abraham, 319
WILLIS, Ann, 228
  Henry, 242, 294, 344
  William, 159, 361
WILLLIAMS, Otho H., 373
  William E., 373
WILLS, Jacob, 334
  Susanna, 334
WILLSON, Thomas P., 58
  William, 77, 319
  William of John, 272
WILLYAR, Nathan, 9
WILLYARD, Jacob, 23
WILSON, Charles, 233
  Edward J., 199, 411
  Hanson, 237
  Hezekiah, 237
  James, 394
  John, 45, 145, 324
  Michael, 304, 306, 321
  Peter, 49, 55
  Samuel, 334
  Susanna, 334
  William of John, 263, 399
WINCHESTER, Stephen, 308
WINDER, Levin, 33
WINDLE, John, 326

WINEBRENNER, Mr., 43
WINEMILLER, 76
  John, 86
WINGER, John, 59
  Mr., 131
WINN, William, 71, 418
WINNULL, Mary, 295
  William, 67, 295
  William L., 298
WINRICH, Adam, 124
WINSON, Alexander, 353
WINSOR, Arnold R., 58
  Arnold T., 77, 232
  Henry, 318
WINTER, B., 286
  Benjamin, 5, 47, 153, 243
  George, 29, 59, 402
  Jane, 269
  John, 29, 308, 402
  Peter, 431
  William, 397
WINTERS, Catharine, 108
  Catherine, 161
  John, 108
WIRGMAN, Peter, 39
WISE, Philip, 43, 426
WISINGER, George, 41
WISSINGER, George, 10
WITHEROW, John, 404
WITMER, Daniel, 202
WOLF, David, 30
  George, 329
  Jacob, 78, 188, 393
  Mary, 360
  Peter, 234, 313, 317

WOLFE, Catharine, 346
  Jacob, 388
  John, 253
  Peter, 346
WOLFENDEN, Charles James, 164
WOLLENDEN, C. J., 155
WOOD, Aaron, 303
  Basil, 242, 248
  Bennett, 265
  H. H., 418
  James, 218, 360, 431
  Joel, 157
  Jonathan, 53, 99, 218, 254, 303, 393
  Joseph, 218, 303, 431
  Richard, 390
  Thomas, 2, 38
  William, 218
WOODS, Pierce, 9, 23
WOODWARD, Abraham B., 24, 199, 226, 403
WOOLFENDEN, C. J., 155
  Charles James, 176
WOOTEN, Singleton, 230
WOOTTEN, Richard, 228
  Singleton, 331
WOOTTON, John, 404
  Singleton, 404
WORMAN, 24
  Moses, 22
  William, 7, 389
WORMLY, Anne B., 13
  Hugh Wallace, 13
  Jane B., 13
  John S., 13
  Mary, 13

Mary W., 13
WORTHINGTON, Charles, 76
  Thomas C., 22, 124, 154, 237
WRIGHT, Benjamin, 23
  Isaac, 283
  Jesse, 14, 25, 239, 308, 399, 406
  Joshua, 259
  Mrs., 27, 367, 410
WYATT, William, 130
WYSONG, Isaac, 97, 391

-Y-

YAGER, Charles, 109
YANTES, George, 21, 403
YANTIS, Daniel, 398
YEAGER, Charles, 113
YEISTER, Barbara, 379
  Daniel, 379
YELLOTT, George, 319
YINGLING, David, 352
  Elizabeth, 347
  Frederick, 251
  Jacob, 80
  John, 80
  Peter, 347
YON, Jacob, 107, 108
YOST, George, 153
YOTER, John, 29
YOUNG, Adam, 121
  Andrew, 39, 42, 162
  Elizabeth, 273
  Lear, 156
  Leonard, 232
  Thomas, 251, 302, 371

William, 212

-Z-

ZANCK, Christopher, 180
ZAPELONE, Barth, 29
ZEALER, George, 22
ZEIGLER, Christopher, 416
ZEPP, Leonard, 67
ZERRICK, Anthony, 149
  John, 149
ZIEGLER, Christopher, 274
ZIMMERMAN, Elizabeth, 77
  George, 13, 238
  Isaac, 1
  John, 6, 273, 296
  Michael, 13, 349
  Nathan, 29, 59, 80, 333
  Peter, 327, 423
ZOCHIE, Nicholas, 196
ZOCKEY, Nicholas, 272
ZOLLIKOFFER, Daniel, 294, 344
ZUCK, Jacob, 47, 279

Other books by F. Edward Wright:

Abstracts of Bucks County, Pennsylvania Wills, 1685-1785
Abstracts of Cumberland County, Pennsylvania Wills, 1750-1785
Abstracts of Cumberland County, Pennsylvania Wills, 1785-1825
Abstracts of Philadelphia County Wills, 1726-1747
Abstracts of Philadelphia County Wills, 1748-1763
Abstracts of Philadelphia County Wills, 1763-1784
Abstracts of Philadelphia County Wills, 1777-1790
Abstracts of Philadelphia County Wills, 1790-1802
Abstracts of Philadelphia County Wills, 1802-1809
Abstracts of Philadelphia County Wills, 1810-1815
Abstracts of Philadelphia County Wills, 1815-1819
Abstracts of Philadelphia County Wills, 1820-1825
Abstracts of Philadelphia County, Pennsylvania Wills, 1682-1726
Abstracts of South Central Pennsylvania Newspapers, Volume 1, 1785-1790
Abstracts of South Central Pennsylvania Newspapers, Volume 3, 1796-1800
Abstracts of the Newspapers of Georgetown and the Federal City, 1789-99
Abstracts of York County, Pennsylvania Wills, 1749-1819
Bucks County, Pennsylvania Church Records of the 17th and 18th Centuries Volume 2: Quaker Records: Falls and Middletown Monthly Meetings
Anna Miller Watring and F. Edward Wright
Caroline County, Maryland Marriages, Births and Deaths, 1850-1880
Citizens of the Eastern Shore of Maryland, 1659-1750
Cumberland County, Pennsylvania Church Records of the 18th Century
Delaware Newspaper Abstracts, Volume 1: 1786-1795
Early Charles County, Maryland Settlers, 1658-1745
Marlene Strawser Bates and F. Edward Wright
Early Church Records of Alexandria City and Fairfax County, Virginia
F. Edward Wright and Wesley E. Pippenger
Early Church Records of New Castle County, Delaware, Volume 1, 1701-1800
Frederick County Militia in the War of 1812
Sallie A. Mallick and F. Edward Wright
Inhabitants of Baltimore County, 1692-1763
Land Records of Sussex County, Delaware, 1769-1782
Land Records of Sussex County, Delaware, 1782-1789
Elaine Hastings Mason and F. Edward Wright
Marriage Licenses of Washington, District of Columbia, 1811-1830
Marriages and Deaths from the Newspapers of Allegany and Washington Counties, Maryland, 1820-1830
Marriages and Deaths from The York Recorder, 1821-1830
Marriages and Deaths in the Newspapers of Frederick and Montgomery Counties, Maryland, 1820-1830

Marriages and Deaths in the Newspapers of Lancaster County, Pennsylvania, 1821-1830
Marriages and Deaths in the Newspapers of Lancaster County, Pennsylvania, 1831-1840
Marriages and Deaths of Cumberland County, [Pennsylvania], 1821-1830
Maryland Calendar of Wills Volume 9: 1744-1749
Maryland Calendar of Wills Volume 10: 1748-1753
Maryland Calendar of Wills Volume 11: 1753-1760
Maryland Calendar of Wills Volume 12: 1759-1764
Maryland Calendar of Wills Volume 13: 1764-1767
Maryland Calendar of Wills Volume 14: 1767-1772
Maryland Calendar of Wills Volume 15: 1772-1774
Maryland Calendar of Wills Volume 16: 1774-1777
Maryland Eastern Shore Newspaper Abstracts, Volume 1: 1790-1805
Maryland Eastern Shore Newspaper Abstracts, Volume 2: 1806-1812
Maryland Eastern Shore Newspaper Abstracts, Volume 3: 1813-1818
Maryland Eastern Shore Newspaper Abstracts, Volume 4: 1819-1824
Maryland Eastern Shore Newspaper Abstracts, Volume 5: Northern Counties, 1825-1829
F. Edward Wright and Irma Harper
Maryland Eastern Shore Newspaper Abstracts, Volume 6: Southern Counties, 1825-1829
Maryland Eastern Shore Newspaper Abstracts, Volume 7: Northern Counties, 1830-1834
Irma Harper and F. Edward Wright
Maryland Eastern Shore Newspaper Abstracts, Volume 8: Southern Counties, 1830-1834
Maryland Militia in the Revolutionary War
S. Eugene Clements and F. Edward Wright
Newspaper Abstracts of Allegany and Washington Counties, 1811-1815
Newspaper Abstracts of Cecil and Harford Counties, [Maryland], 1822-1830
Newspaper Abstracts of Frederick County, [Maryland], 1816-1819
Newspaper Abstracts of Frederick County, 1811-1815
Sketches of Maryland Eastern Shoremen
Tax List of Chester County, Pennsylvania 1768
Tax List of York County, Pennsylvania 1779
Washington County Church Records of the 18th Century, 1768-1800
Western Maryland Newspaper Abstracts, Volume 1: 1786-1798
Western Maryland Newspaper Abstracts, Volume 2: 1799-1805
Western Maryland Newspaper Abstracts, Volume 3: 1806-1810
Wills of Chester County, Pennsylvania, 1766-1778

www.ingramcontent.com/pod-product-compliance
Lightning Source LLC
Chambersburg PA
CBHW051051160426
43193CB00010B/1144